AWS Database Migration Service User Guide

A catalogue record for this book is available from the Hong Kong Public Libraries.

Published in Hong Kong by Samurai Media Limited.

Email: info@samuraimedia.org

ISBN 9789888408245

Contents

6

What Is AWS Database Migration Service?

AWS Database Migration Service (AWS DMS) is a cloud service that makes it easy to migrate relational databases, data warehouses, NoSQL databases, and other types of data stores. You can use AWS DMS to migrate your data into the AWS Cloud, between on-premises instances, or between combinations of cloud and on-premises setups.

With AWS DMS, you can perform one-time migrations, and you can replicate ongoing changes to keep sources and targets in sync. If you want to change database engines, you can use the AWS Schema Conversion Tool (AWS SCT) to translate your database schema to the new platform. You then use AWS DMS to migrate the data. Because AWS DMS is a part of the AWS Cloud, you get the cost efficiency, speed to market, security, and flexibility that AWS services offer.

Migration Tasks That AWS DMS Performs

AWS DMS takes over many of the difficult or tedious tasks involved in a migration project:

- In a traditional solution, you need to perform capacity analysis, procure hardware and software, install and administer systems, and test and debug the installation. AWS DMS automatically manages the deployment, management, and monitoring of all hardware and software needed for your migration. Your migration can be up and running within minutes of starting the AWS DMS configuration process.

- With AWS DMS, you can scale up (or scale down) your migration resources as needed to match your actual workload. For example, if you determine that you need additional storage, you can easily increase your allocated storage and restart your migration, usually within minutes. On the other hand, if you discover that you aren't using all of the resource capacity you configured, you can easily downsize to meet your actual workload.

- AWS DMS uses a pay-as-you-go model. You only pay for AWS DMS resources while you use them, as opposed to traditional licensing models with up-front purchase costs and ongoing maintenance charges.

- AWS DMS automatically manages all of the infrastructure that supports your migration server, including hardware and software, software patching, and error reporting.

- AWS DMS provides automatic failover. If your primary replication server fails for any reason, a backup replication server can take over with little or no interruption of service.

- AWS DMS can help you switch to a modern, perhaps more cost-effective, database engine than the one you are running now. For example, AWS DMS can help you take advantage of the managed database services provided by Amazon RDS or Amazon Aurora. Or it can help you move to the managed data warehouse service provided by Amazon Redshift, NoSQL platforms like Amazon DynamoDB, or low-cost storage platforms like Amazon S3. Conversely, if you want to migrate away from old infrastructure but continue to use the same database engine, AWS DMS also supports that process.

- AWS DMS supports nearly all of today's most popular DBMS engines as data sources, including Oracle, Microsoft SQL Server, MySQL, MariaDB, PostgreSQL, SAP, MongoDB, and Amazon Aurora.

- AWS DMS provides a broad coverage of available target engines including Oracle, Microsoft SQL Server, PostgreSQL, MySQL, Amazon Redshift, SAP ASE, S3, and Amazon DynamoDB.

- You can migrate from any of the supported data sources to any of the supported data targets. AWS DMS supports fully heterogeneous data migrations between the supported engines.

- AWS DMS ensures that your data migration is secure. Data at rest is encrypted with AWS Key Management Service (AWS KMS) encryption. During migration, you can use Secure Socket Layers (SSL) to encrypt your in-flight data as it travels from source to target.

How AWS DMS Works at the Basic Level

At its most basic level, AWS DMS is a server in the AWS Cloud that runs replication software. You create a source and target connection to tell AWS DMS where to extract from and load to. Then you schedule a task that runs on this server to move your data. AWS DMS creates the tables and associated primary keys if they don't exist on the target. You can precreate the target tables manually, if you prefer. Or you can use AWS SCT to create some or all of the target tables, indexes, views, triggers, and so on.

The following diagram illustrates the AWS DMS process.

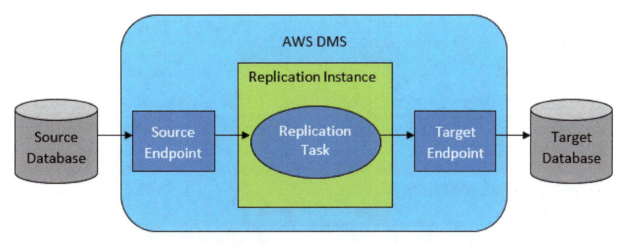

To run the AWS DMS process, start to finish

1. To start a migration project, identify your source and target data stores. These data stores can reside on any of the data engines mentioned preceding.

2. For both the source and target, configure endpoints within AWS DMS that specify the connection information to the databases. The endpoints use the appropriate ODBC drivers to communicate with your source and target.

3. Provision a *replication instance*, which is a server that AWS DMS automatically configures with replication software.

4. Create a *replication task*, which specifies the actual data tables to migrate and data transformation rules to apply. AWS DMS manages running the replication task and provides you status on the migration process.

To learn more, see the following:

- If you are new to AWS DMS but familiar with other AWS services, start with How AWS DMS Works. This section dives into the key components of AWS DMS and the overall process of setting up and running a migration.

- If you want to switch database engines, the AWS Schema Conversion Tool can convert your existing database schema, including tables, indexes, and most application code, to the target platform.

- For information on related AWS services that you might need to design your migration strategy, see AWS Cloud Products.

- Amazon Web Services provides a number of database services. For guidance on which service is best for your environment, see Running Databases on AWS.

- For an overview of all AWS products, see What is Cloud Computing?

How AWS DMS Works

AWS Database Migration Service (AWS DMS) is a web service that you can use to migrate data from a source data store to a target data store. To work with AWS DMS, one of your data stores must be on an AWS service. You can't use AWS DMS to migrate from an on-premises database to another on-premises database.

For information on the cost of database migration, see the AWS Database Migration Service pricing page.

AWS DMS is currently available in the following AWS Regions.

[See the AWS documentation website for more details]

Use the following topics to better understand AWS DMS.

- High-Level View of AWS DMS
- AWS DMS Components
- Sources for AWS Database Migration Service
- Targets for AWS Database Migration Service
- Constructing an Amazon Resource Name (ARN) for AWS DMS
- AWS DMS Support for AWS CloudFormation

High-Level View of AWS DMS

To perform a database migration, AWS DMS connects to the source data store, reads the source data, and formats the data for consumption by the target data store. It then loads the data into the target data store. Most of this processing happens in memory, though large transactions might require some buffering to disk. Cached transactions and log files are also written to disk.

At a high level, when using AWS DMS you do the following:

- Create a replication server.

- Create source and target endpoints that have connection information about your data stores.

- Create one or more tasks to migrate data between the source and target data stores.

A task can consist of three major phases:

- The full load of existing data

- The application of cached changes

- Ongoing replication

During the full load, AWS DMS loads data from tables on the source data store to tables on the target data store. While the full load is in progress, any changes made to the tables being loaded are cached on the replication server; these are the cached changes. It's important to note that AWS DMS doesn't capture changes for a given table until the full load for that table is started. In other words, the point when change capture starts is different for each individual table.

When the full load for a given table is complete, AWS DMS immediately begins to apply the cached changes for that table. When all tables have been loaded, AWS DMS begins to collect changes as transactions for the ongoing replication phase. After AWS DMS applies all cached changes, tables are transactionally consistent. At this point, AWS DMS moves to the ongoing replication phase, applying changes as transactions.

At the start of the ongoing replication phase, a backlog of transactions generally causes some lag between the source and target databases. The migration eventually reaches a steady state after working through this backlog of transactions. At this point, you can shut down your applications, allow any remaining transactions to be applied to the target, and bring your applications up, now pointing at the target database.

AWS DMS creates the target schema objects necessary to perform the migration. However, AWS DMS takes a minimalist approach and creates only those objects required to efficiently migrate the data. In other words, AWS DMS creates tables, primary keys, and in some cases unique indexes, but doesn't create any other objects that are not required to efficiently migrate the data from the source. For example, it doesn't create secondary indexes, nonprimary key constraints, or data defaults.

In most cases, when performing a migration, you also migrate most or all of the source schema. If you are performing a homogeneous migration (between two databases of the same engine type), you migrate the schema by using your engine's native tools to export and import the schema itself, without any data.

If your migration is heterogeneous (between two databases that use different engine types), you can use the AWS Schema Conversion Tool (AWS SCT) to generate a complete target schema for you. If you use the tool, any dependencies between tables such as foreign key constraints need to be disabled during the migration's "full load" and "cached change apply" phases. If performance is an issue, removing or disabling secondary indexes during the migration process helps. For more information on the AWS SCT, see AWS Schema Conversion Tool in the AWS SCT documentation.

AWS DMS Components

The components you work with when using AWS DMS include the following:

** Replication instance **

An AWS DMS replication instance runs on an Amazon Elastic Compute Cloud (Amazon EC2) instance. The replication instance provides high availability and failover support using a Multi-AZ deployment. In a Multi-AZ deployment, AWS DMS automatically provisions and maintains a synchronous standby replica of the replication instance in a different Availability Zone. The primary replication instance is synchronously replicated across Availability Zones to a standby replica. This approach provides data redundancy, eliminates I/O freezes, and minimizes latency spikes during system backups.

AWS DMS uses a replication instance to connect to the source data store, read the source data, and format the data for consumption by the target data store. The replication instance also loads the data into the target data store. Most of this processing happens in memory. However, large transactions might require some buffering on disk. Cached transactions and log files are also written to disk. When creating your replication instance, you should consider the following:

- EC2 instance class – Some of the smaller EC2 instance classes are sufficient for testing the service or for small migrations. If your migration involves a large number of tables, or if you intend to run multiple concurrent replication tasks, you should consider using one of the larger instances. We recommend this approach because AWS DMS can consume a significant amount of memory and CPU.

- Storage – Depending on the EC2 instance class you select, your replication instance comes with either 50 GB or 100 GB of data storage. This storage is used for log files and any cached changes collected during the load. If your source system is busy or takes large transactions, or if you're running multiple tasks on the replication server, you might need to increase this amount of storage. Usually the default amount is sufficient. For more detailed information about the AWS DMS replication instance, see Working with a Replication Instance in AWS Database Migration Service.

** Endpoints **

An endpoint provides connection, data store type, and location information about your data store. AWS DMS uses this information to connect to a data store and migrate data from a source endpoint to a target endpoint. You can specify additional connection attributes for an endpoint by using extra connection attributes. These attributes can control logging, file size, and other parameters; for more information about extra connection attributes, see Using Extra Connection Attributes with AWS Database Migration Service or see the documentation section for your data store. For a list of supported source and target data stores, see Sources for AWS Database Migration Service and Targets for AWS Database Migration Service.

For more detailed information about the AWS DMS replication instance, see Working with Endpoints in AWS Database Migration Service.

Tasks

An AWS DMS task is where all the work happens. You use tasks to migrate data from the source endpoint to the target endpoint, and the task processing is done on the replication instance. You specify what tables and schemas to use for your migration and any special processing, such as logging requirements, control table data, and error handling.

You can create one of three possible types of migration tasks:

- Migrate existing data – If you can afford an outage long enough to copy your existing data, this option is a good one to choose. This option simply migrates the data from your source database to your target database, creating tables when necessary.

- Migrate existing data and replicate ongoing changes – This option performs a full data load while capturing changes on the source. Once the full load is complete, captured changes are applied to the target. Eventually the application of changes reaches a steady state. At this point you can shut down your applications, let the remaining changes flow through to the target, and then restart your applications pointing at the target.

- Replicate data changes only – In some situations it might be more efficient to copy existing data using a method other than AWS DMS. For example, in a homogeneous migration, using native export/import

14

tools might be more efficient at loading the bulk data. In this situation, you can use AWS DMS to replicate changes starting when you start your bulk load to bring and keep your source and target databases in sync. By default AWS DMS starts your task as soon as you create it. However, in some situations, you might want to postpone the start of the task. For example, when using the AWS Command Line Interface (AWS CLI), you might have a process that creates a task and a different process that starts the task based on some triggering event. As needed, you can postpone your task's start.

Ongoing replication, or change data capture (CDC)

AWS DMS can be used to capture ongoing changes to the data store while you are migrating you data. The change capture process that AWS DMS uses when replicating ongoing changes from a source endpoint collects changes to the database logs by using the database engine's native API.

Each source engine has specific configuration requirements for exposing this change stream to a given user account. Most engines require some additional configuration to make the change data consumable in a meaningful way, without data loss, for the capture process. For example, Oracle requires the addition of supplemental logging, and MySQL requires row-level bin logging. When using Amazon RDS as a source, we recommend ensuring that backups are enabled and that the source database is configured to retain change logs for a sufficient time (24 hours is usually enough).

Schema and code migration

AWS DMS doesn't perform schema or code conversion. You can use tools such as Oracle SQL Developer, MySQL Workbench, or pgAdmin III to move your schema if your source and target are the same database engine. If you want to convert an existing schema to a different database engine, you can use AWS SCT. It can create a target schema and also can generate and create an entire schema: tables, indexes, views, and so on. You can also use AWS SCT to convert PL/SQL or TSQL to PgSQL and other formats. For more information on AWS SCT, see AWS Schema Conversion Tool.

Whenever possible, AWS DMS attempts to create the target schema for you. Sometimes, AWS DMS can't create the schema—for example, AWS DMS doesn't create a target Oracle schema for security reasons. For MySQL database targets, you can use extra connection attributes to have AWS DMS migrate all objects to the specified database and schema or create each database and schema for you as it finds the schema on the source.

Sources for AWS Database Migration Service

You can use the following data stores as source endpoints for data migration using AWS Database Migration Service.

On-premises and EC2 instance databases

- Oracle versions 10.2 and later, 11g, and up to 12.1, for the Enterprise, Standard, Standard One, and Standard Two editions
- Microsoft SQL Server versions 2005, 2008, 2008R2, 2012, 2014, and 2016, for the Enterprise, Standard, Workgroup, and Developer editions. The Web and Express editions are not supported.
- MySQL versions 5.5, 5.6, and 5.7
- MariaDB (supported as a MySQL-compatible data source)
- PostgreSQL version 9.4 and later
- MongoDB
- SAP Adaptive Server Enterprise (ASE) versions 12.5, 15, 15.5, 15.7, 16 and later

Microsoft Azure

- Azure SQL Database

Amazon RDS instance databases, and Amazon S3

- Oracle versions 11g (versions 11.2.0.3.v1 and later) and 12c, for the Enterprise, Standard, Standard One, and Standard Two editions
- Microsoft SQL Server versions 2008R2, 2012, and 2014, for the Enterprise, Standard, Workgroup, and Developer editions. The Web and Express editions are not supported.
- MySQL versions 5.5, 5.6, and 5.7
- MariaDB (supported as a MySQL-compatible data source)
- PostgreSQL 9.4 and later. Change data capture (CDC) is only supported for versions 9.4.9 and higher and 9.5.4 and higher. The `rds.logical_replication` parameter, which is required for CDC, is supported only in these versions and later.
- Amazon Aurora (supported as a MySQL-compatible data source)
- Amazon S3

Targets for AWS Database Migration Service

You can use the following data stores as target endpoints for data migration using AWS Database Migration Service.

On-premises and Amazon EC2 instance databases

- Oracle versions 10g, 11g, 12c, for the Enterprise, Standard, Standard One, and Standard Two editions

- Microsoft SQL Server versions 2005, 2008, 2008R2, 2012, 2014, and 2016, for the Enterprise, Standard, Workgroup, and Developer editions. The Web and Express editions are not supported.

- MySQL, versions 5.5, 5.6, and 5.7

- MariaDB (supported as a MySQL-compatible data target)

- PostgreSQL, versions 9.4 and later

- SAP Adaptive Server Enterprise (ASE) versions 15, 15.5, 15.7, 16 and later

Amazon RDS instance databases, Amazon Redshift, Amazon DynamoDB, and Amazon S3

- Oracle versions 11g (versions 11.2.0.3.v1 and later) and 12c, for the Enterprise, Standard, Standard One, and Standard Two editions

- Microsoft SQL Server versions 2008R2, 2012, and 2014, for the Enterprise, Standard, Workgroup, and Developer editions. The Web and Express editions are not supported.

- MySQL, versions 5.5, 5.6, and 5.7

- MariaDB (supported as a MySQL-compatible data target)

- PostgreSQL, versions 9.4 and later

- Amazon Aurora with MySQL compatibility

- Amazon Aurora with PostgreSQL compatibility

- Amazon Redshift

- Amazon S3

- Amazon DynamoDB

Constructing an Amazon Resource Name (ARN) for AWS DMS

If you use the AWS CLI or AWS Database Migration Service API to automate your database migration, then you need to know about working with an Amazon Resource Name (ARN). Resources that are created in Amazon Web Services are identified by an ARN, which is a unique identifier. If you use the AWS CLI or AWS DMS API to set up your database migration, you must supply the ARN of the resource you want to work with.

An ARN for an AWS DMS resource uses the following syntax:

`arn:aws:dms:<region>:<account number>:<resourcetype>:<resourcename>`

In this syntax:

- is the ID of the AWS Region where the AWS DMS resource was created, such as `us-west-2`.

  The following table shows AWS Region names and the values you should use when constructing an ARN. [See the AWS documentation website for more details]

- is your account number with dashes omitted. To find your account number, log in to your AWS account at http://aws/.amazon/.com, choose **My Account/Console**, and then choose **My Account**.

- is the type of AWS DMS resource.

  The following table shows the resource types that you should use when constructing an ARN for a particular AWS DMS resource.
  [See the AWS documentation website for more details]

- is the resource name assigned to the AWS DMS resource. This is a generated arbitrary string.

The following table shows examples of ARNs for AWS DMS resources with an AWS account of 123456789012, which were created in the US East (N. Virginia) region, and has a resource name:

[See the AWS documentation website for more details]

AWS DMS Support for AWS CloudFormation

You can provision AWS Database Migration Service resources using AWS CloudFormation. AWS CloudFormation is a service that helps you model and set up your AWS resources for infrastructure management or deployment. For example, you can provision AWS DMS resources such as replication instances, tasks, certificates, and endpoints. You create a template that describes all the AWS resources that you want and AWS CloudFormation provisions and configures those resources for you.

As a developer or system administrator, you can create and manage collections of these resources that you can then use for repetitive migration tasks or deploying resources to your organization. For more information about AWS CloudFormation, see AWS CloudFormation Concepts in the *AWS CloudFormation User Guide*.

AWS DMS supports creating the following AWS DMS resources using AWS CloudFormation:

- AWS::DMS::Certificate
- AWS::DMS::Endpoint
- AWS::DMS::EventSubscription
- AWS::DMS::ReplicationInstance
- AWS::DMS::ReplicationSubnetGroup
- AWS::DMS::ReplicationTask

Setting Up

Before you use AWS Database Migration Service (AWS DMS) for the first time, you'll need to complete the following tasks:

1. Sign Up for AWS

2. Create an IAM User

3. Migration Planning for AWS Database Migration Service

Sign Up for AWS

When you sign up for Amazon Web Services (AWS), your AWS account is automatically signed up for all services in AWS, including AWS DMS. You are charged only for the services that you use.

With AWS DMS, you pay only for the resources you use. The AWS DMS replication instance that you create will be live (not running in a sandbox). You will incur the standard AWS DMS usage fees for the instance until you terminate it. For more information about AWS DMS usage rates, see the AWS DMS product page. If you are a new AWS customer, you can get started with AWS DMS for free; for more information, see AWS Free Usage Tier.

If you have an AWS account already, skip to the next task. If you don't have an AWS account, use the following procedure to create one.

To create an AWS account

1. Open https://aws.amazon.com/, and then choose **Create an AWS Account**. **Note** This might be unavailable in your browser if you previously signed into the AWS Management Console. In that case, choose **Sign in to a different account**, and then choose **Create a new AWS account**.

2. Follow the online instructions.

   Part of the sign-up procedure involves receiving a phone call and entering a PIN using the phone keypad.

Note your AWS account number, because you'll need it for the next task.

Create an IAM User

Services in AWS, such as AWS DMS, require that you provide credentials when you access them, so that the service can determine whether you have permission to access its resources. The console requires your password. You can create access keys for your AWS account to access the command line interface or API. However, we don't recommend that you access AWS using the credentials for your AWS account; we recommend that you use AWS Identity and Access Management (IAM) instead. Create an IAM user, and then add the user to an IAM group with administrative permissions or and grant this user administrative permissions. You can then access AWS using a special URL and the credentials for the IAM user.

If you signed up for AWS but have not created an IAM user for yourself, you can create one using the IAM console.

To create an IAM user for yourself and add the user to an Administrators group

1. Use your AWS account email address and password to sign in to the AWS Management Console as the *AWS account root user*.

2. In the navigation pane of the console, choose **Users**, and then choose **Add user**.

3. For **User name**, type ** Administrator**.

4. Select the check box next to **AWS Management Console access**, select **Custom password**, and then type the new user's password in the text box. You can optionally select **Require password reset** to force the user to select a new password the next time the user signs in.

5. Choose **Next: Permissions**.

6. On the **Set permissions for user** page, choose **Add user to group**.

7. Choose **Create group**.

8. In the **Create group** dialog box, type ** Administrators**.

9. For **Filter**, choose **Job function**.

10. In the policy list, select the check box for ** AdministratorAccess**. Then choose **Create group**.

11. Back in the list of groups, select the check box for your new group. Choose **Refresh** if necessary to see the group in the list.

12. Choose **Next: Review** to see the list of group memberships to be added to the new user. When you are ready to proceed, choose **Create user**.

You can use this same process to create more groups and users, and to give your users access to your AWS account resources. To learn about using policies to restrict users' permissions to specific AWS resources, go to Access Management and Example Policies.

To sign in as this new IAM user, sign out of the AWS console, then use the following URL, where *your_aws_account_id* is your AWS account number without the hyphens (for example, if your AWS account number is 1234-5678-9012, your AWS account ID is 123456789012):

```
1 https://your_aws_account_id.signin.aws.amazon.com/console/
```

Enter the IAM user name and password that you just created. When you're signed in, the navigation bar displays "*your_user_name @ your_aws_account_id*".

If you don't want the URL for your sign-in page to contain your AWS account ID, you can create an account alias. On the IAM dashboard, choose **Customize** and type an alias, such as your company name. To sign in after you create an account alias, use the following URL.

```
1 https://your_account_alias.signin.aws.amazon.com/console/
```

To verify the sign-in link for IAM users for your account, open the IAM console and check under **AWS Account Alias** on the dashboard.

Migration Planning for AWS Database Migration Service

When planning a database migration using AWS Database Migration Service, consider the following:

- You will need to configure a network that connects your source and target databases to a AWS DMS replication instance. This can be as simple as connecting two AWS resources in the same VPC as the replication instance to more complex configurations such as connecting an on-premises database to an Amazon RDS DB instance over VPN. For more information, see Network Configurations for Database Migration

- **Source and Target Endpoints** – You will need to know what information and tables in the source database need to be migrated to the target database. AWS DMS supports basic schema migration, including the creation of tables and primary keys. However, AWS DMS doesn't automatically create secondary indexes, foreign keys, user accounts, and so on in the target database. Note that, depending on your source and target database engine, you may need to set up supplemental logging or modify other settings for a source or target database. See the Sources for Data Migration and Targets for Data Migration sections for more information.

- **Schema/Code Migration** – AWS DMS doesn't perform schema or code conversion. You can use tools such as Oracle SQL Developer, MySQL Workbench, or pgAdmin III to convert your schema. If you want to convert an existing schema to a different database engine, you can use the AWS Schema Conversion Tool. It can create a target schema and also can generate and create an entire schema: tables, indexes, views, and so on. You can also use the tool to convert PL/SQL or TSQL to PgSQL and other formats. For more information on the AWS Schema Conversion Tool, see AWS Schema Conversion Tool .

- **Unsupported Data Types** – Some source data types need to be converted into the parallel data types for the target database. For tables listing conversions between database data types, see Reference for AWS Database Migration Service Including Data Conversion Reference and Additional Topics.

Getting Started

AWS Database Migration Service (AWS DMS) helps you migrate databases to AWS easily and securely. You can migrate your data to and from most widely used commercial and open-source databases, such as Oracle, MySQL, and PostgreSQL. The service supports homogeneous migrations such as Oracle to Oracle, and also heterogeneous migrations between different database platforms, such as Oracle to PostgreSQL or MySQL to Oracle.

For information on the cost of database migration using AWS Database Migration Service, see the AWS Database Migration Service pricing page.

- Start a Database Migration with AWS Database Migration Service
- Step 1: Welcome
- Step 2: Create a Replication Instance
- Step 3: Specify Source and Target Endpoints
- Step 4: Create a Task
- Monitor Your Task

Start a Database Migration with AWS Database Migration Service

There are several ways to begin a database migration. You can select the AWS DMS console wizard that will walk you through each step of the process, or you can do each step by selecting the appropriate task from the navigation pane. You can also use the AWS CLI; for information on using the CLI with AWS DMS, see AWS CLI for AWS DMS..

To use the wizard, select **Getting started** for from the navigation pane on the AWS DMS console. You can use the wizard to help create your first data migration. Following the wizard process, you allocate a replication instance that performs all the processes for the migration, specify a source and a target database, and then create a task or set of tasks to define what tables and replication processes you want to use. AWS DMS then creates your replication instance and performs the tasks on the data being migrated.

Alternatively, you can create each of the components of an AWS DMS database migration by selecting the items from the navigation pane. For a database migration, you must do the following:

- Complete the tasks outlined in Setting Up

- Allocate a replication instance that performs all the processes for the migration

- Specify a source and a target database endpoint

- Create a task or set of tasks to define what tables and replication processes you want to use

Step 1: Welcome

If you start your database migration using the AWS DMS console wizard, you will see the Welcome page, which explains the process of database migration using AWS DMS.

Welcome to AWS Database Migration Service

AWS Database Migration Service tasks require at least a source, a target, and a replication instance. Your source is the database you wish to move data from and the target is the database you're moving data to. The replication instance processes the migration tasks and requires access to your source and target endpoints inside your VPC. Replication instances come in different sizes depending on your performance needs. If you're migrating to a different database engine, AWS Schema Conversion Tool can generate the new schema for you. Download AWS Schema Conversion Tool

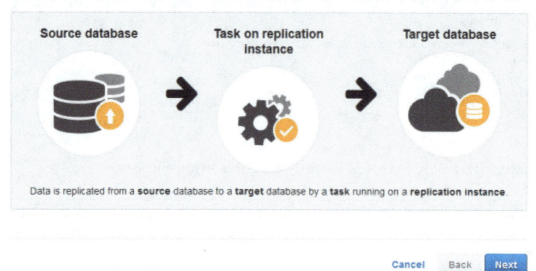

Source database   **Task on replication instance**   **Target database**

Data is replicated from a **source** database to a **target** database by a **task** running on a **replication instance**.

Cancel   Back   Next

To start a database migration from the console's Welcome page

- Choose **Next**.

Step 2: Create a Replication Instance

Your first task in migrating a database is to create a replication instance that has sufficient storage and processing power to perform the tasks you assign and migrate data from your source database to the target database. The required size of this instance varies depending on the amount of data you need to migrate and the tasks that you need the instance to perform. For more information about replication instances, see Working with a Replication Instance in AWS Database Migration Service.

The procedure following assumes that you have chosen the AWS DMS console wizard. Note that you can also do this step by selecting **Replication instances** from the AWS DMS console's navigation pane and then selecting **Create replication instance**.

To create a replication instance by using the AWS console

1. In the navigation pane, click **Replication instances**.

2. Select **Create Replication Instance**.

3. On the **Create replication instance** page, specify your replication instance information. The following table describes the settings.

Create replication instance

A replication instance initiates the connection between the source and target databases, transfers the data, and caches any changes that occur on the source database during the initial data load. Use the fields below to configure the parameters of your new replication instance including network and security information, encryption details, and performance characteristics. We suggest you shut down the replication instance once your migration is complete to prevent further usage charges.

[See the AWS documentation website for more details]

4. Choose the **Advanced** tab, shown following, to set values for network and encryption settings if you need them. The following table describes the settings.

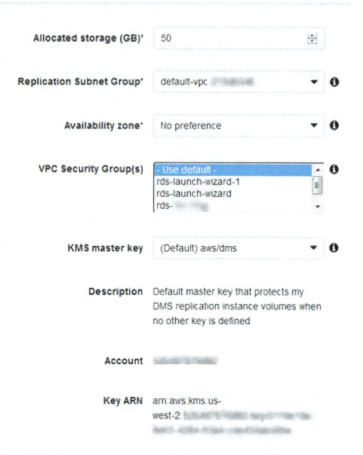

[See the AWS documentation website for more details]

5. Specify the **Maintenance** settings. The following table describes the settings. For more information about maintenance settings, see AWS DMS Maintenance Window

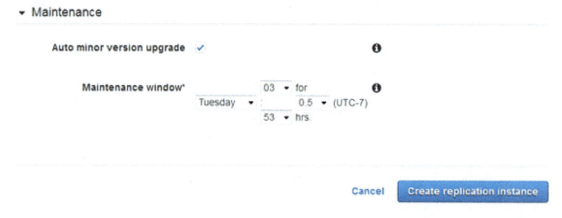

[See the AWS documentation website for more details]

6. Choose **Create replication instance**.

Step 3: Specify Source and Target Endpoints

While your replication instance is being created, you can specify the source and target data stores. The source and target data stores can be on an Amazon Elastic Compute Cloud (Amazon EC2) instance, an Amazon

Relational Database Service (Amazon RDS) DB instance, or an on-premises database.

The procedure following assumes that you have chosen the AWS DMS console wizard. Note that you can also do this step by selecting **Endpoints** from the AWS DMS console's navigation pane and then selecting **Create endpoint**. When using the console wizard, you create both the source and target endpoints on the same page. When not using the console wizard, you create each endpoint separately.

To specify source or target database endpoints using the AWS console

1. On the **Connect source and target database endpoints** page, specify your connection information for the source or target database. The following table describes the settings.

[See the AWS documentation website for more details]

2. Choose the **Advanced** tab, shown following, to set values for connection string and encryption key if you need them. You can test the endpoint connection by choosing **Run test**.

[See the AWS documentation website for more details]

Step 4: Create a Task

Create a task to specify what tables to migrate, to map data using a target schema, and to create new tables on the target database. As part of creating a task, you can choose the type of migration: to migrate existing data, migrate existing data and replicate ongoing changes, or replicate data changes only.

Using AWS DMS, you can specify precise mapping of your data between the source and the target database. Before you specify your mapping, make sure you review the documentation section on data type mapping for your source and your target database.

You can choose to start a task as soon as you finish specifying information for that task on the **Create task** page, or you can start the task from the Dashboard page once you finish specifying task information.

The procedure following assumes that you have chosen the AWS DMS console wizard and specified replication instance information and endpoints using the console wizard. Note that you can also do this step by selecting **Tasks** from the AWS DMS console's navigation pane and then selecting **Create task**.

To create a migration task

1. On the **Create Task** page, specify the task options. The following table describes the settings.

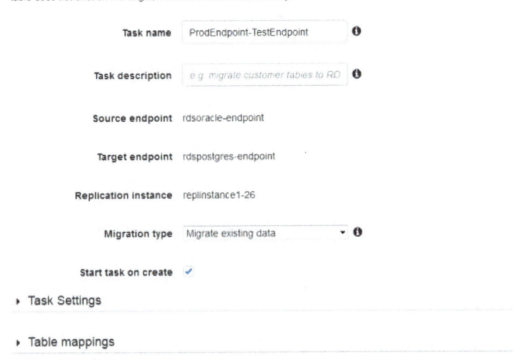

[See the AWS documentation website for more details]

2. Choose the **Task Settings** tab, shown following, and specify values for your target table, LOB support, and to enable logging. The task settings shown depend on the **Migration type** value you select. For example, when you select **Migrate existing data**, the following options are shown:

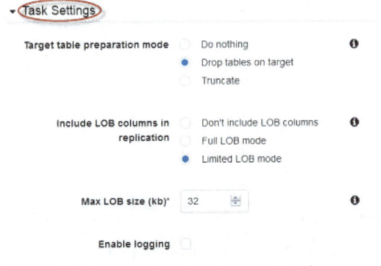

[See the AWS documentation website for more details]

When you select **Migrate existing data and replicate** for **Migration type**, the following options are shown:

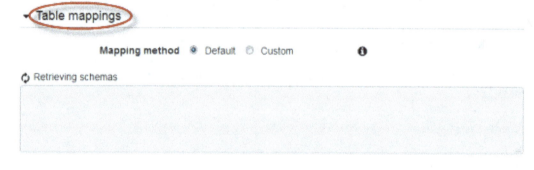

▾ Task Settings

Target table preparation mode	○ Do nothing	❶
	● Drop tables on target	
	○ Truncate	
Stop task after full load completes	● Don't stop	❶
	○ Stop Before Applying Cached Changes	
	○ Stop After Applying Cached Changes	
Include LOB columns in replication	○ Don't include LOB columns	❶
	○ Full LOB mode	
	● Limited LOB mode	
Max LOB size (kb)*	32	❶
Enable logging	☐	

[See the AWS documentation website for more details]

3. Choose the **Table mappings** tab, shown following, to set values for schema mapping and the mapping method. If you choose **Custom**, you can specify the target schema and table values. For more information about table mapping, see Using Table Mapping with a Task to Select and Filter Data.

▾ Table mappings

Mapping method	● Default ○ Custom ❶
↻ Retrieving schemas	

4. Once you have finished with the task settings, choose **Create task**.

Monitor Your Task

If you select **Start task on create** when you create a task, your task begins immediately to migrate your data when you choose **Create task**. You can view statistics and monitoring information for your task by choosing the running task from the AWS Management Console. The following screenshot shows the table statistics of a database migration. For more information about monitoring, see Monitoring AWS Database Migration Service Tasks

task-fkvacppsulxnqyv

Overview Task monitoring Table statistics Logs

Filter: 🔍 Filter									✕
Schema	**Table**	**State**	**Inserts**	**Deletes**	**Updates**	**DDLs**	**Full Load Rows**	**Total**	**Last updated**
aat	T20	Full load	0	0	0	0	16,080,394	16,080,394	3/18/16, 1:18 PM
aat	T21	Full load	0	0	0	0	16,079,437	16,079,437	3/18/16, 1:18 PM
aat	T22	Full load	0	0	0	0	15,804,000	15,804,000	3/18/16, 1:18 PM

Best Practices

To use AWS Database Migration Service (AWS DMS) most effectively, see this section's recommendations on the most efficient way to migrate your data.

- Improving the Performance of an AWS Database Migration Service Migration
- Determining the Optimum Size for a Replication Instance
- Reducing Load on Your Source Database
- Using the Task Log to Troubleshoot Migration Issues
- Schema Conversion
- Migrating Large Binary Objects (LOBs)
- Ongoing Replication
- Changing the User/Schema for an Oracle Target

Improving the Performance of an AWS Database Migration Service Migration

A number of factors affect the performance of your AWS DMS migration:

- Resource availability on the source

- The available network throughput

- The resource capacity of the replication server

- The ability of the target to ingest changes

- The type and distribution of source data

- The number of objects to be migrated

In our tests, we've migrated a terabyte of data in approximately 12 to 13 hours under ideal conditions. These ideal conditions included using source databases running on Amazon Elastic Compute Cloud (Amazon EC2) and in Amazon Relational Database Service (Amazon RDS) with target databases in Amazon RDS. Our source databases contained a representative amount of relatively evenly distributed data with a few large tables containing up to 250 GB of data.

Your migration's performance can be limited by one or more bottlenecks long the way. The following list shows a few things you can do to increase performance:

** Load multiple tables in parallel **
By default, AWS DMS loads eight tables at a time. You might see some performance improvement by increasing this slightly when using a very large replication server, such as a dms.c4.xlarge or larger instance. However, at some point increasing this parallelism reduces performance. If your replication server is relatively small, such as a dms.t2.medium, you'll want to reduce this number.

** Remove bottlenecks on the target **
During the migration, try to remove any processes that might compete with each other for write resources on your target database. As part of this process, disable unnecessary triggers, validation, and secondary indexes. When migrating to an Amazon RDS database, it's a good idea to disable backups and Multi-AZ on the target until you're ready to cut-over. Similarly, when migrating to non-Amazon RDS systems, disabling any logging on the target until cut over is usually a good idea.

** Use multiple tasks **
Sometimes using multiple tasks for a single migration can improve performance. If you have sets of tables that don't participate in common transactions, you might be able to divide your migration into multiple tasks. Transactional consistency is maintained within a task, so it's important that tables in separate tasks don't participate in common transactions. Additionally, each task independently reads the transaction stream, so be careful not to put too much stress on the source system.

Improving LOB performance

For information about improving LOB migration, see Migrating Large Binary Objects (LOBs).

** Optimizing change processing **

By default, AWS DMS processes changes in a *transactional mode,* which preserves transactional integrity. If you can afford temporary lapses in transactional integrity, you can use the *batch optimized apply* option instead. This option efficiently groups transactions and applies them in batches for efficiency purposes. Note that using the *batch optimized apply* option almost certainly violates any referential integrity constraints, so you should disable these during the migration process and enable them again as part of the cut-over process.

Determining the Optimum Size for a Replication Instance

Determining the correct size of your replication instance depends on several factors. The following information can help you understand the migration process and how memory and storage are used.

Tables are loaded individually; by default, eight tables are loaded at a time. While each table is loaded, the transactions for that table are cached in memory. After the available memory is used, transactions are cached to disk. When the table for those transactions is loaded, the transactions and any further transactions on that table are immediately applied to the table.

When all tables have been loaded and all outstanding cached transactions for the individual tables have been applied by AWS DMS, the source and target tables will be in sync. At this point, AWS DMS will apply transactions in a way that maintains transactional consistency. (As you can see, tables will be out of sync during the full load and while cached transactions for individual tables are being applied.)

From the preceding explanation, you can see that relatively little disk space is required to hold cached transactions. The amount of disk space used for a given migration will depend on the following:

- Table size – Large tables take longer to load and so transactions on those tables must be cached until the table is loaded. Once a table is loaded, these cached transactions are applied and are no longer held on disk.

- Data manipulation language (DML) activity – A busy database generates more transactions. These transactions must be cached until the table is loaded. Remember, though, that transactions to an individual table are applied as soon as possible after the table is loaded, until all tables are loaded. At that point, AWS DMS applies all the transactions.

- Transaction size – Data generated by large transactions must be cached. If a table accumulates 10 GB of transactions during the full load process, those transactions will need to be cached until the full load is complete.

- Total size of the migration – Large migrations take longer and the log files that are generated are large.

- Number of tasks – The more tasks, the more caching will likely be required, and the more log files will be generated.

Anecdotal evidence shows that log files consume the majority of space required by AWS DMS. The default storage configurations are usually sufficient. Replication instances that run several tasks might require more disk space. Additionally, if your database includes large and active tables, you may need to account for transactions that are cached to disk during the full load. For example, if your load will take 24 hours and you produce 2GB of transactions per hour, you may want to ensure you have 48GB of space to accommodate cached transactions.

Reducing Load on Your Source Database

During a migration, AWS DMS performs a full table scan of the source table for each table processed in parallel. Additionally, each task will periodically query the source for change information. To perform change processing, you might be required to increase the amount of data written to your databases change log. If you find you are overburdening your source database you can reduce the number of tasks and/or tables per task for your migration. If you prefer not to add load to your source, you might consider performing the migration from a read copy of your source system. However, using a read copy does increase the replication lag.

Using the Task Log to Troubleshoot Migration Issues

At times DMS may encounter issues (warnings or errors) which are only currently visible when viewing the task log. In particular, data truncation issues or row rejections due to foreign key violations are currently only visible via the task log. Therefore, it is important to review the task log when migrating a database.

Schema Conversion

AWS DMS doesn't perform schema or code conversion. You can use tools such as Oracle SQL Developer, MySQL Workbench, or pgAdmin III to move your schema if your source and target are the same database engine. If you want to convert an existing schema to a different database engine, you can use the AWS Schema Conversion Tool. It can create a target schema and also can generate and create an entire schema: tables, indexes, views, and so on. You can also use the tool to convert PL/SQL or TSQL to PgSQL and other formats. For more information on the AWS Schema Conversion Tool, see AWS Schema Conversion Tool .

Migrating Large Binary Objects (LOBs)

Migration of LOB data is done in two phases. First, the row in the LOB column is created in the target table without the LOB data. Next, the row in the target table is updated with the LOB data. This means that during the migration, the LOB columns of a table must be NULLABLE on the target database. If AWS DMS creates the target tables, it sets LOB columns to NULLABLE, even if they are NOT NULLABLE on the source table. If you create the target tables using some other mechanism, such as Import/Export, the LOB columns must be NULLABLE.

Replication tasks, by default, are set to run in **Limited LOB mode** support mode. **Limited LOB mode** typically provides the best performance but you need to ensure that the **Max LOB size** parameter setting is correct. This parameter should be set to the largest LOB size for all your tables. **Full LOB** mode support moves all of the LOBS in your tables, but the process can be slow.

If you have a table that contains a few large LOBs and mostly smaller LOBs, consider breaking up the table before migration and consolidating the table fragments as part of migration. Note that for some database engines, such as PostgreSQL, AWS DMS treats JSON data types as LOBs. Make sure that if you are using **Limited LOB mode** support mode that the **Max LOB size** parameter is set to a value that will not cause the JSON data to be truncated.

AWS Database Migration Service provides full support for using large object data types (BLOBs, CLOBs, and NCLOBs). The following source endpoints have full LOB support:

- Oracle

- Microsoft SQL Server

- ODBC

The following target endpoints have full LOB support:

- Oracle

- Microsoft SQL Server

The following target endpoints have limited LOB support. You cannot use an unlimited LOB size for these target endpoints.

- Amazon Redshift

For endpoints that have full LOB support, you can also set a size limit for LOB data types.

Ongoing Replication

AWS DMS provides comprehensive ongoing replication of data, although it replicates only a limited amount of data definition language (DDL). AWS DMS doesn't propagate items such as indexes, users, privileges, stored procedures, and other database changes not directly related to table data.

If you want to use ongoing replication, you must enable the **Multi-AZ** option on your replication instance. The **Multi-AZ** option provides high availability and failover support for the replication instance.

Changing the User/Schema for an Oracle Target

When using Oracle as a target, we assume the data should be migrated into the schema/user which is used for the target connection. If you want to migrate data to a different schema, you'll need to use a schema transformation to do so. For example, if my target endpoint connects to the user RDSMASTER and you wish to migrate from the user PERFDATA to PERFDATA, you'll need to create a transformation as follows:

```
1  {
2      "rule-type": "transformation",
3      "rule-id": "2",
4      "rule-name": "2",
5      "rule-action": "rename",
6      "rule-target": "schema",
7      "object-locator": {
8      "schema-name": "PERFDATA"
9  },
10 "value": "PERFDATA"
11 }
```

For more information about transformations, see Selection and Transformation Table Mapping using JSON.

Security

AWS Database Migration Service (AWS DMS) uses several processes to secure your data during migration. The service encrypts the storage used by your replication instance and the endpoint connection information using an AWS Key Management Service (AWS KMS) key that is unique to your AWS account. Secure Sockets Layer (SSL) is supported. AWS Database Migration Service also requires that you have the appropriate permissions if you sign in as an AWS Identity and Access Management (IAM) user.

The VPC based on the Amazon Virtual Private Cloud (Amazon VPC) service that you use with your replication instance must be associated with a security group that has rules that allow all traffic on all ports to leave (egress) the VPC. This approach allows communication from the replication instance to your source and target database endpoints, as long as correct ingress is enabled on those endpoints.

If you want to view database migration logs, you need the appropriate Amazon CloudWatch Logs permissions for the IAM role you are using.

- IAM Permissions Needed to Use AWS DMS
- Creating the IAM Roles to Use With the AWS CLI and AWS DMS API
- Fine-Grained Access Control Using Resource Names and Tags
- Setting an Encryption Key and Specifying KMS Permissions
- Network Security for AWS Database Migration Service
- Using SSL With AWS Database Migration Service
- Changing the Database Password

IAM Permissions Needed to Use AWS DMS

You need to use certain IAM permissions and IAM roles to use AWS DMS. If you are signed in as an IAM user and want to use AWS DMS, your account administrator must attach the following policy to the IAM user, group, or role that you use to run AWS DMS. For more information about IAM permissions, see the IAM User Guide.

The following set of permissions gives you access to AWS DMS, and also permissions for certain actions needed from other Amazon services such as AWS KMS, IAM, Amazon Elastic Compute Cloud (Amazon EC2), and Amazon CloudWatch. CloudWatch monitors your AWS DMS migration in real time and collects and tracks metrics that indicate the progress of your migration. You can use CloudWatch Logs to debug problems with a task.

Note
You can further restrict access to AWS DMS resources using tagging. For more information about restricting access to AWS DMS resources using tagging, see Fine-Grained Access Control Using Resource Names and Tags

```
1  {
2      "Version": "2012-10-17",
3      "Statement": [
4          {
5              "Effect": "Allow",
6              "Action": "dms:*",
7              "Resource": "*"
8          },
9          {
10              "Effect": "Allow",
11              "Action": [
12                  "kms:ListAliases",
13                  "kms:DescribeKey"
14              ],
15              "Resource": "*"
16          },
17          {
18              "Effect": "Allow",
19              "Action": [
20                  "iam:GetRole",
21                  "iam:PassRole",
22                  "iam:CreateRole",
23                  "iam:AttachRolePolicy"
24              ],
25              "Resource": "*"
26          },
27          {
28              "Effect": "Allow",
29              "Action": [
30                  "ec2:DescribeVpcs",
31                  "ec2:DescribeInternetGateways",
32                  "ec2:DescribeAvailabilityZones",
33                  "ec2:DescribeSubnets",
34                  "ec2:DescribeSecurityGroups",
35                  "ec2:ModifyNetworkInterfaceAttribute",
36                  "ec2:CreateNetworkInterface",
37                  "ec2:DeleteNetworkInterface"
38              ],
39              "Resource": "*"
```

```
40          },
41          {
42              "Effect": "Allow",
43              "Action": [
44                  "cloudwatch:Get*",
45                  "cloudwatch:List*"
46              ],
47              "Resource": "*"
48          },
49          {

50              "Effect": "Allow",
51              "Action": [
52                  "logs:DescribeLogGroups",
53                  "logs:DescribeLogStreams",
54                  "logs:FilterLogEvents",
55                  "logs:GetLogEvents"
56              ],
57              "Resource": "*"
58          },
59          {

60              "Effect": "Allow",
61              "Action": [
62                  "redshift:Describe*",
63                  "redshift:ModifyClusterIamRoles"
64              ],
65              "Resource": "*"
66          }
67      ]
68 }
```

A breakdown of these permissions might help you better understand why each one is necessary.

This section is required to allow the user to call AWS DMS API operations.

```
1 {
2          "Effect": "Allow",
3          "Action": "dms:*",
4          "Resource": "*"
5 }
```

This section is required to allow the user to list their available KMS Keys and alias for display in the console. This entry is not required if the KMSkey ARN is known and when using only the CLI.

```
1 {
2          "Effect": "Allow",
3          "Action": [
4              "kms:ListAliases",
5              "kms:DescribeKey"
6          ],
7          "Resource": "*"
8      }
```

This section is required for certain endpoint types that require a Role ARN to be passed in with the endpoint. In addition, if the required AWS DMS roles are not created ahead of time, the AWS DMS console has the ability to create the role. If all roles are configured ahead of time, all that is required in iam:GetRole and iam:PassRole. For more information about roles, see Creating the IAM Roles to Use With the AWS CLI and AWS DMS API.

```
 1  {
 2              "Effect": "Allow",
 3              "Action": [
 4                  "iam:GetRole",
 5                  "iam:PassRole",
 6                  "iam:CreateRole",
 7                  "iam:AttachRolePolicy"
 8              ],
 9              "Resource": "*"
10          }
```

This section is required since AWS DMS needs to create the EC2 instance and configure the network for the replication instance that is created. These resources exist in the customer's account, so the ability to perform these actions on behalf of the customer is required.

```
 1  {
 2              "Effect": "Allow",
 3              "Action": [
 4                  "ec2:DescribeVpcs",
 5                  "ec2:DescribeInternetGateways",
 6                  "ec2:DescribeAvailabilityZones",
 7                  "ec2:DescribeSubnets",
 8                  "ec2:DescribeSecurityGroups",
 9                  "ec2:ModifyNetworkInterfaceAttribute",
10                  "ec2:CreateNetworkInterface",
11                  "ec2:DeleteNetworkInterface"
12              ],
13              "Resource": "*"
14          }
```

This section is required to allow the user to be able to view replication instance metrics.

```
 1  {
 2              "Effect": "Allow",
 3              "Action": [
 4                  "cloudwatch:Get*",
 5                  "cloudwatch:List*"
 6              ],
 7              "Resource": "*"
 8          }
```

This section is required to allow the user to view replication logs.

```
 1  {
 2              "Effect": "Allow",
 3              "Action": [
 4                  "logs:DescribeLogGroups",
 5                  "logs:DescribeLogStreams",
 6                  "logs:FilterLogEvents",
 7                  "logs:GetLogEvents"
 8              ],
 9              "Resource": "*"
10          }
```

This section is required when using Redshift as a target. It allows AWS DMS to validate that the Redshift cluster is set up properly for AWS DMS.

```
1  {
2          "Effect": "Allow",
3          "Action": [
4              "redshift:Describe*",
5              "redshift:ModifyClusterIamRoles"
6          ],
7          "Resource": "*"
8      }
```

The AWS DMS console creates several roles that are automatically attached to your AWS account when you use the AWS DMS console. If you use the AWS Command Line Interface (AWS CLI) or the AWS DMS API for your migration, you need to add these roles to your account. For more information on adding these roles, see Creating the IAM Roles to Use With the AWS CLI and AWS DMS API.

Creating the IAM Roles to Use With the AWS CLI and AWS DMS API

If you use the AWS CLI or the AWS DMS API for your database migration, you must add three IAM roles to your AWS account before you can use the features of AWS DMS. Two of these are `dms-vpc-role` and `dms-cloudwatch-logs-role`. If you use Amazon Redshift as a target database, you must also add the IAM role `dms-access-for-endpoint` to your AWS account.

Updates to managed policies are automatic. If you are using a custom policy with the IAM roles, be sure to periodically check for updates to the managed policy in this documentation. You can view the details of the managed policy by using a combination of the `get-policy` and `get-policy-version` commands.

For example, the following `get-policy` command retrieves information on the role.

```
1 aws iam get-policy --policy-arn arn:aws:iam::aws:policy/service-role/AmazonDMSVPCManagementRole
```

The information returned from the command is as follows.

```
1 {
2     "Policy": {
3         "PolicyName": "AmazonDMSVPCManagementRole",
4         "Description": "Provides access to manage VPC settings for AWS managed customer
                configurations",
5         "CreateDate": "2015-11-18T16:33:19Z",
6         "AttachmentCount": 1,
7         "IsAttachable": true,
8         "PolicyId": "ANPAJHKIGMBQI4AEFFSYO",
9         "DefaultVersionId": "v3",
10        "Path": "/service-role/",
11        "Arn": "arn:aws:iam::aws:policy/service-role/AmazonDMSVPCManagementRole",
12        "UpdateDate": "2016-05-23T16:29:57Z"
13    }
14 }
```

The following `get-policy-version` command retrieves policy information.

```
1 aws iam get-policy-version --policy-arn arn:aws:iam::aws:policy/service-role/
      AmazonDMSVPCManagementRole --version-id v3
```

The information returned from the command is as follows.

```
1 {
2     "PolicyVersion": {
3         "CreateDate": "2016-05-23T16:29:57Z",
4         "VersionId": "v3",
5         "Document": {
6         "Version": "2012-10-17",
7         "Statement": [
8             {
9                 "Action": [
10                    "ec2:CreateNetworkInterface",
11                    "ec2:DescribeAvailabilityZones",
12                    "ec2:DescribeInternetGateways",
13                    "ec2:DescribeSecurityGroups",
14                    "ec2:DescribeSubnets",
15                    "ec2:DescribeVpcs",
16                    "ec2:DeleteNetworkInterface",
```

```
17                "ec2:ModifyNetworkInterfaceAttribute"
18            ],
19            "Resource": "*",
20            "Effect": "Allow"
21        }
22      ]
23    },
24    "IsDefaultVersion": true
25    }
26 }
```

The same commands can be used to get information on the `AmazonDMSCloudWatchLogsRole` and the `AmazonDMSRedshiftS3Role` managed policy.

Note

If you use the AWS DMS console for your database migration, these roles are added to your AWS account automatically.

The following procedures create the `dms-vpc-role`, `dms-cloudwatch-logs-role`, and `dms-access-for-endpoint` IAM roles.

To create the `dms-vpc-role` IAM role for use with the AWS CLI or AWS DMS API

1. Create a JSON file with the IAM policy following. Name the JSON file dmsAssumeRolePolicyDocument. json.

```
1  {
2    "Version": "2012-10-17",
3    "Statement": [
4    {
5      "Effect": "Allow",
6      "Principal": {
7        "Service": "dms.amazonaws.com"
8      },
9    "Action": "sts:AssumeRole"
10   }
11  ]
12 }
```

```
1 Create the role using the AWS CLI using the following command\.
```

```
1 aws iam create-role --role-name dms-vpc-role --assume-role-policy-document file://
    dmsAssumeRolePolicyDocument.json
```

1. Attach the `AmazonDMSVPCManagementRole` policy to `dms-vpc-role` using the following command.

```
1 aws iam attach-role-policy --role-name dms-vpc-role --policy-arn arn:aws:iam::aws:policy/service
    -role/AmazonDMSVPCManagementRole
```

To create the `dms-cloudwatch-logs-role` IAM role for use with the AWS CLI or AWS DMS API

1. Create a JSON file with the IAM policy following. Name the JSON file dmsAssumeRolePolicyDocument2 .json.

```
1  {
2    "Version": "2012-10-17",
3    "Statement": [
4    {
5      "Effect": "Allow",
```

```
6        "Principal": {
7          "Service": "dms.amazonaws.com"
8        },
9      "Action": "sts:AssumeRole"
10     }
11   ]
12 }
```

```
1 Create the role using the AWS CLI using the following command\.
```

```
1 aws iam create-role --role-name dms-cloudwatch-logs-role --assume-role-policy-document file://
    dmsAssumeRolePolicyDocument2.json
```

1. Attach the `AmazonDMSCloudWatchLogsRole` policy to `dms-cloudwatch-logs-role` using the following command.

```
1 aws iam attach-role-policy --role-name dms-cloudwatch-logs-role --policy-arn arn:aws:iam::aws:
    policy/service-role/AmazonDMSCloudWatchLogsRole
```

If you use Amazon Redshift as your target database, you must create the IAM role `dms-access-for-endpoint` to provide access to Amazon S3 (S3).

To create the `dms-access-for-endpoint` IAM role for use with Amazon Redshift as a target database

1. Create a JSON file with the IAM policy following. Name the JSON file `dmsAssumeRolePolicyDocument3.json`.

```
1  {
2    "Version": "2012-10-17",
3    "Statement": [
4      {
5        "Sid": "1",
6        "Effect": "Allow",
7        "Principal": {
8          "Service": "dms.amazonaws.com"
9        },
10       "Action": "sts:AssumeRole"
11     },
12     {
13       "Sid": "2",
14       "Effect": "Allow",
15       "Principal": {
16         "Service": "redshift.amazonaws.com"
17       },
18       "Action": "sts:AssumeRole"
19     }
20   ]
21 }
```

2. Create the role using the AWS CLI using the following command.

```
1  aws iam create-role --role-name dms-access-for-endpoint --assume-role-policy-document file://
     dmsAssumeRolePolicyDocument3.json
```

1. Attach the `AmazonDMSRedshiftS3Role` policy to `dms-access-for-endpoint` role using the following command.

```
1 aws iam attach-role-policy --role-name dms-access-for-endpoint \
2     --policy-arn arn:aws:iam::aws:policy/service-role/AmazonDMSRedshiftS3Role
```

You should now have the IAM policies in place to use the AWS CLI or AWS DMS API.

Fine-Grained Access Control Using Resource Names and Tags

You can use ARN-based resource names and resource tags to manage access to AWS DMS resources. You do this by defining permitted action or including conditional statements in IAM policies.

Using Resource Names to Control Access

You can create an IAM user account and assign a policy based on the AWS DMS resource's Amazon Resource Name (ARN).

The following policy denies access to the AWS DMS replication instance with the ARN *arn:aws:dms:us-east-1:152683116:rep:DOH67ZTOXGLIXMIHKITV*:

```
1  {
2      "Version": "2012-10-17",
3      "Statement": [
4          {
5              "Action": [
6                  "dms:*"
7              ],
8              "Effect": "Deny",
9              "Resource": "arn:aws:dms:us-east-1:152683116:rep:DOH67ZTOXGLIXMIHKITV"
10         }
11     ]
12 }
```

For example, the following commands would fail when the policy is in effect:

```
1  $ aws dms delete-replication-instance
2    --replication-instance-arn "arn:aws:dms:us-east-1:152683116:rep:DOH67ZTOXGLIXMIHKITV"
3
4  A client error (AccessDeniedException) occurred when calling the DeleteReplicationInstance
5  operation: User: arn:aws:iam::152683116:user/dmstestusr is not authorized to perform:
6  dms:DeleteReplicationInstance on resource: arn:aws:dms:us-east-1:152683116:rep:
     DOH67ZTOXGLIXMIHKITV
7
8  $ aws dms modify-replication-instance
9    --replication-instance-arn "arn:aws:dms:us-east-1:152683116:rep:DOH67ZTOXGLIXMIHKITV"
10
11 A client error (AccessDeniedException) occurred when calling the ModifyReplicationInstance
12 operation: User: arn:aws:iam::152683116:user/dmstestusr is not authorized to perform:
13 dms:ModifyReplicationInstance on resource: arn:aws:dms:us-east-1:152683116:rep:
     DOH67ZTOXGLIXMIHKITV
```

You can also specify IAM policies that limit access to AWS DMS endpoints and replication tasks.

The following policy limits access to an AWS DMS endpoint using the endpoint's ARN:

```
1  {
2      "Version": "2012-10-17",
3      "Statement": [
4          {
5              "Action": [
6                  "dms:*"
7              ],
8              "Effect": "Deny",
```

```
9            "Resource": "arn:aws:dms:us-east-1:152683116:endpoint:D6E37YBXTNHOA6XRQSZCUGX"
10        }
11    ]
12 }
```

For example, the following commands would fail when the policy using the endpoint's ARN is in effect:

```
1 $ aws dms delete-endpoint
2    --endpoint-arn "arn:aws:dms:us-east-1:152683116:endpoint:D6E37YBXTNHOA6XRQSZCUGX"
3
4 A client error (AccessDeniedException) occurred when calling the DeleteEndpoint operation:
5 User: arn:aws:iam::152683116:user/dmstestusr is not authorized to perform: dms:DeleteEndpoint
6 on resource: arn:aws:dms:us-east-1:152683116:endpoint:D6E37YBXTNHOA6XRQSZCUGX
7
8 $ aws dms modify-endpoint
9    --endpoint-arn "arn:aws:dms:us-east-1:152683116:endpoint:D6E37YBXTNHOA6XRQSZCUGX"
10
11 A client error (AccessDeniedException) occurred when calling the ModifyEndpoint operation:
12 User: arn:aws:iam::152683116:user/dmstestusr is not authorized to perform: dms:ModifyEndpoint
13 on resource: arn:aws:dms:us-east-1:152683116:endpoint:D6E37YBXTNHOA6XRQSZCUGX
```

The following policy limits access to an AWS DMS task using the task's ARN:

```
1 {
2    "Version": "2012-10-17",
3    "Statement": [
4        {
5            "Action": [
6                "dms:*"
7            ],
8            "Effect": "Deny",
9            "Resource": "arn:aws:dms:us-east-1:152683116:task:UO3YR4N47DXH3ATT4YMWOIT"
10        }
11    ]
12 }
```

For example, the following commands would fail when the policy using the task's ARN is in effect:

```
1 $ aws dms delete-replication-task
2    --replication-task-arn "arn:aws:dms:us-east-1:152683116:task:UO3YR4N47DXH3ATT4YMWOIT"
3
4 A client error (AccessDeniedException) occurred when calling the DeleteReplicationTask operation
     :
5 User: arn:aws:iam::152683116:user/dmstestusr is not authorized to perform: dms:
     DeleteReplicationTask
6 on resource: arn:aws:dms:us-east-1:152683116:task:UO3YR4N47DXH3ATT4YMWOIT
```

Using Tags to Control Access

AWS DMS defines a set of common key/value pairs that are available for use in customer defined policies without any additional tagging requirements. For more information about tagging AWS DMS resources, see Tagging AWS Database Migration Service Resources.

The following lists the standard tags available for use with AWS DMS:

- aws:CurrentTime – Represents the request date and time, allowing the restriction of access based on temporal criteria.

- aws:EpochTime – This tag is similar to the aws:CurrentTime tag above, except that the current time is represented as the number of seconds elapsed since the Unix Epoch.

- aws:MultiFactorAuthPresent – This is a boolean tag that indicates whether or not the request was signed via multi-factor authentication.

- aws:MultiFactorAuthAge – Provides access to the age of the multi-factor authentication token (in seconds).

- aws:principaltype - Provides access to the type of principal (user, account, federated user, etc.) for the current request.

- aws:SourceIp - Represents the source ip address for the user issuing the request.

- aws:UserAgent – Provides information about the client application requesting a resource.

- aws:userid – Provides access to the ID of the user issuing the request.

- aws:username – Provides access to the name of the user issuing the request.

- dms:InstanceClass – Provides access to the compute size of the replication instance host(s).

- dms:StorageSize - Provides access to the storage volume size (in GB).

You can also define your own tags. Customer-defined tags are simple key/value pairs that are persisted in the AWS Tagging service and can be added to AWS DMS resources, including replication instances, endpoints, and tasks. These tags are matched via IAM "Conditional" statements in policies, and are referenced using a specific conditional tag. The tag keys are prefixed with "dms", the resource type, and the "tag" prefix. The following shows the tag format:

```
1 dms:{resource type}-tag/{tag key}={tag value}
```

For example, suppose you want to define a policy that only allows an API call to succeed for a replication instance that contains the tag "stage=production". The following conditional statement would match a resource with the given tag:

```
1 "Condition":
2 {
3     "streq":
4         {
5             "dms:rep-tag/stage":"production"
6         }
7 }
```

You would add the following tag to a replication instance that would match this policy condition:

```
1 stage production
```

In addition to tags already assigned to AWS DMS resources, policies can also be written to limit the tag keys and values that may be applied to a given resource. In this case, the tag prefix would be "req".

For example, the following policy statement would limit the tags that a user can assign to a given resource to a specific list of allowed values:

```
1 "Condition":
2 {
3     "streq":
4         {
5             "dms:req-tag/stage": [ "production", "development", "testing" ]
6         }
7 }
```

The following policy examples limit access to an AWS DMS resource based on resource tags.

The following policy limits access to a replication instance where the tag value is "Desktop" and the tag key is "Env":

```
1  {
2      "Version": "2012-10-17",
3      "Statement": [
4          {
5              "Action": [
6                  "dms:*"
7              ],
8              "Effect": "Deny",
9              "Resource": "*",
10             "Condition": {
11                 "StringEquals": {
12                     "dms:rep-tag/Env": [
13                         "Desktop"
14                     ]
15                 }
16             }
17         }
18     ]
19 }
```

The following commands succeed or fail based on the IAM policy that restricts access when the tag value is "Desktop" and the tag key is "Env":

```
1  $ aws dms list-tags-for-resource
2      --resource-name arn:aws:dms:us-east-1:152683116:rep:46DHOU7JOJYOJXWDOZNFEN
3      --endpoint-url http://localhost:8000
4  {
5      "TagList": [
6          {
7              "Value": "Desktop",
8              "Key": "Env"
9          }
10     ]
11 }
12
13 $ aws dms delete-replication-instance
14     --replication-instance-arn "arn:aws:dms:us-east-1:152683116:rep:46DHOU7JOJYOJXWDOZNFEN"
15 A client error (AccessDeniedException) occurred when calling the DeleteReplicationInstance
16 operation: User: arn:aws:iam::152683116:user/dmstestusr is not authorized to perform:
17 dms:DeleteReplicationInstance on resource: arn:aws:dms:us-east-1:152683116:rep:46
       DHOU7JOJYOJXWDOZNFEN
18
19 $ aws dms modify-replication-instance
20     --replication-instance-arn "arn:aws:dms:us-east-1:152683116:rep:46DHOU7JOJYOJXWDOZNFEN"
21
22 A client error (AccessDeniedException) occurred when calling the ModifyReplicationInstance
23 operation: User: arn:aws:iam::152683116:user/dmstestusr is not authorized to perform:
24 dms:ModifyReplicationInstance on resource: arn:aws:dms:us-east-1:152683116:rep:46
       DHOU7JOJYOJXWDOZNFEN
25
26 $ aws dms add-tags-to-resource
```

```
27    --resource-name arn:aws:dms:us-east-1:152683116:rep:46DHOU7JOJYOJXWDOZNFEN
28    --tags Key=CostCenter,Value=1234
29
30 A client error (AccessDeniedException) occurred when calling the AddTagsToResource
31 operation: User: arn:aws:iam::152683116:user/dmstestusr is not authorized to perform:
32 dms:AddTagsToResource on resource: arn:aws:dms:us-east-1:152683116:rep:46DHOU7JOJYOJXWDOZNFEN
33
34 $ aws dms remove-tags-from-resource
35    --resource-name arn:aws:dms:us-east-1:152683116:rep:46DHOU7JOJYOJXWDOZNFEN
36    --tag-keys Env
37
38 A client error (AccessDeniedException) occurred when calling the RemoveTagsFromResource
39 operation: User: arn:aws:iam::152683116:user/dmstestusr is not authorized to perform:
40 dms:RemoveTagsFromResource on resource: arn:aws:dms:us-east-1:152683116:rep:46
       DHOU7JOJYOJXWDOZNFEN
```

The following policy limits access to a AWS DMS endpoint where the tag value is "Desktop" and the tag key is "Env":

```
1  {
2      "Version": "2012-10-17",
3      "Statement": [
4          {
5              "Action": [
6                  "dms:*"
7              ],
8              "Effect": "Deny",
9              "Resource": "*",
10             "Condition": {
11                 "StringEquals": {
12                     "dms:endpoint-tag/Env": [
13                         "Desktop"
14                     ]
15                 }
16             }
17         }
18     ]
19 }
```

The following commands succeed or fail based on the IAM policy that restricts access when the tag value is "Desktop" and the tag key is "Env":

```
1  $ aws dms list-tags-for-resource
2      --resource-name arn:aws:dms:us-east-1:152683116:endpoint:J2YCZPNGOLFY52344IZWA6I
3  {
4      "TagList": [
5          {
6              "Value": "Desktop",
7              "Key": "Env"
8          }
9      ]
10 }
11
12 $ aws dms delete-endpoint
13     --endpoint-arn "arn:aws:dms:us-east-1:152683116:endpoint:J2YCZPNGOLFY52344IZWA6I"
14
```

```
15 A client error (AccessDeniedException) occurred when calling the DeleteEndpoint
16 operation: User: arn:aws:iam::152683116:user/dmstestusr is not authorized to perform:
17 dms:DeleteEndpoint on resource: arn:aws:dms:us-east-1:152683116:endpoint:J2YCZPNGOLFY52344IZWA6I
18
19 $ aws dms modify-endpoint
20     --endpoint-arn "arn:aws:dms:us-east-1:152683116:endpoint:J2YCZPNGOLFY52344IZWA6I"
21
22 A client error (AccessDeniedException) occurred when calling the ModifyEndpoint
23 operation: User: arn:aws:iam::152683116:user/dmstestusr is not authorized to perform:
24 dms:ModifyEndpoint on resource: arn:aws:dms:us-east-1:152683116:endpoint:J2YCZPNGOLFY52344IZWA6I
25
26 $ aws dms add-tags-to-resource
27     --resource-name arn:aws:dms:us-east-1:152683116:endpoint:J2YCZPNGOLFY52344IZWA6I
28     --tags Key=CostCenter,Value=1234
29
30 A client error (AccessDeniedException) occurred when calling the AddTagsToResource
31 operation: User: arn:aws:iam::152683116:user/dmstestusr is not authorized to perform:
32 dms:AddTagsToResource on resource: arn:aws:dms:us-east-1:152683116:endpoint:
        J2YCZPNGOLFY52344IZWA6I
33
34 $ aws dms remove-tags-from-resource
35     --resource-name arn:aws:dms:us-east-1:152683116:endpoint:J2YCZPNGOLFY52344IZWA6I
36     --tag-keys Env
37
38 A client error (AccessDeniedException) occurred when calling the RemoveTagsFromResource
39 operation: User: arn:aws:iam::152683116:user/dmstestusr is not authorized to perform:
40 dms:RemoveTagsFromResource on resource: arn:aws:dms:us-east-1:152683116:endpoint:
        J2YCZPNGOLFY52344IZWA6I
```

The following policy limits access to a replication task where the tag value is "Desktop" and the tag key is "Env":

```
1  {
2      "Version": "2012-10-17",
3      "Statement": [
4          {
5              "Action": [
6                  "dms:*"
7              ],
8              "Effect": "Deny",
9              "Resource": "*",
10             "Condition": {
11                 "StringEquals": {
12                     "dms:task-tag/Env": [
13                         "Desktop"
14                     ]
15                 }
16             }
17         }
18     ]
19 }
```

The following commands succeed or fail based on the IAM policy that restricts access when the tag value is "Desktop" and the tag key is "Env":

```
1 $ aws dms list-tags-for-resource
2     --resource-name arn:aws:dms:us-east-1:152683116:task:RB7N24J2XBUPS3RFABZTG3
```

```
 3 {
 4     "TagList": [
 5         {
 6             "Value": "Desktop",
 7             "Key": "Env"
 8         }
 9     ]
10 }
11
12 $ aws dms delete-replication-task
13     --replication-task-arn "arn:aws:dms:us-east-1:152683116:task:RB7N24J2XBUPS3RFABZTG3"
14
15 A client error (AccessDeniedException) occurred when calling the DeleteReplicationTask
16 operation: User: arn:aws:iam::152683116:user/dmstestusr is not authorized to perform:
17 dms:DeleteReplicationTask on resource: arn:aws:dms:us-east-1:152683116:task:
       RB7N24J2XBUPS3RFABZTG3
18
19 $ aws dms add-tags-to-resource
20     --resource-name arn:aws:dms:us-east-1:152683116:task:RB7N24J2XBUPS3RFABZTG3
21     --tags Key=CostCenter,Value=1234
22
23 A client error (AccessDeniedException) occurred when calling the AddTagsToResource
24 operation: User: arn:aws:iam::152683116:user/dmstestusr is not authorized to perform:
25 dms:AddTagsToResource on resource: arn:aws:dms:us-east-1:152683116:task:RB7N24J2XBUPS3RFABZTG3
26
27 $ aws dms remove-tags-from-resource
28     --resource-name arn:aws:dms:us-east-1:152683116:task:RB7N24J2XBUPS3RFABZTG3
29     --tag-keys Env
30
31 A client error (AccessDeniedException) occurred when calling the RemoveTagsFromResource
32 operation: User: arn:aws:iam::152683116:user/dmstestusr is not authorized to perform:
33 dms:RemoveTagsFromResource on resource: arn:aws:dms:us-east-1:152683116:task:
       RB7N24J2XBUPS3RFABZTG3
```

Setting an Encryption Key and Specifying KMS Permissions

AWS DMS encrypts the storage used by a replication instance and the endpoint connection information. To encrypt the storage used by a replication instance, AWS DMS uses an AWS Key Management Service (KMS) key that is unique to your AWS account. You can view and manage this key with KMS. You can use the default KMS key in your account (**aws/dms**) or you can create a custom KMS key. If you have an existing KMS key, you can also use that key for encryption.

The default KMS key (**aws/dms**) is created when you first launch a replication instance and you have not selected a custom KMS master key from the **Advanced** section of the **Create Replication Instance** page. If you use the default KMS key, the only permissions you need to grant to the IAM user account you are using for migration are **kms:ListAliases** and **kms:DescribeKey**. For more information about using the default KMS key, see IAM Permissions Needed to Use AWS DMS.

To use a custom KMS key, assign permissions for the custom KMS key using one of the following options.

- Add the IAM user account used for the migration as a Key Administrator/Key User for the KMS custom key. This will ensure that necessary KMS permissions are granted to the IAM user account. Note that this action is in addition to the IAM permissions that you must grant to the IAM user account to use AWS DMS. For more information about granting permissions to a key user, see Allows Key Users to Use the CMK.

- If you do not want to add the IAM user account as a Key Administrator/Key User for your custom KMS key, then add the following additional permissions to the IAM permissions that you must grant to the IAM user account to use AWS DMS.

```
1  {
2          "Effect": "Allow",
3          "Action": [
4              "kms:ListAliases",
5              "kms:DescribeKey",
6              "kms:CreateGrant",
7              "kms:Encrypt",
8              "kms:ReEncrypt*"
9          ],
10         "Resource": "*"
11     },
```

AWS DMS does not work with KMS Key Aliases, but you can use the KMS key's Amazon Resource Number (ARN) when specifying the KMS key information. For more information on creating your own KMS keys and giving users access to a KMS key, see the *KMS Developer Guide*.

If you don't specify a KMS key identifier, then AWS DMS uses your default encryption key. KMS creates the default encryption key for AWS DMS for your AWS account. Your AWS account has a different default encryption key for each AWS region.

To manage the KMS keys used for encrypting your AWS DMS resources, you use KMS. You can find KMS in the AWS Management Console by choosing **Identity & Access Management** on the console home page and then choosing **Encryption Keys** on the navigation pane. KMS combines secure, highly available hardware and software to provide a key management system scaled for the cloud. Using KMS, you can create encryption keys and define the policies that control how these keys can be used. KMS supports AWS CloudTrail, so you can audit key usage to verify that keys are being used appropriately. Your KMS keys can be used in combination with AWS DMS and supported AWS services such as Amazon RDS, Amazon Simple Storage Service (Amazon S3), Amazon Redshift, and Amazon Elastic Block Store (Amazon EBS).

Once you have created your AWS DMS resources with the KMS key, you cannot change the encryption key for those resources. Make sure to determine your encryption key requirements before you create your AWS DMS resources.

Network Security for AWS Database Migration Service

The security requirements for the network you create when using AWS Database Migration Service depend on how you configure the network. The general rules for network security for AWS DMS are as follows:

- The replication instance must have access to the source and target endpoints. The security group for the replication instance must have network ACLs or rules that allow egress from the instance out on the database port to the database endpoints.

- Database endpoints must include network ACLs and security group rules that allow incoming access from the replication instance. You can achieve this using the replication instance's security group, the private IP address, the public IP address, or the NAT gateway's public address, depending on your configuration.

- If your network uses a VPN Tunnel, the EC2 instance acting as the NAT Gateway must use a security group that has rules that allow the replication instance to send traffic through it.

By default, the VPC security group used by the AWS DMS replication instance has rules that allow egress to 0.0.0.0/0 on all ports. If you modify this security group or use your own security group, egress must, at a minimum, be permitted to the source and target endpoints on the respective database ports.

The network configurations you can use for database migration each require specific security considerations:

- Configuration with All Database Migration Components in One VPC — The security group used by the endpoints must allow ingress on the database port from the replication instance. Ensure that the security group used by the replication instance has ingress to the endpoints, or you can create a rule in the security group used by the endpoints that allows the private IP address of the replication instance access.

- Configuration with Two VPCs — The security group used by the replication instance must have a rule for the VPC range and the DB port on the database.

- Configuration for a Network to a VPC Using AWS Direct Connect or a VPN — a VPN tunnel allowing traffic to tunnel from the VPC into an on- premises VPN. In this configuration, the VPC includes a routing rule that sends traffic destined for a specific IP address or range to a host that can bridge traffic from the VPC into the on-premises VPN. If this case, the NAT host includes its own Security Group settings that must allow traffic from the Replication Instance's private IP address or security group into the NAT instance.

- Configuration for a Network to a VPC Using the Internet — The VPC security group must include routing rules that send traffic not destined for the VPC to the Internet gateway. In this configuration, the connection to the endpoint appears to come from the public IP address on the replication instance.

- Configuration with an Amazon RDS DB instance not in a VPC to a DB instance in a VPC Using ClassicLink — When the source or target Amazon RDS DB instance is not in a VPC and does not share a security group with the VPC where the replication instance is located, you can setup a proxy server and use ClassicLink to connect the source and target databases.

- **Source endpoint is outside the VPC used by the replication instance and uses a NAT gateway** — You can configure a network address translation (NAT) gateway using a single Elastic IP Address bound to a single Elastic Network Interface, which then receives a NAT identifier (nat-#####). If the VPC includes a default route to that NAT Gateway instead of the Internet Gateway, the replication instance will instead appear to contact the Database Endpoint using the public IP address of the Internet Gateway. In this case, the ingress to the Database Endpoint outside the VPC needs to allow ingress from the NAT address instead of the Replication Instance's public IP Address.

Using SSL With AWS Database Migration Service

You can encrypt connections for source and target endpoints by using Secure Sockets Layer (SSL). To do so, you can use the AWS DMS Management Console or AWS DMS API to assign a certificate to an endpoint. You can also use the AWS DMS console to manage your certificates.

Not all databases use SSL in the same way. Amazon Aurora with MySQL compatibility uses the server name, the endpoint of the primary instance in the cluster, as the endpoint for SSL. An Amazon Redshift endpoint already uses an SSL connection and does not require an SSL connection set up by AWS DMS. An Oracle endpoint requires additional steps; for more information, see SSL Support for an Oracle Endpoint.

- Limitations on Using SSL with AWS Database Migration Service
- Managing Certificates
- Enabling SSL for a MySQL-compatible, PostgreSQL, or SQL Server Endpoint
- SSL Support for an Oracle Endpoint

To assign a certificate to an endpoint, you provide the root certificate or the chain of intermediate CA certificates leading up to the root (as a certificate bundle), that was used to sign the server SSL certificate that is deployed on your endpoint. Certificates are accepted as PEM formatted X509 files, only. When you import a certificate, you receive an Amazon Resource Name (ARN) that you can use to specify that certificate for an endpoint. If you use Amazon RDS, you can download the root CA and certificate bundle provided by Amazon RDS at https://s3.amazonaws.com/rds-downloads/rds-combined-ca-bundle.pem.

You can choose from several SSL modes to use for your SSL certificate verification.

- **none** – The connection is not encrypted. This option is not secure, but requires less overhead.

- **require** – The connection is encrypted using SSL (TLS) but no CA verification is made. This option is more secure, and requires more overhead.

- **verify-ca** – The connection is encrypted. This option is more secure, and requires more overhead. This option verifies the server certificate.

- **verify-full** – The connection is encrypted. This option is more secure, and requires more overhead. This option verifies the server certificate and verifies that the server hostname matches the hostname attribute for the certificate.

Not all SSL modes work with all database endpoints. The following table shows which SSL modes are supported for each database engine.

DB Engine	none	require	verify-ca	verify-full
MySQL/MariaDB/Amazon Aurora MySQL	Default	Not supported	Supported	Supported
Microsoft SQL Server	Default	Supported	Not Supported	Supported
PostgreSQL	Default	Supported	Supported	Supported
Amazon Redshift	Default	SSL not enabled	SSL not enabled	SSL not enabled
Oracle	Default	Not supported	Supported	Not Supported
SAP ASE	Default	SSL not enabled	SSL not enabled	Supported
MongoDB	Default	Supported	Not Supported	Supported

Limitations on Using SSL with AWS Database Migration Service

- SSL connections to Amazon Redshift target endpoints are not supported. AWS DMS uses an S3 bucket to transfer data to the Redshift database. This transmission is encrypted by Amazon Redshift by default.

- SQL timeouts can occur when performing CDC tasks with SSL-enabled Oracle endpoints. If you have this issue, where CDC counters don't reflect the expected numbers, set the `MinimumTransactionSize` parameter from the `ChangeProcessingTuning` section of task settings to a lower value, starting with a value as low as 100. For more information about the `MinimumTransactionSize` parameter, see Change Processing Tuning Settings.

- Certificates can only be imported in the .PEM and .SSO (Oracle wallet) formats.

- If your server SSL certificate is signed by an intermediate CA, make sure the entire certificate chain leading from the intermediate CA up to the root CA is imported as a single .PEM file.

- If you are using self-signed certificates on your server, choose **require** as your SSL mode. The **require** SSL mode implicitly trusts the server's SSL certificate and will not try to validate that the certificate was signed by a CA.

Managing Certificates

You can use the DMS console to view and manage your SSL certificates. You can also import your certificates using the DMS console.

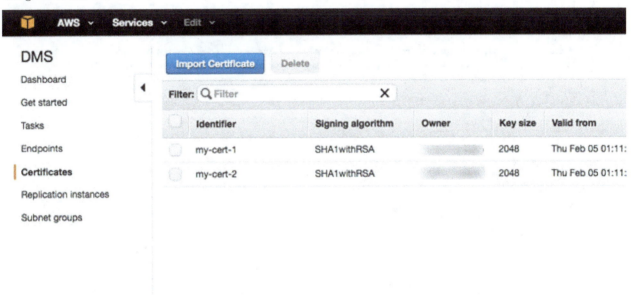

Enabling SSL for a MySQL-compatible, PostgreSQL, or SQL Server Endpoint

You can add an SSL connection to a newly created endpoint or to an existing endpoint.

To create an AWS DMS endpoint with SSL

1. Sign in to the AWS Management Console and choose AWS Database Migration Service. **Note** If you are signed in as an AWS Identity and Access Management (IAM) user, you must have the appropriate permissions to access AWS DMS. For more information on the permissions required for database migration, see IAM Permissions Needed to Use AWS DMS.

2. In the navigation pane, choose **Certificates**.

3. Choose **Import Certificate**.

4. Upload the certificate you want to use for encrypting the connection to an endpoint. **Note** You can also upload a certificate using the AWS DMS console when you create or modify an endpoint by selecting **Add new CA certificate** on the **Create database endpoint** page.

5. Create an endpoint as described in Step 3: Specify Source and Target Endpoints

To modify an existing AWS DMS endpoint to use SSL:

1. Sign in to the AWS Management Console and choose AWS Database Migration Service. **Note** If you are signed in as an AWS Identity and Access Management (IAM) user, you must have the appropriate permissions to access AWS DMS. For more information on the permissions required for database migration, see IAM Permissions Needed to Use AWS DMS.

2. In the navigation pane, choose **Certificates**.

3. Choose **Import Certificate**.

4. Upload the certificate you want to use for encrypting the connection to an endpoint. **Note** You can also upload a certificate using the AWS DMS console when you create or modify an endpoint by selecting **Add new CA certificate** on the **Create database endpoint** page.

5. In the navigation pane, choose **Endpoints**, select the endpoint you want to modify, and choose **Modify**.

6. Choose an **SSL mode**.

   If you select either the **verify-ca** or **verify-full** mode, you must specify the **CA certificate** that you want to use, as shown following.

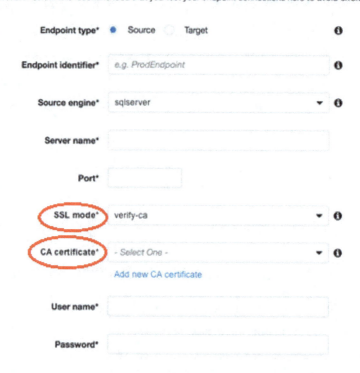

7. Choose **Modify**.

8. When the endpoint has been modified, select the endpoint and choose **Test connection** to determine if the SSL connection is working.

After you create your source and target endpoints, create a task that uses these endpoints. For more information on creating a task, see Step 4: Create a Task.

SSL Support for an Oracle Endpoint

Oracle endpoints in AWS DMS support `none` and `verify-ca` SSL modes. To use SSL with an Oracle endpoint, you must upload the Oracle wallet for the endpoint instead of .pem certificate files.

- Using an Existing Certificate for Oracle SSL
- Using a Self-Signed Certificate for Oracle SSL

Using an Existing Certificate for Oracle SSL

To use an existing Oracle client installation to create the Oracle wallet file from the CA certificate file, do the following steps.

To use an existing Oracle client installation for Oracle SSL with AWS DMS

1. Set the ORACLE_HOME system variable to the location of your dbhome_1 directory by running the following command:

```
1 prompt>export ORACLE_HOME=/home/user/app/user/product/12.1.0/dbhome_1
```

2. Append $ORACLE_HOME/lib to the LD_LIBRARY_PATH system variable.

```
1 prompt>export LD_LIBRARY_PATH=$LD_LIBRARY_PATH:$ORACLE_HOME/lib
```

3. Create a directory for the Oracle wallet at $ORACLE_HOME/ssl_wallet.

```
1 prompt>mkdir $ORACLE_HOME/ssl_wallet
```

4. Put the CA certificate .pem file in the ssl_wallet directory. Amazon RDS customers can download the RDS CA certificates file from https://s3.amazonaws.com/rds-downloads/rds-ca-2015-root.pem.

5. Run the following commands to create the Oracle wallet:

```
1 prompt>orapki wallet create -wallet $ORACLE_HOME/ssl_wallet -auto_login_only
2
3 prompt>orapki wallet add -wallet $ORACLE_HOME/ssl_wallet -trusted_cert -cert
4    $ORACLE_HOME/ssl_wallet/ca-cert.pem -auto_login_only
```

When you have completed the steps previous, you can import the wallet file with the ImportCertificate API by specifying the certificate-wallet parameter. You can then use the imported wallet certificate when you select `verify-ca` as the SSL mode when creating or modifying your Oracle endpoint.

Note
Oracle wallets are binary files. AWS DMS accepts these files as-is.

Using a Self-Signed Certificate for Oracle SSL

To use a self-signed certificate for Oracle SSL, do the following.

To use a self-signed certificate for Oracle SSL with AWS DMS

1. Create a directory you will use to work with the self-signed certificate.

```
1 mkdir <SELF_SIGNED_CERT_DIRECTORY>
```

2. Change into the directory you created in the previous step.

```
1 cd <SELF_SIGNED_CERT_DIRECTORY>
```

3. Create a root key.

```
1 openssl genrsa -out self-rootCA.key 2048
```

4. Self sign a root certificate using the root key you created in the previous step.

```
1 openssl req -x509 -new -nodes -key self-rootCA.key
2     -sha256 -days 1024 -out self-rootCA.pem
```

5. Create an Oracle wallet directory for the Oracle database.

```
1 mkdir $ORACLE_HOME/self_signed_ssl_wallet
```

6. Create a new Oracle wallet.

```
1 orapki wallet create -wallet $ORACLE_HOME/self_signed_ssl_wallet
2     -pwd <password> -auto_login_local
```

7. Add the root certificate to the Oracle wallet.

```
1 orapki wallet add -wallet $ORACLE_HOME/self_signed_ssl_wallet
2     -trusted_cert -cert self-rootCA.pem -pwd <password>
```

8. List the contents of the Oracle wallet. The list should include the root certificate.

```
1 orapki wallet display -wallet $ORACLE_HOME/self_signed_ssl_wallet
```

9. Generate the Certificate Signing Request (CSR) using the ORAPKI utility.

```
1 orapki wallet add -wallet $ORACLE_HOME/self_signed_ssl_wallet
2     -dn "CN=`hostname`, OU=Sample Department, O=Sample Company,
3     L=NYC, ST=NY, C=US" -keysize 1024 -pwd <password>
```

10. List the contents of the Oracle wallet. The list should include the CSR.

```
1 orapki wallet display -wallet $ORACLE_HOME/self_signed_ssl_wallet
```

11. Export the CSR from the Oracle wallet.

```
1 orapki wallet export -wallet $ORACLE_HOME/self_signed_ssl_wallet
2     -dn "CN=`hostname`, OU=Sample Department, O=Sample Company,
3     L=NYC, ST=NY, C=US" -request self-signed-oracle.csr -pwd <password>
```

12. Sign the CSR using the root certificate.

```
1 openssl x509 -req -in self-signed-oracle.csr -CA self-rootCA.pem
2     -CAkey self-rootCA.key -CAcreateserial -out self-signed-oracle.crt
3     -days 365 -sha256
```

13. Add the Client certificate to the server wallet.

```
1 orapki wallet add -wallet $ORACLE_HOME/self_signed_ssl_wallet
2     -user_cert -cert self-signed-oracle.crt -pwd <password>
```

14. List the content of the Oracle wallet.

```
1 orapki wallet display -wallet $ORACLE_HOME/self_signed_ssl_wallet
```

15. Configure *sqlnet.ora* file ($ORACLE_HOME/network/admin/sqlnet.ora).

```
1 WALLET_LOCATION =
2   (SOURCE =
3     (METHOD = FILE)
4     (METHOD_DATA =
5       (DIRECTORY = <ORACLE_HOME>/self_signed_ssl_wallet)
6     )
7   )
8
9 SQLNET.AUTHENTICATION_SERVICES = (NONE)
10 SSL_VERSION = 1.0
11 SSL_CLIENT_AUTHENTICATION = FALSE
12 SSL_CIPHER_SUITES = (SSL_RSA_WITH_AES_256_CBC_SHA)
```

16. Stop the Oracle listener.

```
1 lsnrctl stop
```

17. Add entries for SSL in the *listener.ora* file (($ORACLE_HOME/network/admin/listener.ora).

```
1 SSL_CLIENT_AUTHENTICATION = FALSE
2 WALLET_LOCATION =
3   (SOURCE =
4     (METHOD = FILE)
5     (METHOD_DATA =
6       (DIRECTORY = <ORACLE_HOME>/self_signed_ssl_wallet)
7     )
8   )
9
10 SID_LIST_LISTENER =
11   (SID_LIST =
12   (SID_DESC =
13     (GLOBAL_DBNAME = <SID>)
14     (ORACLE_HOME = <ORACLE_HOME>)
15     (SID_NAME = <SID>)
16   )
17   )
18
19 LISTENER =
20   (DESCRIPTION_LIST =
21     (DESCRIPTION =
22       (ADDRESS = (PROTOCOL = TCP)(HOST = localhost.localdomain)(PORT = 1521))
23       (ADDRESS = (PROTOCOL = TCPS)(HOST = localhost.localdomain)(PORT = 1522))
24       (ADDRESS = (PROTOCOL = IPC)(KEY = EXTPROC1521))
25     )
26   )
```

18. Configure the* tnsnames.ora* file ($ORACLE_HOME/network/admin/tnsnames.ora).

```
1 <SID>=
2 (DESCRIPTION=
3         (ADDRESS_LIST =
4                 (ADDRESS=(PROTOCOL = TCP)(HOST = localhost.localdomain)(PORT = 1521))
5         )
6         (CONNECT_DATA =
7                 (SERVER = DEDICATED)
8                 (SERVICE_NAME = <SID>)
```

```
 9            )
10 )
11
12 <SID>_ssl=
13 (DESCRIPTION=
14           (ADDRESS_LIST =
15                   (ADDRESS=(PROTOCOL = TCPS)(HOST = localhost.localdomain)(PORT = 1522))
16           )
17           (CONNECT_DATA =
18                   (SERVER = DEDICATED)
19                   (SERVICE_NAME = <SID>)
20           )
21 )
```

19. Restart the Oracle listener.

```
1 lsnrctl start
```

20. Show the Oracle listener status.

```
1 lsnrctl status
```

21. Test the SSL connection to the database from localhost using sqlplus and the SSL tnsnames entry.

```
1 sqlplus -L <ORACLE_USER>@<SID>_ssl
```

22. Verify that you successfully connected using SSL.

```
1 SELECT SYS_CONTEXT('USERENV', 'network_protocol') FROM DUAL;
2
3 SYS_CONTEXT('USERENV','NETWORK_PROTOCOL')
4 --------------------------------------------------------------------------------
5 tcps
```

23. Change directory to the directory with the self-signed certificate.

```
1 cd <SELF_SIGNED_CERT_DIRECTORY>
```

24. Create a new client Oracle wallet that AWS DMS will use.

```
1 orapki wallet create -wallet ./ -auto_login_only
```

25. Add the self-signed root certificate to the Oracle wallet.

```
1 orapki wallet add -wallet ./ -trusted_cert -cert rootCA.pem -auto_login_only
```

26. List the contents of the Oracle wallet that AWS DMS will use. The list should include the self-signed root certificate.

```
1 orapki wallet display -wallet ./
```

27. Upload the Oracle wallet you just created to AWS DMS.

Changing the Database Password

In most situations, changing the database password for your source or target endpoint is straightforward. If you need to change the database password for an endpoint that you are currently using in a migration or replication task, the process is slightly more complex. The procedure following shows how to do this.

To change the database password for an endpoint in a migration or replication task

1. Sign in to the AWS Management Console and choose AWS DMS. Note that if you are signed in as an AWS Identity and Access Management (IAM) user, you must have the appropriate permissions to access AWS DMS. For more information on the permissions required, see IAM Permissions Needed to Use AWS DMS.

2. In the navigation pane, choose **Tasks**.

3. Choose the task that uses the endpoint you want to change the database password for, and then choose **Stop**.

4. While the task is stopped, you can change the password of the database for the endpoint using the native tools you use to work with the database.

5. Return to the DMS Management Console and choose **Endpoints** from the navigation pane.

6. Choose the endpoint for the database you changed the password for, and then choose **Modify**.

7. Type the new password in the **Password** box, and then choose **Modify**.

8. Choose **Tasks** from the navigation pane.

9. Choose the task that you stopped previously, and choose **Start/Resume**.

10. Choose either **Start** or **Resume**, depending on how you want to continue the task, and then choose **Start task**.

Limits for AWS Database Migration Service

This topic describes the resource limits and naming constraints for AWS Database Migration Service (AWS DMS).

The maximum size of a database that AWS DMS can migrate depends on your source environment, the distribution of data in your source database, and how busy your source system is. The best way to determine whether your particular system is a candidate for AWS DMS is to test it out. Start slowly so you can get the configuration worked out, then add some complex objects, and finally, attempt a full load as a test.

Limits for AWS Database Migration Service

Each AWS account has limits, per region, on the number of AWS DMS resources that can be created. Once a limit for a resource has been reached, additional calls to create that resource will fail with an exception.

The 6 TB limit for storage applies to the DMS replication instance. This storage is used to cache changes if the target cannot keep up with the source and for storing log information. This limit does not apply to the target size; target endpoints can be larger than 6 TB.

The following table lists the AWS DMS resources and their limits per region.

Resource	Default Limit
Replication instances	20
Total amount of storage	6 TB
Event subscriptions	100
Replication subnet groups	20
Subnets per replication subnet group	20
Endpoints	100
Tasks	200
Endpoints per instance	20

AWS Database Migration Service Components

AWS Database Migration Service (AWS DMS) is made up of several components. The following sections provide more in-depth information on using these components for data migration.

- Working with a Replication Instance in AWS Database Migration Service
- Working with Endpoints in AWS Database Migration Service
- Working with AWS DMS Tasks

Working with a Replication Instance in AWS Database Migration Service

The first step in migrating data using AWS Database Migration Service is to create a replication instance. An *AWS DMS replication instance* runs on an Amazon Elastic Compute Cloud (Amazon EC2) instance. A replication instance provides high availability and failover support using a Multi-AZ deployment.

In a Multi-AZ deployment, AWS DMS automatically provisions and maintains a synchronous standby replica of the replication instance in a different Availability Zone. The primary replication instance is synchronously replicated across Availability Zones to a standby replica. This approach provides data redundancy, eliminates I/O freezes, and minimizes latency spikes during system backups.

AWS DMS uses a replication instance that connects to the source data store, reads the source data, and formats the data for consumption by the target data store. A replication instance also loads the data into the target data store. Most of this processing happens in memory. However, large transactions might require some buffering on disk. Cached transactions and log files are also written to disk.

Following, you can find out more details about replication instances.

- AWS DMS Replication Instances in Depth
- Public and Private Replication Instances
- AWS DMS Maintenance
- Working with Replication Engine Versions
- Setting Up a Network for a Replication Instance
- Setting an Encryption Key for a Replication Instance
- Creating a Replication Instance
- Modifying a Replication Instance
- Rebooting a Replication Instance
- DDL Statements Supported by AWS DMS

AWS DMS Replication Instances in Depth

AWS DMS creates a replication instance that runs on an Amazon Elastic Compute Cloud (Amazon EC2) instance in a VPC based on the Amazon Virtual Private Cloud (Amazon VPC) service. You use this replication instance to perform your database migration. The replication instance provides high availability and failover support using a Multi-AZ deployment when you select the **Multi-AZ** option.

In a Multi-AZ deployment, AWS DMS automatically provisions and maintains a synchronous standby replica of the replication instance in a different Availability Zone. The primary replication instance is synchronously replicated across Availability Zones to a standby replica to provide data redundancy, eliminate I/O freezes, and minimize latency spikes.

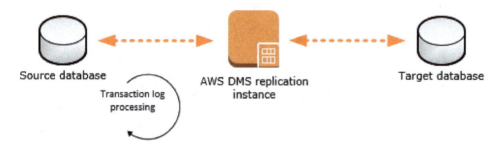

AWS DMS currently supports the T2 and C4 instance classes for replication instances. The T2 instance classes are low-cost standard instances designed to provide a baseline level of CPU performance with the ability to burst above the baseline. They are suitable for developing, configuring, and testing your database migration process, and for periodic data migration tasks that can benefit from the CPU burst capability. The C4 instance classes are designed to deliver the highest level of processor performance. They achieve significantly higher packet per second (PPS) performance, lower network jitter, and lower network latency. You should use C4 instance classes if you are migrating large databases and want to minimize the migration time.

Each replication instance has a specific configuration of memory and vCPU. The following table shows the configuration for each replication instance type. For pricing information, see the AWS Database Migration Service pricing page.

Replication Instance Type	vCPU	Memory (GB)
General Purpose		
dms.t2.micro	1	1
dms.t2.small	1	2
dms.t2.medium	2	4
dms.t2.large	2	8
Compute Optimized		
dms.c4.large	2	3.75
dms.c4.xlarge	4	7.5
dms.c4.2xlarge	8	15
dms.c4.4xlarge	16	30

Public and Private Replication Instances

You can specify whether a replication instance has a public or private IP address that the instance uses to connect to the source and target databases.

A private replication instance has a private IP address that you can't access outside the replication network. A replication instance should have a private IP address when both source and target databases are in the same network that is connected to the replication instance's VPC by using a VPN, AWS Direct Connect, or VPC peering.

A *VPC peering* connection is a networking connection between two VPCs that enables routing using each VPC's private IP addresses as if they were in the same network. For more information about VPC peering, see VPC Peering in the *Amazon VPC User Guide*.

AWS DMS Maintenance

Periodically, AWS DMS performs maintenance on AWS DMS resources. Maintenance most often involves updates to the replication instance or the replication instance's operating system (OS). You can manage the time period for your maintenance window and see maintenance updates using the AWS CLI or AWS DMS API. The AWS DMS console is not currently supported for this work.

Maintenance items require that AWS DMS take your replication instance offline for a short time. Maintenance that requires a resource to be offline includes required operating system or instance patching. Required patching is automatically scheduled only for patches that are related to security and instance reliability. Such patching occurs infrequently (typically once or twice a year) and seldom requires more than a fraction of your maintenance window. You can have minor version updates applied automatically by choosing the **Auto minor version upgrade** console option.

AWS DMS Maintenance Window

Every AWS DMS replication instance has a weekly maintenance window during which any available system changes are applied. You can think of the maintenance window as an opportunity to control when modifications and software patching occurs.

If AWS DMS determines that maintenance is required during a given week, the maintenance occurs during the 30-minute maintenance window you chose when you created the replication instance. AWS DMS completes most maintenance during the 30-minute maintenance window. However, a longer time might be required for larger changes.

The 30-minute maintenance window that you selected when you created the replication instance is from an 8-hour block of time allocated for each AWS Region. If you don't specify a preferred maintenance window when you create your replication instance, AWS DMS assigns one on a randomly selected day of the week. For a replication instance that uses a Multi-AZ deployment, a failover might be required for maintenance to be completed.

The following table lists the maintenance window for each AWS Region that supports AWS DMS.

[See the AWS documentation website for more details]

Changing the Maintenance Window Using the Console

You can change the maintenance window time frame using the AWS Management Console, the AWS CLI, or the AWS DMS API.

To change the preferred maintenance window using the console

1. Sign in to the AWS Management Console and choose AWS DMS.

2. In the navigation pane, choose **Replication instances**.

3. Choose the replication instance you want to modify and choose **Modify**.

4. Expand the **Maintenance** section and choose a date and time for your maintenance window.

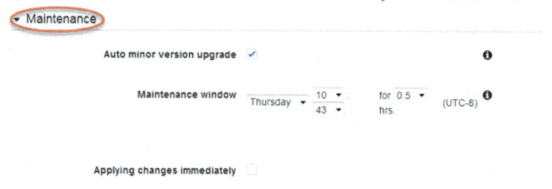

5. Choose **Apply changes immediately**.

6. Choose **Modify**.

Changing the Maintenance Window Setting Using the CLI

To adjust the preferred maintenance window, use the AWS CLI http://docs.aws.amazon.com/cli/latest/reference/rds/modify-db-instance.html command with the following parameters.

- `--replication-instance-identifier`

- `--preferred-maintenance-window`

Example
The following AWS CLI example sets the maintenance window to Tuesdays from 4:00–4:30 a.m. UTC.

```
1 aws dms modify-replication-instance \
2 --replication-instance-identifier myrepinstance \
```

```
3 --preferred-maintenance-window Tue:04:00-Tue:04:30
```

Changing the Maintenance Window Setting Using the API

To adjust the preferred maintenance window, use the AWS DMS API http://docs.aws.amazon.com/AmazonRDS/latest/APIReference/API_ModifyDBInstance.html action with the following parameters.

- `ReplicationInstanceIdentifier = myrepinstance`

- `PreferredMaintenanceWindow = Tue:04:00-Tue:04:30`

Example

The following code example sets the maintenance window to Tuesdays from 4:00–4:30 a.m. UTC.

```
1  1. https://dms.us-west-2.amazonaws.com/
2  2. ?Action=ModifyReplicationInstance
3  3. &DBInstanceIdentifier=myrepinstance
4  4. &PreferredMaintenanceWindow=Tue:04:00-Tue:04:30
5  5. &SignatureMethod=HmacSHA256
6  6. &SignatureVersion=4
7  7. &Version=2014-09-01
8  8. &X-Amz-Algorithm=AWS4-HMAC-SHA256
9  9. &X-Amz-Credential=AKIADQKE4SARGYLE/20140425/us-east-1/dms/aws4_request
10  10. &X-Amz-Date=20140425T192732Z
11  11. &X-Amz-SignedHeaders=content-type;host;user-agent;x-amz-content-sha256;x-amz-date
12  12. &X-Amz-Signature=1dc9dd716f4855e9bdf188c70f1cf9f6251b070b68b81103b59ec70c3e7854b3
```

Effect of Maintenance on Existing Migration Tasks

When an AWS DMS migration task is running on an instance, the following events occur when a patch is applied:

- If the tables in the migration task are in the replicating ongoing changes phase (CDC), AWS DMS pauses the task for a moment while the patch is applied. The migration then continues from where it was interrupted when the patch was applied.

- If AWS DMS is migrating a table when the patch is applied, AWS DMS restarts the migration for the table.

Working with Replication Engine Versions

The *replication engine* is the core AWS DMS software that runs on your replication instance and performs the migration tasks you specify. AWS periodically releases new versions of the AWS DMS replication engine software, with new features and performance improvements. Each version of the replication engine software has its own version number, to distinguish it from other versions.

When you launch a new replication instance, it runs the latest AWS DMS engine version unless you specify otherwise. For more information, see Working with a Replication Instance in AWS Database Migration Service.

If you have a replication instance that is currently running, you can upgrade it to a more recent engine version. (AWS DMS doesn't support engine version downgrades.) For more information, including a list of replication engine versions, see the following section.

Deprecating a Replication Instance Version

Occasionally AWS DMS deprecates older versions of the replication instance. Beginning April 2, 2018, AWS DMS will disable creation of any new replication instance version 1.9.0. This version was initially supported in

AWS DMS on March 15, 2016, and has since been replaced by subsequent versions containing improvements to functionality, security, and reliability.

Beginning on May 7, 2018, at 0:00 UTC, all DMS replication instances running version 1.9.0 will be scheduled for automatic upgrade to the latest available version during the maintenance window specified for each instance. We recommend that you upgrade your instances before that at your convenience.

You can initiate an upgrade of your replication instance by using the instructions in the following section, Upgrading the Engine Version of a Replication Instance .

For migration tasks that are running when you choose to upgrade the replication instance, tables in the full load phase at the time of the upgrade are reloaded from the start once the upgrade is complete. Replication for all other tables should resume without interruption once the upgrade is complete. We recommend testing all current migration tasks on the latest available version of AWS DMS replication instance before upgrading the instances from version 1.9.0.

Upgrading the Engine Version of a Replication Instance

AWS periodically releases new versions of the AWS DMS replication engine software, with new features and performance improvements. The following is a summary of available AWS DMS engine versions.

Version	Summary
2.4.x	[See the AWS documentation website for more details]
2.3.x	[See the AWS documentation website for more details]
2.2.x	[See the AWS documentation website for more details]
1.9.x	Cumulative release of AWS DMS replication engine software.

Upgrading the Engine Version Using the Console

You can upgrade an AWS DMS replication instance using the AWS Management Console.

To upgrade a replication instance using the console

1. Open the AWS DMS console at https://console.aws.amazon.com/dms/.

2. In the navigation pane, choose **Replication instances**.

3. Choose your replication engine, and then choose **Modify**.

4. For **Replication engine version**, choose the version number you want, and then choose **Modify**.

Note
Upgrading the replication instance takes several minutes. When the instance is ready, its status changes to **available**.

Upgrading the Engine Version Using the CLI

You can upgrade an AWS DMS replication instance using the AWS CLI, as follows.

To upgrade a replication instance using the AWS CLI

1. Determine the Amazon Resource Name (ARN) of your replication instance by using the following command.

```
1 aws dms describe-replication-instances \
2 --query "ReplicationInstances[*].[ReplicationInstanceIdentifier,ReplicationInstanceArn,
    ReplicationInstanceClass]"
```

In the output, take note of the ARN for the replication instance you want to upgrade, for example: arn:aws:dms:us-east-1:123456789012:rep:6EFQQO6U6EDPRCPKLNPL2SCEEY

2. Determine which replication instance versions are available by using the following command.

```
1 aws dms describe-orderable-replication-instances \
2 --query "OrderableReplicationInstances[*].[ReplicationInstanceClass,EngineVersion]"
```

In the output, take note of the engine version number or numbers that are available for your replication instance class. You should see this information in the output from step 1.

3. Upgrade the replication instance by using the following command.

```
1 aws dms modify-replication-instance \
2 --replication-instance-arn arn \
3 --engine-version n.n.n
```

Replace *arn* in the preceding with the actual replication instance ARN from the previous step.

Replace *n.n.n *with the engine version number that you want, for example: 2.2.1

Note

Upgrading the replication instance takes several minutes. You can view the replication instance status using the following command.

```
1 aws dms describe-replication-instances \
2 --query "ReplicationInstances[*].[ReplicationInstanceIdentifier,ReplicationInstanceStatus]"
```

When the replication instance is ready, its status changes to **available**.

Setting Up a Network for a Replication Instance

AWS DMS always creates the replication instance in a VPC based on Amazon Virtual Private Cloud (Amazon VPC). You specify the VPC where your replication instance is located. You can use your default VPC for your account and AWS Region, or you can create a new VPC. The VPC must have two subnets in at least one Availability Zone.

The Elastic Network Interface (ENI) allocated for the replication instance in your VPC must be associated with a security group that has rules that allow all traffic on all ports to leave (egress) the VPC. This approach allows communication from the replication instance to your source and target database endpoints, as long as correct egress rules are enabled on the endpoints. We recommend that you use the default settings for the endpoints, which allows egress on all ports to all addresses.

The source and target endpoints access the replication instance that is inside the VPC either by connecting to the VPC or by being inside the VPC. The database endpoints must include network access control lists (ACLs) and security group rules (if applicable) that allow incoming access from the replication instance. Depending on the network configuration you are using, you can use the replication instance VPC security group, the replication instance's private or public IP address, or the NAT gateway's public IP address. These connections form a network that you use for data migration.

Network Configurations for Database Migration

You can use several different network configurations with AWS Database Migration Service. The following are common configurations for a network used for database migration.

- Configuration with All Database Migration Components in One VPC
- Configuration with Two VPCs
- Configuration for a Network to a VPC Using AWS Direct Connect or a VPN
- Configuration for a Network to a VPC Using the Internet
- Configuration with an Amazon RDS DB instance not in a VPC to a DB instance in a VPC Using ClassicLink

Configuration with All Database Migration Components in One VPC

The simplest network for database migration is for the source endpoint, the replication instance, and the target endpoint to all be in the same VPC. This configuration is a good one if your source and target endpoints are on an Amazon RDS DB instance or an Amazon EC2 instance.

The following illustration shows a configuration where a database on an Amazon EC2 instance connects to the replication instance and data is migrated to an Amazon RDS DB instance.

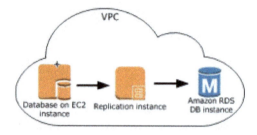

The VPC security group used in this configuration must allow ingress on the database port from the replication instance. You can do this by either ensuring that the security group used by the replication instance has ingress to the endpoints, or by explicitly allowing the private IP address of the replication instance.

Configuration with Two VPCs

If your source endpoint and target endpoints are in different VPCs, you can create your replication instance in one of the VPCs and then link the two VPCs by using VPC peering.

A VPC peering connection is a networking connection between two VPCs that enables routing using each VPC's private IP addresses as if they were in the same network. We recommend this method for connecting VPCs within an AWS Region. You can create VPC peering connections between your own VPCs or with a VPC in another AWS account within the same AWS Region. For more information about VPC peering, see VPC Peering in the *Amazon VPC User Guide*.

The following illustration shows an example configuration using VPC peering. Here, the source database on an Amazon EC2 instance in a VPC connects by VPC peering to a VPC. This VPC contains the replication instance and the target database on an Amazon RDS DB instance.

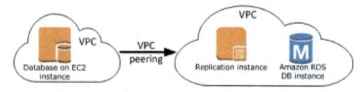

The VPC security groups used in this configuration must allow ingress on the database port from the replication instance.

Configuration for a Network to a VPC Using AWS Direct Connect or a VPN

Remote networks can connect to a VPC using several options such as AWS Direct Connect or a software or hardware VPN connection. These options are often used to integrate existing on-site services, such as monitoring, authentication, security, data, or other systems, by extending an internal network into the AWS cloud. By using this type of network extension, you can seamlessly connect to AWS-hosted resources such as a VPC.

The following illustration shows a configuration where the source endpoint is an on-premises database in a corporate data center. It is connected by using AWS Direct Connect or a VPN to a VPC that contains the replication instance and a target database on an Amazon RDS DB instance.

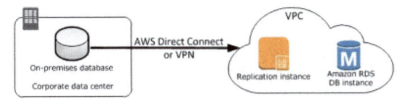

In this configuration, the VPC security group must include a routing rule that sends traffic destined for a specific IP address or range to a host. This host must be able to bridge traffic from the VPC into the on-premises VPN. In this case, the NAT host includes its own security group settings that must allow traffic from the replication instance's private IP address or security group into the NAT instance.

Configuration for a Network to a VPC Using the Internet

If you don't use a VPN or AWS Direct Connect to connect to AWS resources, you can use the Internet to migrate a database to an Amazon EC2 instance or Amazon RDS DB instance. This configuration involves a public replication instance in a VPC with an internet gateway that contains the target endpoint and the replication instance.

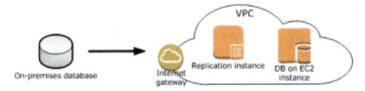

To add an Internet gateway to your VPC, see Attaching an Internet Gateway in the *Amazon VPC User Guide*.

The VPC security group must include routing rules that send traffic not destined for the VPC by default to the Internet gateway. In this configuration, the connection to the endpoint appears to come from the public IP address of the replication instance, not the private IP address.

Configuration with an Amazon RDS DB instance not in a VPC to a DB instance in a VPC Using ClassicLink

You can use ClassicLink with a proxy server to connect an Amazon RDS DB instance that is not in a VPC to an AWS DMS replication server and DB instance that reside in a VPC.

ClassicLink allows you to link an EC2-Classic DB instance to a VPC in your account, within the same AWS Region. After you've created the link, the source DB instance can communicate with the replication instance inside the VPC using their private IP addresses.

Because the replication instance in the VPC cannot directly access the source DB instance on the EC2-Classic platform using ClassicLink, you must use a proxy server. The proxy server connects the source DB instance to the VPC containing the replication instance and target DB instance. The proxy server uses ClassicLink to connect to the VPC. Port forwarding on the proxy server allows communication between the source DB instance and the target DB instance in the VPC.

For step-by-step instructions on creating a ClassicLink for use with AWS DMS, see Using ClassicLink with AWS Database Migration Service.

Creating a Replication Subnet Group

As part of the network to use for database migration, you need to specify what subnets in your Amazon Virtual Private Cloud (Amazon VPC) you plan to use. A *subnet* is a range of IP addresses in your VPC in a given Availability Zone. These subnets can be distributed among the Availability Zones for the AWS Region where your VPC is located.

You create a replication instance in a subnet that you select, and you can manage what subnet a source or target endpoint uses by using the AWS DMS console.

You create a replication subnet group to define which subnets to use. You must specify at least one subnet in two different Availability Zones.

To create a replication subnet group

1. Sign in to the AWS Management Console and choose AWS Database Migration Service. If you are signed in as an AWS Identity and Access Management (IAM) user, you must have the appropriate permissions to access AWS DMS. For more information on the permissions required for database migration, see IAM Permissions Needed to Use AWS DMS.

2. In the navigation pane, choose **Subnet Groups**.

3. Choose **Create Subnet Group**.

4. On the **Edit Replication Subnet Group** page, shown following, specify your replication subnet group information. The following table describes the settings.

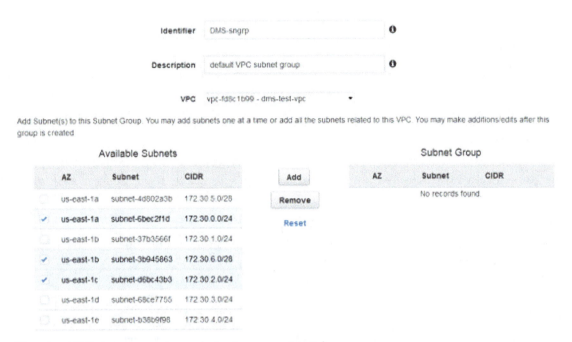

Edit Replication Subnet Group

Identifier   DMS-sngrp   ⓘ

Description   default VPC subnet group   ⓘ

VPC   vpc-fd8c1b99 - dms-test-vpc   ▾

Add Subnet(s) to this Subnet Group. You may add subnets one at a time or add all the subnets related to this VPC. You may make additions/edits after this group is created

Available Subnets

	AZ	Subnet	CIDR
○	us-east-1a	subnet-4d802a3b	172.30.5.0/28
✓	us-east-1a	subnet-6bec2f1d	172.30.0.0/24
○	us-east-1b	subnet-37b3566f	172.30.1.0/24
✓	us-east-1b	subnet-3b945863	172.30.6.0/28
✓	us-east-1c	subnet-d6bc43b3	172.30.2.0/24
○	us-east-1d	subnet-68ce7755	172.30.3.0/24
○	us-east-1e	subnet-b38b9f98	172.30.4.0/24

Add
Remove
Reset

Subnet Group

AZ	Subnet	CIDR
No records found.		

[See the AWS documentation website for more details]

5. Choose **Add** to add the subnets to the replication subnet group.

6. Choose **Create**.

Setting an Encryption Key for a Replication Instance

AWS DMS encrypts the storage used by a replication instance and the endpoint connection information. To encrypt the storage used by a replication instance, AWS DMS uses a master key that is unique to your AWS account. You can view and manage this master key with AWS Key Management Service (AWS KMS). You can use the default master key in your account (`aws/dms`) or a custom master key that you create. If you have an existing AWS KMS encryption key, you can also use that key for encryption.

You can specify your own encryption key by supplying a KMS key identifier to encrypt your AWS DMS resources. When you specify your own encryption key, the user account used to perform the database migration must have access to that key. For more information on creating your own encryption keys and giving users access to an encryption key, see the *AWS KMS Developer Guide*.

If you don't specify a KMS key identifier, then AWS DMS uses your default encryption key. KMS creates the default encryption key for AWS DMS for your AWS account. Your AWS account has a different default encryption key for each AWS Region.

To manage the keys used for encrypting your AWS DMS resources, you use KMS. You can find KMS in the AWS Management Console by choosing **Identity & Access Management** on the console home page and then choosing **Encryption Keys** on the navigation pane.

KMS combines secure, highly available hardware and software to provide a key management system scaled for the cloud. Using KMS, you can create encryption keys and define the policies that control how these keys can be used. KMS supports AWS CloudTrail, so you can audit key usage to verify that keys are being used appropriately. Your KMS keys can be used in combination with AWS DMS and supported AWS services such as Amazon RDS, S3, Amazon Elastic Block Store (Amazon EBS), and Amazon Redshift.

When you have created your AWS DMS resources with a specific encryption key, you can't change the encryption key for those resources. Make sure to determine your encryption key requirements before you create your AWS DMS resources.

Creating a Replication Instance

Your first task in migrating a database is to create a replication instance that has sufficient storage and processing power to perform the tasks you assign and migrate data from your source database to the target database. The required size of this instance varies depending on the amount of data you need to migrate and the tasks that you need the instance to perform. For more information about replication instances, see Working with a Replication Instance in AWS Database Migration Service.

The procedure following assumes that you have chosen the AWS DMS console wizard. You can also do this step by selecting **Replication instances** from the AWS DMS console's navigation pane and then selecting **Create replication instance.**

To create a replication instance by using the AWS console

1. On the **Create replication instance** page, specify your replication instance information. The following table describes the settings.

[See the AWS documentation website for more details]

2. Choose the **Advanced** tab, shown following, to set values for network and encryption settings if you need them. The following table describes the settings.

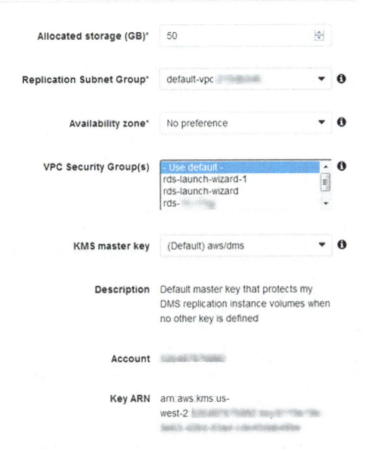

[See the AWS documentation website for more details]

3. Specify the **Maintenance** settings. The following table describes the settings. For more information about maintenance settings, see AWS DMS Maintenance Window.

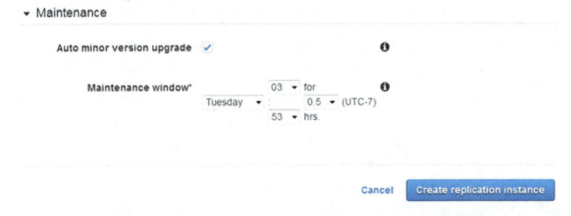

[See the AWS documentation website for more details]

4. Choose **Create replication instance**.

Modifying a Replication Instance

You can modify the settings for a replication instance to, for example, change the instance class or to increase storage.

When you modify a replication instance, you can apply the changes immediately. To apply changes immediately, you select the **Apply changes immediately** option in the AWS Management Console, you use the `--apply-immediately` parameter when calling the AWS CLI, or you set the `ApplyImmediately` parameter to `true` when using the AWS DMS API.

If you don't choose to apply changes immediately, the changes are put into the pending modifications queue. During the next maintenance window, any pending changes in the queue are applied.

Note
If you choose to apply changes immediately, any changes in the pending modifications queue are also applied. If any of the pending modifications require downtime, choosing **Apply changes immediately** can cause unexpected downtime.

To modify a replication instance by using the AWS console

1. Sign in to the AWS Management Console and select AWS DMS.

2. In the navigation pane, choose **Replication instances**.

3. Choose the replication instance you want to modify. The following table describes the modifications you can make.
   [See the AWS documentation website for more details]

Rebooting a Replication Instance

You can reboot an AWS DMS replication instance to restart the replication engine. A reboot results in a momentary outage for the replication instance, during which the instance status is set to **Rebooting**. If the AWS DMS instance is configured for Multi-AZ, the reboot can be conducted with a failover. An AWS DMS event is created when the reboot is completed.

If your AWS DMS instance is a Multi-AZ deployment, you can force a failover from one AWS Availability Zone to another when you reboot. When you force a failover of your AWS DMS instance, AWS DMS automatically switches to a standby instance in another Availability Zone. Rebooting with failover is beneficial when you want to simulate a failure of an AWS DMS instance for testing purposes.

If there are migration tasks running on the replication instance when a reboot occurs, no data loss occurs and the task resumes once the reboot is completed. If the tables in the migration task are in the middle of a bulk load (full load phase), DMS restarts the migration for those tables from the beginning. If tables in the migration task are in the ongoing replication phase, the task resumes once the reboot is completed.

You can't reboot your AWS DMS replication instance if its status is not in the **Available** state. Your AWS DMS instance can be unavailable for several reasons, such as a previously requested modification or a maintenance-window action. The time required to reboot an AWS DMS replication instance is typically small (under 5 minutes).

To reboot a replication instance using the AWS console

1. Sign in to the AWS Management Console and select AWS DMS.

2. In the navigation pane, choose **Replication instances**.

3. Choose the replication instance you want to reboot.

4. Choose **Reboot**.

5. In the **Reboot replication instance** dialog box, choose **Reboot With Failover?** if you have configured your replication instance for Multi-AZ deployment and you want to fail over to another AWS Availability Zone.

6. Choose **Reboot**.

Rebooting a Replication Instance Using the CLI

To reboot a replication instance, use the AWS CLI http://docs.aws.amazon.com/cli/latest/reference/rds/modify-db-instance.html command with the following parameter:

- `--replication-instance-arn`

Example Example Simple Reboot
The following AWS CLI example reboots a replication instance.

```
1 aws dms reboot-replication-instance \
2 --replication-instance-arn arnofmyrepinstance
```

Example Example Simple Reboot with Failover
The following AWS CLI example reboots a replication instance with failover.

```
1 aws dms reboot-replication-instance \
2 --replication-instance-arn arnofmyrepinstance \
3 --force-failover
```

Rebooting a Replication Instance Using the API

To reboot a replication instance, use the AWS DMS API http://docs.aws.amazon.com/AmazonRDS/latest/APIReference/API_ModifyDBInstance.html action with the following parameters:

- `ReplicationInstanceArn = arnofmyrepinstance`

Example Example Simple Reboot
The following code example reboots a replication instance.

```
1  1. https://dms.us-west-2.amazonaws.com/
2  2. ?Action=RebootReplicationInstance
3  3. &DBInstanceArn=arnofmyrepinstance
4  4. &SignatureMethod=HmacSHA256
5  5. &SignatureVersion=4
6  6. &Version=2014-09-01
7  7. &X-Amz-Algorithm=AWS4-HMAC-SHA256
8  8. &X-Amz-Credential=AKIADQKE4SARGYLE/20140425/us-east-1/dms/aws4_request
9  9. &X-Amz-Date=20140425T192732Z
10 10. &X-Amz-SignedHeaders=content-type;host;user-agent;x-amz-content-sha256;x-amz-date
11 11. &X-Amz-Signature=1dc9dd716f4855e9bdf188c70f1cf9f6251b070b68b81103b59ec70c3e7854b3
```

Example Example Simple Reboot with Failover
The following code example reboots a replication instance and fails over to another AWS Availability Zone.

```
1   1. https://dms.us-west-2.amazonaws.com/
2   2. ?Action=RebootReplicationInstance
3   3. &DBInstanceArn=arnofmyrepinstance
4   4. &ForceFailover=true
5   5. &SignatureMethod=HmacSHA256
6   6. &SignatureVersion=4
7   7. &Version=2014-09-01
8   8. &X-Amz-Algorithm=AWS4-HMAC-SHA256
9   9. &X-Amz-Credential=AKIADQKE4SARGYLE/20140425/us-east-1/dms/aws4_request
10 10. &X-Amz-Date=20140425T192732Z
11 11. &X-Amz-SignedHeaders=content-type;host;user-agent;x-amz-content-sha256;x-amz-date
12 12. &X-Amz-Signature=1dc9dd716f4855e9bdf188c70f1cf9f6251b070b68b81103b59ec70c3e7854b3
```

DDL Statements Supported by AWS DMS

You can execute data definition language (DDL) statements on the source database during the data migration process. These statements are replicated to the target database by the replication server.

Supported DDL statements include the following:

- Create table
- Drop table
- Rename table
- Add column
- Drop column
- Rename column
- Change column data type

For information about which DDL statements are supported for a specific source, see the topic describing that source.

Working with Endpoints in AWS Database Migration Service

An endpoint provides connection, data store type, and location information about your data store. AWS Database Migration Service uses this information to connect to a data store and migrate data from a source endpoint to a target endpoint. You can specify additional connection attributes for an endpoint by using extra connection attributes. These attributes can control logging, file size, and other parameters; for more information about extra connection attributes, see Using Extra Connection Attributes with AWS Database Migration Service or see the documentation section for your data store.

Following, you can find out more details about endpoints.

- Sources for Data Migration
- Targets for Data Migration
- Creating Source and Target Endpoints

Creating Source and Target Endpoints

While your replication instance is being created, you can specify the source and target data stores. The source and target data stores can be on an Amazon Elastic Compute Cloud (Amazon EC2) instance, an Amazon Relational Database Service (Amazon RDS) DB instance, or an on-premises database.

The procedure following assumes that you have chosen the AWS DMS console wizard. Note that you can also do this step by selecting **Endpoints** from the AWS DMS console's navigation pane and then selecting **Create endpoint**. When using the console wizard, you create both the source and target endpoints on the same page. When not using the console wizard, you create each endpoint separately.

To specify source or target database endpoints using the AWS console

1. On the **Connect source and target database endpoints** page, specify your connection information for the source or target database. The following table describes the settings.

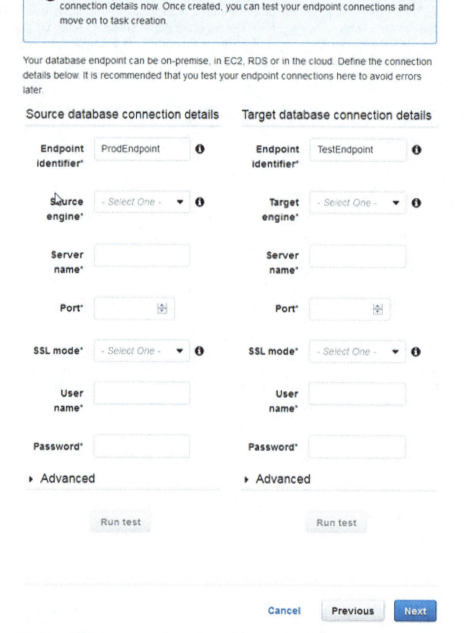

Connect source and target database endpoints

> ⟳ Your replication instance is being created. You can start entering your endpoint connection details now. Once created, you can test your endpoint connections and move on to task creation.

Your database endpoint can be on-premise, in EC2, RDS or in the cloud. Define the connection details below. It is recommended that you test your endpoint connections here to avoid errors later.

Source database connection details	Target database connection details
Endpoint identifier* ProdEndpoint ℹ	**Endpoint identifier*** TestEndpoint ℹ
Source engine* - Select One - ▼ ℹ	**Target engine*** - Select One - ▼ ℹ
Server name*	**Server name***
Port* ⇕	**Port*** ⇕
SSL mode* - Select One - ▼ ℹ	**SSL mode*** - Select One - ▼ ℹ
User name*	**User name***
Password*	**Password***
▸ Advanced	▸ Advanced
Run test	Run test

Cancel   Previous   Next

[See the AWS documentation website for more details]

2. Choose the **Advanced** tab, shown following, to set values for connection string and encryption key if you need them. You can test the endpoint connection by choosing **Run test**.

▾ Advanced

Extra
connection
attributes

KMS
master
key

(Default) aws/... ▾ ❶

Description   Default master key
that protects my DMS
replication instance
volumes when no
other key is defined

Account

Key ARN   arn:aws:kms:us-
west-2:   key/7944f0ec-

Run test

▾ Advanced

Extra
connection
attributes

KMS
master
key

(Default) aws/... ▾ ❶

Description   Default master key
that protects my DMS
replication instance
volumes when no
other key is defined

Account

Key ARN   arn:aws:kms:us-
west-2:   key/7944

Run test

Cancel   Previous   Next

[See the AWS documentation website for more details]

Sources for Data Migration

AWS Database Migration Service (AWS DMS) can use many of the most popular data engines as a source for data replication. The database source can be a self-managed engine running on an Amazon Elastic Compute Cloud (Amazon EC2) instance or an on-premises database. Or it can be a data source on an Amazon-managed service such as Amazon Relational Database Service (Amazon RDS) or Amazon S3.

Valid sources for AWS DMS include the following:

On-premises and Amazon EC2 instance databases

- Oracle versions 10.2 and later, 11g, and up to 12.2, for the Enterprise, Standard, Standard One, and Standard Two editions.
- Microsoft SQL Server versions 2005, 2008, 2008R2, 2012, 2014, and 2016, for the Enterprise, Standard, Workgroup, and Developer editions. The Web and Express editions are not supported.
- MySQL versions 5.5, 5.6, and 5.7.
- MariaDB (supported as a MySQL-compatible data source).
- PostgreSQL 9.4 and later.
- SAP Adaptive Server Enterprise (ASE) versions 12.5, 15, 15.5, 15.7, 16 and later.
- MongoDB versions 2.6.x and 3.x and later.

Microsoft Azure

- AWS DMS supports full data load when using Azure SQL Database as a source. Change data capture (CDC) is not supported.

Amazon RDS instance databases

- Oracle versions 11g (versions 11.2.0.3.v1 and later), and 12c, for the Enterprise, Standard, Standard One, and Standard Two editions.
- Microsoft SQL Server versions 2008R2, 2012, and 2014, f2016, and 2017 for both the Enterprise and Standard editions. CDC is supported for all versions of Enterprise Edition. CDC is only supported for Standard Edition version 2016 SP1 and later. The Web, Workgroup, Developer, and Express editions are not supported by AWS DMS.
- MySQL versions 5.5, 5.6, and 5.7. Change data capture (CDC) is only supported for versions 5.6 and later.
- PostgreSQL 9.4 and later. CDC is only supported for versions 9.4.9 and higher and 9.5.4 and higher. The `rds.logical_replication` parameter, which is required for CDC, is supported only in these versions and later.
- MariaDB, supported as a MySQL-compatible data source.
- Amazon Aurora with MySQL compatibility.

Amazon S3

- AWS DMS supports full data load and change data capture (CDC) when using Amazon S3 as a source.
- Using an Oracle Database as a Source for AWS DMS
- Using a Microsoft SQL Server Database as a Source for AWS DMS
- Using Microsoft Azure SQL Database as a Source for AWS DMS
- Using a PostgreSQL Database as a Source for AWS DMS
- Using a MySQL-Compatible Database as a Source for AWS DMS
- Using a SAP ASE Database as a Source for AWS DMS

- Using MongoDB as a Source for AWS DMS
- Using Amazon S3 as a Source for AWS DMS

Using an Oracle Database as a Source for AWS DMS

You can migrate data from one or many Oracle databases using AWS DMS. With an Oracle database as a source, you can migrate data to any of the targets supported by AWS DMS.

For self-managed Oracle databases, AWS DMS supports all Oracle database editions for versions 10.2 and later, 11g, and up to 12.2 for self-managed databases as sources. For Amazon-managed Oracle databases provided by Amazon RDS, AWS DMS supports all Oracle database editions for versions 11g (versions 11.2.0.3.v1 and later) and up to 12.2.

You can use SSL to encrypt connections between your Oracle endpoint and the replication instance. For more information on using SSL with an Oracle endpoint, see Using SSL With AWS Database Migration Service.

The steps to configure an Oracle database as a source for AWS DMS source are as follows:

1. If you want to create a CDC-only or full load plus CDC task, then you must choose either Oracle LogMiner or Oracle Binary Reader to capture data changes. Choosing LogMiner or Binary Reader determines some of the subsequent permission and configuration tasks. For a comparison of LogMiner and Binary Reader, see the next section.

2. Create an Oracle user with the appropriate permissions for AWS DMS. If you are creating a full-load-only task, then no further configuration is needed.

3. If you are creating a full load plus CDC task or a CDC-only task, configure Oracle for LogMiner or Binary Reader.

4. Create a DMS endpoint that conforms with your chosen configuration.

For additional details on working with Oracle databases and AWS DMS, see the following sections.

- Using Oracle LogMiner or Oracle Binary Reader for Change Data Capture (CDC)
- Working with a Self-Managed Oracle Database as a Source for AWS DMS
- Working with an Amazon-Managed Oracle Database as a Source for AWS DMS
- Limitations on Using Oracle as a Source for AWS DMS
- Extra Connection Attributes When Using Oracle as a Source for AWS DMS
- Source Data Types for Oracle

Using Oracle LogMiner or Oracle Binary Reader for Change Data Capture (CDC)

Oracle offers two methods for reading the redo logs when doing change processing: Oracle LogMiner and Oracle Binary Reader. Oracle LogMiner provides a SQL interface to Oracle's online and archived redo log files. Binary Reader is an AWS DMS feature that reads and parses the raw redo log files directly.

By default, AWS DMS uses Oracle LogMiner for change data capture (CDC). The advantages of using LogMiner with AWS DMS include the following:

- LogMiner supports most Oracle options, such as encryption options and compression options. Binary Reader doesn't support all Oracle options, in particular options for encryption and compression.

- LogMiner offers a simpler configuration, especially compared to Oracle Binary Reader's direct access setup or if the redo logs are on Automatic Storage Management (ASM).

- LogMiner fully supports most Oracle encryption options, including Oracle Transparent Data Encryption (TDE).

- LogMiner supports the following HCC compression types for both full load and on-going replication (CDC):
  - QUERY HIGH
  - ARCHIVE HIGH

- ARCHIVE LOW

- QUERY LOW

Binary Reader supports QUERY LOW compression only for full load replications, not ongoing (CDC) replications.

- LogMiner supports table clusters for use by AWS DMS. Binary Reader does not.

The advantages to using Binary Reader with AWS DMS, instead of LogMiner, include the following:

- For migrations with a high volume of changes, LogMiner might have some I/O or CPU impact on the computer hosting the Oracle source database. Binary Reader has less chance of having I/O or CPU impact because the archive logs are copied to the replication instance and minded there.

- For migrations with a high volume of changes, CDC performance is usually much better when using Binary Reader compared with using Oracle LogMiner.

- Binary Reader supports CDC for LOBS in Oracle version 12c. LogMiner does not.

- Binary Reader supports the following HCC compression types for both full load and continuous replication (CDC):

  - QUERY HIGH

  - ARCHIVE HIGH

  - ARCHIVE LOW

  The QUERY LOW compression type is only supported for full load migrations.

In general, use Oracle LogMiner for migrating your Oracle database unless you have one of the following situations:

- You need to run several migration tasks on the source Oracle database.

- The volume of changes or the redo log volume on the source Oracle database is high.

- You are migrating LOBs from an Oracle 12.2 or later source endpoint.

- If your workload includes UPDATE statements that update only LOB columns you must use Binary Reader. These update statements are not supported by Oracle LogMiner.

- If your source is Oracle version 11 and you perform UPDATE statements on XMLTYPE and LOB columns, you must use Binary Reader. These statements are not supported by Oracle LogMiner.

- On Oracle 12c, LogMiner does not support LOB columns. You must use Binary Reader if you are migrating LOB columns from Oracle 12c.

Configuration for Change Data Capture (CDC) on an Oracle Source Database

When you use Oracle as a source endpoint either for full-load and change data capture (CDC) or just for CDC, you must set an extra connection attribute. This attribute specifies whether to use LogMiner or Binary Reader to access the transaction logs. You specify an extra connection attribute when you create the source endpoint. Multiple extra connection attribute settings should be separated by a semicolon.

LogMiner is used by default, so you don't have to explicitly specify its use. The enable Binary Reader to access the transaction logs, add the following extra connection attribute.

```
1 useLogMinerReader=N; useBfile=Y
```

If the Oracle source database is using Oracle Automatic Storage Management (ASM), the extra connection attribute needs to include the ASM user name and ASM server address. When you create the source endpoint, the password field needs to have both passwords, the source user password and the ASM password.

For example, the following extra connection attribute format is used to access a server that uses Oracle ASM.

```
1 useLogMinerReader=N;asm_user=<asm_username>;asm_server=<first_RAC_server_ip_address>/+ASM
```

If the Oracle source database is using Oracle ASM, the source endpoint password field must have both the Oracle user password and the ASM password, separated by a comma. For example, the following works in the password field.

```
1 <oracle_user_password>,<asm_user_password>
```

Limitations for CDC on an Oracle Source Database

The following limitations apply when using an Oracle database as a source for AWS DMS change data capture:

- AWS DMS doesn't capture changes made by the Oracle DBMS_REDEFINITION package, such as changes to table metadata and the OBJECT_ID value.
- AWS DMS doesn't support index-organized tables with an overflow segment in CDC mode when using BFILE. An example is when you access the redo logs without using LogMiner.

Working with a Self-Managed Oracle Database as a Source for AWS DMS

A self-managed database is a database that you configure and control, either a local on-premises database instance or a database on Amazon EC2. Following, you can find out about the privileges and configurations you need to set up when using a self-managed Oracle database with AWS DMS.

User Account Privileges Required on a Self-Managed Oracle Source for AWS DMS

To use an Oracle database as a source in an AWS DMS task, the user specified in the AWS DMS Oracle database definitions must be granted the following privileges in the Oracle database.

When granting privileges, use the actual name of objects (for example, V_$OBJECT including the underscore), not the synonym for the object (for example, V$OBJECT without the underscore).

- Grant SELECT ANY TRANSACTION to <dms_user>
- Grant SELECT on V_$ARCHIVED_LOG to <dms_user>
- Grant SELECT on V_$LOG to <dms_user>
- Grant SELECT on V_$LOGFILE to <dms_user>
- Grant SELECT on V_$DATABASE to <dms_user>
- Grant SELECT on V_$THREAD to <dms_user>
- Grant SELECT on V_$PARAMETER to <dms_user>
- Grant SELECT on V_$NLS_PARAMETERS to <dms_user>
- Grant SELECT on V_$TIMEZONE_NAMES to <dms_user>
- Grant SELECT on V_$TRANSACTION to <dms_user>
- Grant SELECT on ALL_INDEXES to <dms_user>
- Grant SELECT on ALL_OBJECTS to <dms_user>
- Grant SELECT on DBA_OBJECTS to <dms_user> (required if the Oracle version is earlier than 11.2.0.3)
- Grant SELECT on ALL_TABLES to <dms_user>

- Grant SELECT on ALL_USERS to <dms_user>

- Grant SELECT on ALL_CATALOG to <dms_user>

- Grant SELECT on ALL_CONSTRAINTS to <dms_user>

- Grant SELECT on ALL_CONS_COLUMNS to <dms_user>

- Grant SELECT on ALL_TAB_COLS to <dms_user>

- Grant SELECT on ALL_IND_COLUMNS to <dms_user>

- Grant SELECT on ALL_LOG_GROUPS to <dms_user>

- Grant SELECT on SYS.DBA_REGISTRY to <dms_user>

- Grant SELECT on SYS.OBJ$ to <dms_user>

- Grant SELECT on DBA_TABLESPACES to <dms_user>

- Grant SELECT on ALL_TAB_PARTITIONS to <dms_user>

- Grant SELECT on ALL_ENCRYPTED_COLUMNS to <dms_user>

If you are using any of the additional features noted following, the given additional permissions are required:

- If views are exposed, grant SELECT on ALL_VIEWS to <dms_user>.

- If you use a pattern to match table names in your replication task, grant SELECT ANY TABLE.

- If you specify a table list in your replication task, grant SELECT on each table in the list.

- If you add supplemental logging, grant ALTER ANY TABLE.

- If you add supplemental logging and you use a specific table list, grant ALTER for each table in the list.

- If you are migrating from Oracle RAC, grant SELECT permissions on materialized views with the prefixes g_$ and v_$.

Configuring a Self-Managed Oracle Source for AWS DMS

Before using a self-managed Oracle database as a source for AWS DMS, you need to perform several tasks:

- Provide Oracle account access – You must provide an Oracle user account for AWS DMS. The user account must have read/write privileges on the Oracle database, as specified in the previous section.

- Ensure that ARCHIVELOG mode is on – Oracle can run in two different modes, the ARCHIVELOG mode and the NOARCHIVELOG mode. To use Oracle with AWS DMS, the source database must be in ARCHIVELOG mode.

- Set up supplemental logging – If you are planning to use the source in a CDC or full-load plus CDC task, then you need to set up supplemental logging to capture the changes for replication.

There are two steps to enable supplemental logging for Oracle. First, you need to enable database-level supplemental logging. Doing this ensures that the LogMiner has the minimal information to support various table structures such as clustered and index-organized tables. Second, you need to enable table-level supplemental logging for each table to be migrated.

To enable database-level supplemental logging

1. Run the following query to determine if database-level supplemental logging is already enabled. The return result should be from GE to 9.0.0.

```
1 SELECT name, value, description FROM v$parameter WHERE name = 'compatible';
```

2. Run the following query. The returned result should be YES or IMPLICIT.

```
1 SELECT supplemental_log_data_min FROM v$database;
```

3. Run the following query to enable database-level supplemental logging.

```
1 ALTER DATABASE ADD SUPPLEMENTAL LOG DATA;
```

There are two methods to enable table-level supplemental logging. In the first one, if your database user account has ALTER TABLE privileges on all tables to be migrated, you can use the extra connection parameter `addSupplementalLogging` as described following. Otherwise, you can use the steps following for each table in the migration.

To enable table-level supplemental logging

1. If the table has a primary key, add PRIMARY KEY supplemental logging for the table by running the following command.

```
1 ALTER TABLE <table_name> ADD SUPPLEMENTAL LOG DATA (PRIMARY KEY) COLUMNS;
```

2. If no primary key exists and the table has multiple unique indexes, then AWS DMS uses the first unique index in alphabetical order of index name.

   Create a supplemental log group as shown preceding on that index's columns.

3. If there is no primary key and no unique index, supplemental logging must be added on all columns. Run the following query to add supplemental logging to all columns.

```
1 ALTER TABLE <table_name> ADD SUPPLEMENTAL LOG DATA (ALL) COLUMNS;
```

In some cases, the target table primary key or unique index is different than the source table primary key or unique index. In these cases, add supplemental logging on the source table columns that make up the target table primary key or unique index. If you change the target table primary key, you should add supplemental logging on the selected index's columns, instead of the columns of the original primary key or unique index.

Add additional logging if needed, such as if a filter is defined for a table. If a table has a unique index or a primary key, you need to add supplemental logging on each column that is involved in a filter if those columns are different than the primary key or unique index columns. However, if ALL COLUMNS supplemental logging has been added to the table, you don't need to add any additional logging.

```
1 ALTER TABLE <table_name> ADD SUPPLEMENTAL LOG GROUP <group_name> (<column_list>) ALWAYS;
```

Working with an Amazon-Managed Oracle Database as a Source for AWS DMS

An Amazon-managed database is a database that is on an Amazon service such as Amazon RDS, Amazon Aurora, or Amazon S3. Following, you can find the privileges and configurations you need to set up when using an Amazon-managed Oracle database with AWS DMS.

User Account Privileges Required on an Amazon-Managed Oracle Source for AWS DMS

To grant privileges on Oracle databases on Amazon RDS, use the stored procedure `rdsadmin.rdsadmin_util.grant_sys_object`. For more information, see Granting SELECT or EXECUTE privileges to SYS Objects.

Grant the following to the AWS DMS user account used to access the source Oracle endpoint.

- Grant SELECT ANY TABLE to <dms_user>;
- Grant SELECT on ALL_VIEWS to <dms_user>;
- Grant SELECT ANY TRANSACTION to <dms_user>;

- Run the following: exec rdsadmin.rdsadmin_util.grant_sys_object('V_$ARCHIVED_LOG','<dms_user>','SELECT');

- Run the following: exec rdsadmin.rdsadmin_util.grant_sys_object('V_$LOG','<dms_user>','SELECT');

- Run the following: exec rdsadmin.rdsadmin_util.grant_sys_object('V_$LOGFILE','<dms_user>','SELECT');

- Run the following: exec rdsadmin.rdsadmin_util.grant_sys_object('V_$DATABASE','<dms_user>','SELECT');

- Run the following: exec rdsadmin.rdsadmin_util.grant_sys_object('V_$THREAD','<dms_user>','SELECT');

- Run the following: exec rdsadmin.rdsadmin_util.grant_sys_object('V_$PARAMETER','<dms_user>','SELECT');

- Run the following: exec rdsadmin.rdsadmin_util.grant_sys_object('V_$NLS_PARAMETERS','<dms_user>','SELECT');

- Run the following: exec rdsadmin.rdsadmin_util.grant_sys_object('V_$TIMEZONE_NAMES','<dms_user>','SELECT');

- Run the following: exec rdsadmin.rdsadmin_util.grant_sys_object('V_$TRANSACTION','<dms_user>','SELECT');

- Grant SELECT on ALL_INDEXES to <dms_user>;

- Grant SELECT on ALL_OBJECTS to <dms_user>;

- Grant SELECT on ALL_TABLES to <dms_user>;

- Grant SELECT on ALL_USERS to <dms_user>;

- Grant SELECT on ALL_CATALOG to <dms_user>;

- Grant SELECT on ALL_CONSTRAINTS to <dms_user>;

- Grant SELECT on ALL_CONS_COLUMNS to <dms_user>;

- Grant SELECT on ALL_TAB_COLS to <dms_user>;

- Grant SELECT on ALL_IND_COLUMNS to <dms_user>;

- Grant SELECT on ALL_LOG_GROUPS to <dms_user>;

- Run the following: exec rdsadmin.rdsadmin_util.grant_sys_object('DBA_REGISTRY','<dms_user>','SELECT');

- Run the following: exec rdsadmin.rdsadmin_util.grant_sys_object('OBJ$','<dms_user>','SELECT');

- Grant SELECT on DBA_TABLESPACES to <dms_user>;

- Grant SELECT on ALL_TAB_PARTITIONS to <dms_user>;

- Run the following: exec rdsadmin.rdsadmin_util.grant_sys_object('ALL_ENCRYPTED_COLUMNS','<dms_user>','SELECT');

- Run the following: exec rdsadmin.rdsadmin_util.grant_sys_object('V_$LOGMNR_LOGS','<dms_user>','SELECT');

- Run the following: exec rdsadmin.rdsadmin_util.grant_sys_object('V_$LOGMNR_CONTENTS','<dms_user>','SELECT');

- Run the following: `exec rdsadmin.rdsadmin_util.grant_sys_object('DBMS_LOGMNR','<dms_user>','EXECUTE');`

Configuring an Amazon-Managed Oracle Source for AWS DMS

Before using an Amazon-managed Oracle database as a source for AWS DMS, you need to perform several tasks:

- Provide Oracle account access – You must provide an Oracle user account for AWS DMS. The user account must have read/write privileges on the Oracle database, as specified in the previous section.

- Set the backup retention period for your Amazon RDS database to one day or longer – Setting the backup retention period ensures that the database is running in ARCHIVELOG mode. For more information about setting the backup retention period, see the Working with Automated Backups in the* Amazon Relational Database Service User Guide.*

- Set up archive retention – Run the following to retain archived redo logs of your Oracle database instance. Running this command lets AWS DMS retrieve the log information using LogMiner. Make sure that you have enough storage for the archived redo logs during the migration period.

  In the following example, logs are kept for 24 hours.

  ```
  1 exec rdsadmin.rdsadmin_util.set_configuration('archivelog retention hours',24);
  ```

- Set up supplemental logging – If you are planning to use the source in a CDC or full-load plus CDC task, then set up supplemental logging to capture the changes for replication.

  There are two steps to enable supplemental logging for Oracle. First, you need to enable database-level supplemental logging. Doing this ensures that the LogMiner has the minimal information to support various table structures such as clustered and index-organized tables. Second, you need to enable table-level supplemental logging for each table to be migrated.

To enable database-level supplemental logging

- Run the following query to enable database-level supplemental logging.

  ```
  1 exec rdsadmin.rdsadmin_util.alter_supplemental_logging('ADD');
  ```

To enable table-level supplemental logging

- Run the following command to enable PRIMARY KEY logging for tables that have primary keys.

  ```
  1 exec rdsadmin.rdsadmin_util.alter_supplemental_logging('ADD','PRIMARY KEY');
  ```

For tables that don't have primary keys, use the following command to add supplemental logging.

```
1 alter table <table_name> add supplemental log data (ALL) columns;
```

If you create a table without a primary key, you should either include a supplemental logging clause in the create statement or alter the table to add supplemental logging. The following command creates a table and adds supplemental logging.

```
1 create table <table_name> (<column_list>, supplemental log data (ALL) columns);
```

If you create a table and later add a primary key, you need to add supplemental logging to the table. Add supplemental logging to the table using the following command.

```
1 alter table <table_name> add supplemental log data (PRIMARY KEY) columns;
```

Limitations on Using Oracle as a Source for AWS DMS

The following limitations apply when using an Oracle database as a source for AWS DMS:

- AWS DMS supports Oracle transparent data encryption (TDE) tablespace encryption and AWS Key Management Service (AWS KMS) encryption when used with Oracle LogMiner. All other forms of encryption are not supported.

- Tables with LOBs must have a primary key to use CDC.

- AWS DMS supports the `rename table <table name> to <new table name>` syntax with Oracle version 11 and higher.

- Oracle source databases columns created using explicit CHAR semantics are transferred to a target Oracle database using BYTE semantics. You must create tables containing columns of this type on the target Oracle database before migrating.

- AWS DMS doesn't replicate data changes resulting from partition or subpartition operations—data definition language (DDL) operations such as ADD, DROP, EXCHANGE, or TRUNCATE. To replicate such changes, you must reload the table being replicated. AWS DMS replicates any future data changes to newly added partitions without you having to reload the table. However, UPDATE operations on old data records in partitions fail and generate a `0 rows affected` warning.

- The DDL statement `ALTER TABLE ADD <column> <data_type> DEFAULT <>` doesn't replicate the default value to the target. The new column in the target is set to NULL. If the new column is nullable, Oracle updates all the table rows before logging the DDL itself. As a result, AWS DMS captures the changes to the counters but doesn't update the target. Because the new column is set to NULL, if the target table has no primary key or unique index, subsequent updates generate a `0 rows affected` warning.

- Data changes resulting from the `CREATE TABLE AS` statement are not supported. However, the new table is created on the target.

- When limited-size LOB mode is enabled, AWS DMS replicates empty LOBs on the Oracle source as NULL values in the target.

- When AWS DMS begins CDC, it maps a timestamp to the Oracle system change number (SCN). By default, Oracle keeps only five days of the timestamp to SCN mapping. Oracle generates an error if the timestamp specified is too old (greater than the five-day retention period). For more information, see the Oracle documentation.

- AWS DMS doesn't support connections to an Oracle source by using an ASM proxy.

- AWS DMS doesn't support virtual columns.

Extra Connection Attributes When Using Oracle as a Source for AWS DMS

You can use extra connection attributes to configure your Oracle source. You specify these settings when you create the source endpoint. Multiple extra connection attribute settings should be separated from each other by semicolons.

The following table shows the extra connection attributes you can use to configure an Oracle database as a source for AWS DMS.

Name	Description
addSupplementalLogging	Set this attribute to set up table-level supplemental logging for the Oracle database. This attribute enables PRIMARY KEY supplemental logging on all tables selected for a migration task. Default value: N Valid values: Y/N Example: `addSupplementalLogging=Y` If you use this option, you still need to enable database-level supplemental logging as discussed previously.
additionalArchivedLogDestId	Set this attribute with `archivedLogDestId` in a primary/standby setup. This attribute is useful in the case of a failover. In this case, AWS DMS needs to know which destination to get archive redo logs from to read changes, because the previous primary instance is now a standby instance after failover.
useLogminerReader	Set this attribute to Y to capture change data using the LogMiner utility (the default). Set this option to N if you want AWS DMS to access the redo logs as a binary file. When set to N, you must also add the setting useBfile=Y. For more information, see Using Oracle LogMiner or Oracle Binary Reader for Change Data Capture (CDC). Default value: Y Valid values: Y/N Example: `useLogminerReader=N; useBfile=Y` If the Oracle source database is using Oracle Automatic Storage Management (ASM), the extra connection parameter needs to include the ASM user name and ASM server address. The password field also needs to have both passwords, the source user password and the ASM password, separated from each other by a comma. Example: `useLogminerReader=N ;asm_user=<asm_username>; asm_server =<first_RAC_server_ip_address>/+ASM`
retryInterval	Specifies the number of seconds that the system waits before resending a query. Default value: 5 Valid values: Numbers starting from 1 Example: `retryInterval=6`
archivedLogDestId	Specifies the destination of the archived redo logs. The value should be the same as the DEST_ID number in the $archived_log table. When working with multiple log destinations (DEST_ID), we recommend that you to specify an archived redo logs location identifier. Doing this improves performance by ensuring that the correct logs are accessed from the outset. Default value:0 Valid values: Number Example: `archivedLogDestId=1`

Name	Description
`archivedLogsOnly`	When this field is set to Y, AWS DMS only accesses the archived redo logs. If the archived redo logs are stored on Oracle ASM only, the AWS DMS user account needs to be granted ASM privileges. Default value: N Valid values: Y/N Example: `archivedLogsOnly=Y`
`numberDataTypeScale`	Specifies the number scale. You can select a scale up to 38, or you can select FLOAT. By default, the NUMBER data type is converted to precision 38, scale 10. Default value: 10 Valid values: -1 to 38 (-1 for FLOAT) Example: `numberDataTypeScale =12`
afterConnectScript	Specifies a script to run immediately after AWS DMS connects to the endpoint. Valid values: Any SQL statement set off by a semicolon. Example: `afterConnectScript=ALTER SESSION SET CURRENT_SCHEMA = system;`
`failTasksOnLobTruncation`	When set to `true`, this attribute causes a task to fail if the actual size of an LOB column is greater than the specified `LobMaxSize`. If a task is set to limited LOB mode and this option is set to `true`, the task fails instead of truncating the LOB data. Default value: false Valid values: Boolean Example: `failTasksOnLobTruncation=true`
`readTableSpaceName`	When set to `true`, this attribute supports tablespace replication. The ability to migrate tablespaces from an Oracle source eliminates the need to precreate tablespaces in the target before migration. Default value: false Valid values: Boolean Example: `readTableSpaceName =true`

Source Data Types for Oracle

The Oracle endpoint for AWS DMS supports most Oracle data types. The following table shows the Oracle source data types that are supported when using AWS DMS and the default mapping to AWS DMS data types.

For information on how to view the data type that is mapped in the target, see the section for the target endpoint you are using.

For additional information about AWS DMS data types, see Data Types for AWS Database Migration Service.

Oracle Data Type	AWS DMS Data Type
BINARY_FLOAT	REAL4
BINARY_DOUBLE	REAL8
BINARY	BYTES
FLOAT (P)	If precision is less than or equal to 24, use REAL4. If precision is greater than 24, use REAL8.
NUMBER (P,S)	When scale is less than 0, use REAL8

Oracle Data Type	AWS DMS Data Type
NUMBER according to the "Expose number as" property in the Oracle source database settings.	When scale is 0: [See the AWS documentation website for more details] In all other cases, use REAL8.
DATE	DATETIME
INTERVAL_YEAR TO MONTH	STRING (with interval year_to_month indication)
INTERVAL_DAY TO SECOND	STRING (with interval day_to_second indication)
TIME	DATETIME
TIMESTAMP	DATETIME
TIMESTAMP WITH TIME ZONE	STRING (with timestamp_with_timezone indication)
TIMESTAMP WITH LOCAL TIME ZONE	STRING (with timestamp_with_local_timezone indication)
CHAR	STRING
VARCHAR2	STRING
NCHAR	WSTRING
NVARCHAR2	WSTRING
RAW	BYTES
REAL	REAL8
BLOB	BLOB To use this data type with AWS DMS, you must enable the use of BLOB data types for a specific task. AWS DMS supports BLOB data types only in tables that include a primary key.
CLOB	CLOB To use this data type with AWS DMS, you must enable the use of CLOB data types for a specific task. During change data capture (CDC), AWS DMS supports CLOB data types only in tables that include a primary key.
NCLOB	NCLOB To use this data type with AWS DMS, you must enable the use of NCLOB data types for a specific task. During CDC, AWS DMS supports NCLOB data types only in tables that include a primary key.
LONG	CLOB The LONG data type is not supported in batch-optimized apply mode (TurboStream CDC mode). To use this data type with AWS DMS, you must enable the use of LOBs for a specific task. During CDC, AWS DMS supports LOB data types only in tables that have a primary key.
LONG RAW	BLOB The LONG RAW data type is not supported in batch-optimized apply mode (TurboStream CDC mode). To use this data type with AWS DMS, you must enable the use of LOBs for a specific task. During CDC, AWS DMS supports LOB data types only in tables that have a primary key.

Oracle Data Type	AWS DMS Data Type
XMLTYPE	CLOB Support for the XMLTYPE data type requires the full Oracle Client (as opposed to the Oracle Instant Client). When the target column is a CLOB, both full LOB mode and limited LOB mode are supported (depending on the target).

Oracle tables used as a source with columns of the following data types are not supported and cannot be replicated. Replicating columns with these data types result in a null column.

- BFILE
- ROWID
- REF
- UROWID
- Nested Table
- User-defined data types
- ANYDATA

Note
Virtual columns are not supported.

Using a Microsoft SQL Server Database as a Source for AWS DMS

You can migrate data from one or many Microsoft SQL Server databases using AWS DMS (AWS DMS). With a SQL Server database as a source, you can migrate data to either another SQL Server database or one of the other supported databases.

AWS DMS supports, as a source, on-premises and Amazon EC2 instance databases for Microsoft SQL Server versions 2005, 2008, 2008R2, 2012, 2014, and 2016. The Enterprise, Standard, Workgroup, and Developer editions are supported. The Web and Express editions are not supported.

AWS DMS supports, as a source, Amazon RDS DB instance databases for SQL Server versions 2008R2, 2012, and 2014, and 2016. The Enterprise and Standard editions are supported. The Web, Workgroup, Developer, and Express editions are not supported.

You can have the source SQL Server database installed on any computer in your network. A SQL Server account with the appropriate access privileges to the source database for the type of task you chose is also required for use with AWS DMS.

AWS DMS supports migrating data from named instances of SQL Server. You can use the following notation in the server name when you create the source endpoint.

```
1  IPAddress\InstanceName
```

For example, the following is a correct source endpoint server name. Here, the first part of the name is the IP address of the server, and the second part is the SQL Server instance name (in this example, SQLTest).

```
1  10.0.0.25\SQLTest
```

You can use SSL to encrypt connections between your SQL Server endpoint and the replication instance. For more information on using SSL with a SQL Server endpoint, see Using SSL With AWS Database Migration Service.

To capture changes from a source SQL Server database, the database must be configured for full backups and must be either the Enterprise, Developer, or Standard Edition.

For additional details on working with SQL Server source databases and AWS DMS, see the following.

- Limitations on Using SQL Server as a Source for AWS DMS
- Using Ongoing Replication (CDC) from a SQL Server Source
- Supported Compression Methods
- Working with SQL Server AlwaysOn Availability Groups
- Configuring a SQL Server Database as a Replication Source for AWS DMS
- Extra Connection Attributes When Using SQL Server as a Source for AWS DMS
- Source Data Types for SQL Server

Limitations on Using SQL Server as a Source for AWS DMS

The following limitations apply when using a SQL Server database as a source for AWS DMS:

- The identity property for a column is not migrated to a target database column.

- In AWS DMS engine versions before version 2.4.x, changes to rows with more than 8000 bytes of information, including header and mapping information, are not processed correctly due to limitations in the SQL Server TLOG buffer size. Use the latest AWS DMS version to avoid this issue.

- The SQL Server endpoint does not support the use of sparse tables.

- Windows Authentication is not supported.

- Changes to computed fields in a SQL Server are not replicated.

- SQL Server partition switching is not supported.

- A clustered index on the source is created as a nonclustered index on the target.

- When using the WRITETEXT and UPDATETEXT utilities, AWS DMS does not capture events applied on the source database.

- The following data manipulation language (DML) pattern is not supported:

```
1 SELECT <*> INTO <new_table> FROM <existing_table>
```

- When using SQL Server as a source, column-level encryption is not supported.

- Due to a known issue with SQL Server 2008 and 2008 R2, AWS DMS doesn't support server level audits on SQL Server 2008 and SQL Server 2008 R2 as a source endpoint.

  For example, running the following command causes AWS DMS to fail:

```
1 USE [master]
2 GO
3 ALTER SERVER AUDIT [my_audit_test-20140710] WITH (STATE=on)
4 GO
```

Using Ongoing Replication (CDC) from a SQL Server Source

You can use ongoing replication (change data capture, or CDC) for a self-managed SQL Server database on-premises or on Amazon EC2, or an Amazon-managed database on Amazon RDS.

AWS DMS supports ongoing replication for these SQL Server configurations:

- For source SQL Server instances that are on-premises or on Amazon EC2, AWS DMS supports ongoing replication for SQL Server Enterprise, Standard, and Developer Edition.

- For source SQL Server instances running on Amazon RDS, AWS DMS supports ongoing replication for SQL Server Enterprise through SQL Server 2016 SP1. Beyond this version, AWS DMS supports CDC for both SQL Server Enterprise and Standard editions.

If you want AWS DMS to automatically set up the ongoing replication, the AWS DMS user account that you use to connect to the source database must have the sysadmin fixed server role. If you don't want to assign the sysadmin role to the user account you use, you can still use ongoing replication by following the series of manual steps discussed following.

The following requirements apply specifically when using ongoing replication with a SQL Server database as a source for AWS DMS:

- SQL Server must be configured for full backups, and you must perform a backup before beginning to replicate data.

- The recovery model must be set to **Bulk logged** or **Full**.

- SQL Server backup to multiple disks isn't supported. If the backup is defined to write the database backup to multiple files over different disks, AWS DMS can't read the data and the AWS DMS task fails.

- For self-managed SQL Server sources, be aware that SQL Server Replication Publisher definitions for the source database used in a DMS CDC task aren't removed when you remove a task. A SQL Server system administrator must delete these definitions from SQL Server for self-managed sources.

- During CDC, AWS DMS needs to look up SQL Server transaction log backups to read changes. AWS DMS doesn't support using SQL Server transaction log backups that were created using third-party backup software.

- For self-managed SQL Server sources, be aware that SQL Server doesn't capture changes on newly created tables until they've been published. When tables are added to a SQL Server source, AWS DMS manages creating the publication. However, this process might take several minutes. Operations made to newly created tables during this delay aren't captured or replicated to the target.

- AWS DMS change data capture requires FULLLOGGING to be turned on in SQL Server. To turn on FULLLOGGING in SQL Server, either enable MS-REPLICATION or CHANGE DATA CAPTURE (CDC).

- You can't reuse the SQL Server *tlog* until the changes have been processed.

- CDC operations aren't supported on memory-optimized tables. This limitation applies to SQL Server 2014 (when the feature was first introduced) and later.

Capturing Data Changes for SQL Server

For a self-managed SQL Server source, AWS DMS uses the following:

- MS-Replication, to capture changes for tables with primary keys. You can configure this automatically by giving the AWS DMS endpoint user sysadmin privileges on the source SQL Server instance. Alternatively, you can follow the steps provided in this section to prepare the source and use a non-sysadmin user for the AWS DMS endpoint.

- MS-CDC, to capture changes for tables without primary keys. MS-CDC must be enabled at the database level, and for all of the tables individually.

For a SQL Server source running on Amazon RDS, AWS DMS uses MS-CDC to capture changes for tables, with or without primary keys. MS-CDC must be enabled at the database level, and for all of the tables individually, using the Amazon RDS-specific stored procedures described in this section.

There are several ways you can use a SQL Server database for ongoing replication (CDC):

- Set up ongoing replication using the sysadmin role. (This applies only to self-managed SQL Server sources.)

- Set up ongoing replication to not use the sysadmin role. (This applies only to self-managed SQL Server sources.)

- Set up ongoing replication for an Amazon RDS for SQL Server DB instance.

Setting Up Ongoing Replication Using the sysadmin Role

For tables with primary keys, AWS DMS can configure the required artifacts on the source. For tables without primary keys, you need to set up MS-CDC.

First, enable MS-CDC for the database by running the following command. Use an account that has the sysadmin role assigned to it.

```
1 use [DBname]
2 EXEC sys.sp_cdc_enable_db
```

Next, enable MS-CDC for each of the source tables by running the following command.

```
1 EXECUTE sys.sp_cdc_enable_table @source_schema = N'MySchema', @source_name =
2 N'MyTable', @role_name = NULL;
```

For more information on setting up MS-CDC for specific tables, see the SQL Server documentation.

Setting Up Ongoing Replication Without Assigning the sysadmin Role

You can set up ongoing replication for a SQL Server database source that doesn't require the user account to have sysadmin privileges.

To set up a SQL Server database source for ongoing replication without using the sysadmin role

1. Create a new SQL Server account with password authentication using SQL Server Management Studio (SSMS). In this example, we use an account called `dmstest`.

2. In the **User Mappings** section of SSMS, choose the MSDB and MASTER databases (which gives public permission) and assign the DB_OWNER role for the database you want to use ongoing replication.

3. Open the context (right-click) menu for the new account, choose **Security** and explicitly grant the Connect SQL privilege.

4. Run the following grant commands.

```
1 GRANT SELECT ON FN_DBLOG TO dmstest;
2 GRANT SELECT ON FN_DUMP_DBLOG TO dmstest;
3 GRANT VIEW SERVER STATE TO dmstest;
4 use msdb;
5 GRANT EXECUTE ON MSDB.DBO.SP_STOP_JOB TO dmstest;
6 GRANT EXECUTE ON MSDB.DBO.SP_START_JOB TO dmstest;
7 GRANT SELECT ON MSDB.DBO.BACKUPSET TO dmstest;
8 GRANT SELECT ON MSDB.DBO.BACKUPMEDIAFAMILY TO dmstest;
9 GRANT SELECT ON MSDB.DBO.BACKUPFILE TO dmstest;
```

5. In SSMS, open the context (right-click) menu for the **Replication** folder, and then choose **Configure Distribution**. Follow all default steps and configure this SQL Server instance for distribution. A distribution database is created under databases.

6. Enable the database for replication using the following command.

```
1 exec sp_replicationdboption @dbname = N'<database name>', @optname = 'publish', @value = '
    true';
```

7. Create a new AWS DMS task with SQL Server as the source endpoint using the user account you created.

Note
The steps in this procedure apply only for tables with primary keys. You still need to enable MS-CDC for tables without primary keys.

Setting Up Ongoing Replication on an Amazon RDS for SQL Server DB Instance

Amazon RDS for SQL Server supports MS-CDC for all versions of Amazon RDS for SQL Server Enterprise editions up to SQL Server 2016 SP1. Later versions of SQL Server 2016 SP1 support MS-CDC for standard editions of Amazon RDS for SQL Server.

Unlike self-managed SQL Server sources, Amazon RDS for SQL Server doesn't support MS-Replication. Therefore, AWS DMS needs to use MS-CDC for tables with or without primary keys.

Amazon RDS does not grant sysadmin privileges for setting replication artifacts that AWS DMS uses for on-going changes in a source SQL Server instance. You must enable MS-CDC on the Amazon RDS instance using master user privileges in the following procedure.

To enable MS-CDC on an RDS for SQL Server DB instance

1. Run the following query at the database level.

```
1 exec msdb.dbo.rds_cdc_enable_db '<DB instance name>'
```

2. Run the following query for each table to enable MS-CDC.

```
1 exec sys.sp_cdc_enable_table
2 @source_schema = N'db_name',
3 @source_name = N'table_name',
4 @role_name = NULL,
5 @supports_net_changes = 1
6 GO
```

3. Set the retention period for changes to be available on the source using the following command.

```
1 EXEC sys.sp_cdc_change_job @job_type = 'capture' ,@pollinginterval = 86400
```

The parameter `@pollinginterval` is measured in seconds. The preceding command retains changes for one day. AWS recommends a one day retention period when using MS-CDC with AWS DMS.

Supported Compression Methods

The following table shows the compression methods that AWS DMS supports for each SQL Server version.

SQL Server Version	Row/Page Compression (at Partition Level)	Vardecimal Storage Format
2005	No	No
2008	Yes	No
2012	Yes	No
2014	Yes	No

Note
Sparse columns and columnar structure compression are not supported.

Working with SQL Server AlwaysOn Availability Groups

The SQL Server AlwaysOn Availability Groups feature is a high-availability and disaster-recovery solution that provides an enterprise-level alternative to database mirroring.

To use AlwaysOn Availability Groups as a source in AWS DMS, do the following:

- Enable the Distribution option on all SQL Server instances in your Availability Replicas.

- In the AWS DMS console, open the SQL Server source database settings. For **Server Name**, specify the Domain Name Service (DNS) name or IP address that was configured for the Availability Group Listener.

When you start an AWS DMS task for the first time, it might take longer than usual to start because the creation of the table articles is being duplicated by the Availability Groups Server.

Configuring a SQL Server Database as a Replication Source for AWS DMS

You can configure a SQL Server database as a replication source for AWS DMS (AWS DMS). For the most complete replication of changes, we recommend that you use the Enterprise, Standard, or Developer edition of SQL Server. One of these versions is required because these are the only versions that include MS-Replication(EE,SE) and MS-CDC(EE,DEV). The source SQL Server must also be configured for full backups. In addition, AWS DMS must connect with a user (a SQL Server instance login) that has the sysadmin fixed server role on the SQL Server database you are connecting to.

Following, you can find information about configuring SQL Server as a replication source for AWS DMS.

Extra Connection Attributes When Using SQL Server as a Source for AWS DMS

You can use extra connection attributes to configure your SQL Server source. You specify these settings when you create the source endpoint. Multiple extra connection attribute settings should be separated by a semicolon.

The following table shows the extra connection attributes you can use with SQL Server as a source:

Name	Description
safeguardPolicy	For optimal performance, AWS DMS tries to capture all unread changes from the active transaction log (TLOG). However, sometimes due to truncation, the active TLOG might not contain all of the unread changes. When this occurs, AWS DMS accesses the backup log to capture the missing changes. To minimize the need to access the backup log, AWS DMS prevents truncation using one of the following methods: 1. **Start transactions in the database:** This is the default method. When this method is used, AWS DMS prevents TLOG truncation by mimicking a transaction in the database. As long as such a transaction is open, changes that appear after the transaction started aren't truncated. If you need Microsoft Replication to be enabled in your database, then you must choose this method. 2.** Exclusively use sp_repldone within a single task:** When this method is used, AWS DMS reads the changes and then uses sp_repldone to mark the TLOG transactions as ready for truncation. Although this method does not involve any transactional activities, it can only be used when Microsoft Replication is not running. Also, when using this method, only one AWS DMS task can access the database at any given time. Therefore, if you need to run parallel AWS DMS tasks against the same database, use the default method. Default value: `RELY_ON_SQL_SERVER_REPLICATION_AGENT` Valid values: `{EXCLUSIVE_AUTOMATIC_TRUNCATION, RELY_ON_SQL_SERVER_REPLICATION_AGENT }` Example: `safeguardPolicy= RELY_ON_SQL_SERVER_REPLICATION_AGENT`

Source Data Types for SQL Server

Data migration that uses SQL Server as a source for AWS DMS supports most SQL Server data types. The following table shows the SQL Server source data types that are supported when using AWS DMS and the default mapping from AWS DMS data types.

For information on how to view the data type that is mapped in the target, see the section for the target endpoint you are using.

For additional information about AWS DMS data types, see Data Types for AWS Database Migration Service.

SQL Server Data Types	AWS DMS Data Types
BIGINT	INT8
BIT	BOOLEAN
DECIMAL	NUMERIC
INT	INT4
MONEY	NUMERIC
NUMERIC (p,s)	NUMERIC
SMALLINT	INT2
SMALLMONEY	NUMERIC
TINYINT	UINT1
REAL	REAL4
FLOAT	REAL8
DATETIME	DATETIME
DATETIME2 (SQL Server 2008 and later)	DATETIME
SMALLDATETIME	DATETIME
DATE	DATE
TIME	TIME
DATETIMEOFFSET	WSTRING
CHAR	STRING
VARCHAR	STRING
VARCHAR (max)	CLOB TEXT To use this data type with AWS DMS, you must enable the use of CLOB data types for a specific task. For SQL Server tables, AWS DMS updates LOB columns in the target even for UPDATE statements that don't change the value of the LOB column in SQL Server. During CDC, AWS DMS supports CLOB data types only in tables that include a primary key.
NCHAR	WSTRING
NVARCHAR (length)	WSTRING
NVARCHAR (max)	NCLOB NTEXT To use this data type with AWS DMS, you must enable the use of NCLOB data types for a specific task. For SQL Server tables, AWS DMS updates LOB columns in the target even for UPDATE statements that don't change the value of the LOB column in SQL Server. During CDC, AWS DMS supports CLOB data types only in tables that include a primary key.
BINARY	BYTES
VARBINARY	BYTES

SQL Server Data Types	AWS DMS Data Types
VARBINARY (max)	BLOB IMAGE For SQL Server tables, AWS DMS updates LOB columns in the target even for UPDATE statements that don't change the value of the LOB column in SQL Server. To use this data type with AWS DMS, you must enable the use of BLOB data types for a specific task. AWS DMS supports BLOB data types only in tables that include a primary key.
TIMESTAMP	BYTES
UNIQUEIDENTIFIER	STRING
HIERARCHYID	Use HIERARCHYID when replicating to a SQL Server target endpoint. Use WSTRING (250) when replicating to all other target endpoints.
XML	NCLOB For SQL Server tables, AWS DMS updates LOB columns in the target even for UPDATE statements that don't change the value of the LOB column in SQL Server. To use this data type with AWS DMS, you must enable the use of NCLOB data types for a specific task. During CDC, AWS DMS supports NCLOB data types only in tables that include a primary key.
GEOMETRY	Use GEOMETRY when replicating to target endpoints that support this data type. Use CLOB when replicating to target endpoints that don't support this data type.
GEOGRAPHY	Use GEOGRAPHY when replicating to target endpoints that support this data type. Use CLOB when replicating to target endpoints that do not support this data type.

AWS DMS does not support tables that include fields with the following data types:

- CURSOR
- SQL_VARIANT
- TABLE

Note

User-defined data types are supported according to their base type. For example, a user-defined data type based on DATETIME is handled as a DATETIME data type.

Using Microsoft Azure SQL Database as a Source for AWS DMS

With AWS DMS, you can use Microsoft Azure SQL Database as a source in much the same way as you do SQL Server. AWS DMS supports, as a source, the same list of database versions that are supported for SQL Server running on-premises or on an Amazon EC2 instance.

For more information, see Using a Microsoft SQL Server Database as a Source for AWS DMS.

Note
AWS DMS doesn't support change data capture operations (CDC) with Azure SQL Database.

Using a PostgreSQL Database as a Source for AWS DMS

You can migrate data from one or many PostgreSQL databases using AWS DMS (AWS DMS). With a PostgreSQL database as a source, you can migrate data to either another PostgreSQL database or one of the other supported databases. AWS DMS supports a PostgreSQL version 9.4 database as a source for on-premises databases, databases on an EC2 instance, and databases on an Amazon RDS DB instance.

You can use SSL to encrypt connections between your PostgreSQL endpoint and the replication instance. For more information on using SSL with a PostgreSQL endpoint, see Using SSL With AWS Database Migration Service.

For a homogeneous migration from a PostgreSQL database to a PostgreSQL database on AWS, the following is true:

- JSONB columns on the source are migrated to JSONB columns on the target.

- JSON columns are migrated as JSON columns on the target.

- HSTORE columns are migrated as HSTORE columns on the target.

For a heterogeneous migration with PostgreSQL as the source and a different database engine as the target, the situation is different. In this case, JSONB, JSON, and HSTORE columns are converted to the AWS DMS intermediate type of NCLOB and then translated to the corresponding NCLOB column type on the target. In this case, AWS DMS treats JSONB data as if it were a LOB column. During the full load phase of a migration, the target column must be nullable.

AWS DMS supports change data capture (CDC) for PostgreSQL tables with primary keys. If a table doesn't have a primary key, the write-ahead logs (WAL) don't include a before image of the database row and AWS DMS can't update the table.

AWS DMS supports CDC on Amazon RDS PostgreSQL databases when the DB instance is configured to use logical replication. Amazon RDS supports logical replication for a PostgreSQL DB instance version 9.4.9 and higher and 9.5.4 and higher.

For additional details on working with PostgreSQL databases and AWS DMS, see the following sections.

- Prerequisites for Using a PostgreSQL Database as a Source for AWS DMS
- Security Requirements When Using a PostgreSQL Database as a Source for AWS DMS
- Limitations on Using a PostgreSQL Database as a Source for AWS DMS
- Setting Up an Amazon RDS PostgreSQL DB Instance as a Source
- Removing AWS DMS Artifacts from a PostgreSQL Source Database
- Additional Configuration Settings When Using a PostgreSQL Database as a Source for AWS DMS
- Extra Connection Attributes When Using PostgreSQL as a Source for AWS DMS
- Source Data Types for PostgreSQL

Prerequisites for Using a PostgreSQL Database as a Source for AWS DMS

For a PostgreSQL database to be a source for AWS DMS, you should do the following:

- Use a PostgreSQL database that is version 9.4.x or later.

- Grant superuser permissions for the user account specified for the PostgreSQL source database.

- Add the IP address of the AWS DMS replication server to the `pg_hba.conf` configuration file.

- Set the following parameters and values in the `postgresql.conf` configuration file:

  - Set `wal_level = logical`

- Set `max_replication_slots >=1`

  The `max_replication_slots` value should be set according to the number of tasks that you want to run. For example, to run five tasks you need to set a minimum of five slots. Slots open automatically as soon as a task starts and remain open even when the task is no longer running. You need to manually delete open slots.

- Set `max_wal_senders >=1`

  The `max_wal_senders` parameter sets the number of concurrent tasks that can run.

- Set `wal_sender_timeout =0`

  The `wal_sender_timeout` parameter terminates replication connections that are inactive longer than the specified number of milliseconds. Although the default is 60 seconds, we recommend that you set this parameter to zero, which disables the timeout mechanism.

Security Requirements When Using a PostgreSQL Database as a Source for AWS DMS

The only security requirement when using PostgreSQL as a source is that the user account specified must be a registered user in the PostgreSQL database.

Limitations on Using a PostgreSQL Database as a Source for AWS DMS

The following change data capture (CDC) limitations apply when using PostgreSQL as a source for AWS DMS:

- A captured table must have a primary key. If a table doesn't have a primary key, AWS DMS ignores DELETE and UPDATE record operations for that table.

- AWS DMS ignores an attempt to update a primary key segment. In these cases, the target identifies the update as one that didn't update any rows. However, because the results of updating a primary key in PostgreSQL are unpredictable, no records are written to the exceptions table.

- AWS DMS doesn't support the **Start Process Changes from Timestamp** run option.

- AWS DMS supports full load and change processing on Amazon RDS for PostgreSQL. For information on how to prepare a PostgreSQL DB instance and to set it up for using CDC, see Setting Up an Amazon RDS PostgreSQL DB Instance as a Source.

- Replication of multiple tables with the same name but where each name has a different case (for example table1, TABLE1, and Table1) can cause unpredictable behavior, and therefore AWS DMS doesn't support it.

- AWS DMS supports change processing of CREATE, ALTER, and DROP DDL statements for tables unless the tables are held in an inner function or procedure body block or in other nested constructs.

  For example, the following change is not captured:

```
1 CREATE OR REPLACE FUNCTION attu.create_distributors1() RETURNS void
2 LANGUAGE plpgsql
3 AS $$
4 BEGIN
5 create table attu.distributors1(did serial PRIMARY KEY,name
6 varchar(40) NOT NULL);
7 END;
8 $$;
```

- AWS DMS doesn't support change processing of TRUNCATE operations.

- AWS DMS doesn't support change processing to set column default values (using the ALTER COLUMN SET DEFAULT clause on ALTER TABLE statements).

- AWS DMS doesn't support change processing to set column nullability (using the ALTER COLUMN [SET|DROP] NOT NULL clause on ALTER TABLE statements).

- AWS DMS doesn't support replication of partitioned tables. When a partitioned table is detected, the following occurs:

  - The endpoint reports a list of parent and child tables.

  - AWS DMS creates the table on the target as a regular table with the same properties as the selected tables.

  - If the parent table in the source database has the same primary key value as its child tables, a "duplicate key" error is generated.

Note

To replicate partitioned tables from a PostgreSQL source to a PostgreSQL target, you first need to manually create the parent and child tables on the target. Then you define a separate task to replicate to those tables. In such a case, you set the task configuration to **Truncate before loading**.

Setting Up an Amazon RDS PostgreSQL DB Instance as a Source

You can use an Amazon RDS for PostgreSQL DB instance or Read Replica as a source for AWS DMS. A DB instance can be used for both full-load and CDC (ongoing replication); a Read Replica can only be used for full-load tasks and cannot be used for CDC.

You use the AWS master user account for the PostgreSQL DB instance as the user account for the PostgreSQL source endpoint for AWS DMS. The master user account has the required roles that allow it to set up change data capture (CDC). If you use an account other than the master user account, the account must have the rds_superuser role and the rds_replication role. The rds_replication role grants permissions to manage logical slots and to stream data using logical slots.

If you don't use the master user account for the DB instance, you must create several objects from the master user account for the account that you use. For information about creating the needed objects, see Migrating an Amazon RDS for PostgreSQL Database Without Using the Master User Account.

Using CDC with an RDS for PostgreSQL DB Instance

You can use PostgreSQL's native logical replication feature to enable CDC during a database migration of an Amazon RDS PostgreSQL DB instance. This approach reduces downtime and ensures that the target database is in sync with the source PostgreSQL database. Amazon RDS supports logical replication for a PostgreSQL DB instance version 9.4.9 and higher and 9.5.4 and higher.

Note

Amazon RDS for PostgreSQL Read Replicas cannot be used for CDC (ongoing replication).

To enable logical replication for an RDS PostgreSQL DB instance, do the following:

- In general, use the AWS master user account for the PostgreSQL DB instance as the user account for the PostgreSQL source endpoint. The master user account has the required roles that allow it to set up CDC. If you use an account other than the master user account, you must create several objects from the master account for the account that you use. For more information, see Migrating an Amazon RDS for PostgreSQL Database Without Using the Master User Account.

- Set the `rds.logical_replication` parameter in your DB parameter group to 1. This is a static parameter that requires a reboot of the DB instance for the parameter to take effect. As part of applying this parameter, AWS DMS sets the `wal_level`, `max_wal_senders`, `max_replication_slots`, and `max_connections` parameters. These parameter changes can increase WAL generation, so you should only set the `rds.logical_replication` parameter when you are using logical slots.

Migrating an Amazon RDS for PostgreSQL Database Without Using the Master User Account

If you don't use the master user account for the Amazon RDS PostgreSQL DB instance that you are using as a source, you need to create several objects to capture data definition language (DDL) events. You create these objects in the account other than the master account and then create a trigger in the master user account.

Note
If you set the `captureDDL` parameter to N on the source endpoint, you don't have to create the following table and trigger on the source database.

Use the following procedure to create these objects. The user account other than the master account is referred to as the `NoPriv` account in this procedure.

To create objects

1. Choose the schema where the objects are to be created. The default schema is `public`. Ensure that the schema exists and is accessible by the `NoPriv` account.

2. Log in to the PostgreSQL DB instance using the `NoPriv` account.

3. Create the table `awsdms_ddl_audit` by running the following command, replacing `<objects_schema>` in the code following with the name of the schema to use.

```
1  create table <objects_schema>.awsdms_ddl_audit
2  (
3    c_key     bigserial primary key,
4    c_time    timestamp,     -- Informational
5    c_user    varchar(64),   -- Informational: current_user
6    c_txn     varchar(16),   -- Informational: current transaction
7    c_tag     varchar(24),   -- Either 'CREATE TABLE' or 'ALTER TABLE' or 'DROP TABLE'
8    c_oid     integer,       -- For future use - TG_OBJECTID
9    c_name    varchar(64),   -- For future use - TG_OBJECTNAME
10   c_schema  varchar(64),   -- For future use - TG_SCHEMANAME. For now - holds current_schema
11   c_ddlqry  text           -- The DDL query associated with the current DDL event
12 )
```

4. Create the function `awsdms_intercept_ddl` by running the following command, replacing `<objects_schema>` in the code following with the name of the schema to use.

```
1  CREATE OR REPLACE FUNCTION <objects_schema>.awsdms_intercept_ddl()
2    RETURNS event_trigger
3  LANGUAGE plpgsql
4  SECURITY DEFINER
5    AS $$
6    declare _qry text;
7  BEGIN
8    if (tg_tag='CREATE TABLE' or tg_tag='ALTER TABLE' or tg_tag='DROP TABLE') then
9          SELECT current_query() into _qry;
10         insert into <objects_schema>.awsdms_ddl_audit
11         values
12         (
13         default,current_timestamp,current_user,cast(TXID_CURRENT()as varchar(16)),tg_tag
                ,0,'',current_schema,_qry
14         );
15         delete from <objects_schema>.awsdms_ddl_audit;
```

```
16 end if;
17 END;
18 $$;
```

5. Log out of the `NoPriv` account and log in with an account that has the **rds_superuser** role assigned to it.

6. Create the event trigger `awsdms_intercept_ddl` by running the following command.

```
1 CREATE EVENT TRIGGER awsdms_intercept_ddl ON ddl_command_end
2 EXECUTE PROCEDURE <objects_schema>.awsdms_intercept_ddl();
```

When you have completed the procedure preceding, you can create the AWS DMS source endpoint using the `NoPriv` account.

Using CDC with an Amazon RDS for PostgreSQL DB Instance

You can use PostgreSQL's native logical replication feature to enable CDC during a database migration of an Amazon RDS PostgreSQL DB instance. This approach reduces downtime and ensures that the target database is in sync with the source PostgreSQL database. Amazon RDS supports logical replication for a PostgreSQL DB instance version 9.4.9 and higher and 9.5.4 and higher.

To enable logical replication for an RDS PostgreSQL DB instance, do the following:

- In general, use the AWS master user account for the PostgreSQL DB instance as the user account for the PostgreSQL source endpoint. The master user account has the required roles that allow the it to set up CDC. If you use an account other than the master user account, you must create several objects from the master account for the account that you use. For more information, see Migrating an Amazon RDS for PostgreSQL Database Without Using the Master User Account.

- Set the `rds.logical_replication` parameter in your DB parameter group to 1. This is a static parameter that requires a reboot of the DB instance for the parameter to take effect. As part of applying this parameter, AWS DMS sets the `wal_level`, `max_wal_senders`, `max_replication_slots`, and `max_connections` parameters. These parameter changes can increase WAL generation, so you should only set the `rds.logical_replication` parameter when you are using logical slots.

Removing AWS DMS Artifacts from a PostgreSQL Source Database

To capture DDL events, AWS DMS creates various artifacts in the PostgreSQL database when a migration task starts. When the task completes, you might want to remove these artifacts. To remove the artifacts, issue the following statements (in the order they appear), where {AmazonRDSMigration} is the schema in which the artifacts were created:

```
1 drop event trigger awsdms_intercept_ddl;
```

The event trigger doesn't belong to a specific schema.

```
1 drop function {AmazonRDSMigration}.awsdms_intercept_ddl()
2 drop table {AmazonRDSMigration}.awsdms_ddl_audit
3 drop schema {AmazonRDSMigration}
```

Note
Dropping a schema should be done with extreme caution, if at all. Never drop an operational schema, especially not a public one.

Additional Configuration Settings When Using a PostgreSQL Database as a Source for AWS DMS

You can add additional configuration settings when migrating data from a PostgreSQL database in two ways:

- You can add values to the extra connection attribute to capture DDL events and to specify the schema in which the operational DDL database artifacts are created. For more information, see Extra Connection Attributes When Using PostgreSQL as a Source for AWS DMS.

- You can override connection string parameters. Select this option if you need to do either of the following:

  - Specify internal AWS DMS parameters. Such parameters are rarely required and are therefore not exposed in the user interface.

  - Specify pass-through (passthru) values for the specific database client. AWS DMS includes pass-through parameters in the connection sting passed to the database client.

Extra Connection Attributes When Using PostgreSQL as a Source for AWS DMS

You can use extra connection attributes to configure your PostgreSQL source. You specify these settings when you create the source endpoint. Multiple extra connection attribute settings should be separated by a semicolon.

The following table shows the extra connection attributes you can use when using PostgreSQL as a source for AWS DMS:

[See the AWS documentation website for more details]

Source Data Types for PostgreSQL

The following table shows the PostgreSQL source data types that are supported when using AWS DMS and the default mapping to AWS DMS data types.

For information on how to view the data type that is mapped in the target, see the section for the target endpoint you are using.

For additional information about AWS DMS data types, see Data Types for AWS Database Migration Service.

PostgreSQL Data Types	AWS DMS Data Types
INTEGER	INT4
SMALLINT	INT2
BIGINT	INT8
NUMERIC (p,s)	If precision is from 0 through 38, then use NUMERIC. If precision is 39 or greater, then use STRING.
DECIMAL(P,S)	If precision is from 0 through 38, then use NUMERIC. If precision is 39 or greater, then use STRING.
REAL	REAL4
DOUBLE	REAL8
SMALLSERIAL	INT2
SERIAL	INT4
BIGSERIAL	INT8
MONEY	NUMERIC(38,4) Note: The MONEY data type is mapped to FLOAT in SQL Server.
CHAR	WSTRING (1)
CHAR(N)	WSTRING (n)

PostgreSQL Data Types	AWS DMS Data Types
VARCHAR(N)	WSTRING (n)
TEXT	NCLOB
BYTEA	BLOB
TIMESTAMP	TIMESTAMP
TIMESTAMP (z)	TIMESTAMP
TIMESTAMP with time zone	Not supported
DATE	DATE
TIME	TIME
TIME (z)	TIME
INTERVAL	STRING (128)—1 YEAR, 2 MONTHS, 3 DAYS, 4 HOURS, 5 MINUTES, 6 SECONDS
BOOLEAN	CHAR (5) false or true
ENUM	STRING (64)
CIDR	STRING (50)
INET	STRING (50)
MACADDR	STRING (18)
BIT (n)	STRING (n)
BIT VARYING (n)	STRING (n)
UUID	STRING
TSVECTOR	CLOB
TSQUERY	CLOB
XML	CLOB
POINT	STRING (255) "(x,y)"
LINE	STRING (255) "(x,y,z)"
LSEG	STRING (255) "((x1,y1),(x2,y2))"
BOX	STRING (255) "((x1,y1),(x2,y2))"
PATH	CLOB "((x1,y1),(xn,yn))"
POLYGON	CLOB "((x1,y1),(xn,yn))"
CIRCLE	STRING (255) "(x,y),r"
JSON	NCLOB
JSONB	NCLOB
ARRAY	NCLOB
COMPOSITE	NCLOB
HSTORE	NCLOB
INT4RANGE	STRING (255)
INT8RANGE	STRING (255)
NUMRANGE	STRING (255)
STRRANGE	STRING (255)

Using a MySQL-Compatible Database as a Source for AWS DMS

You can migrate data from any MySQL-compatible database (MySQL, MariaDB, or Amazon Aurora MySQL) using AWS Database Migration Service. MySQL versions 5.5, 5.6, and 5.7, and also MariaDB and Amazon Aurora MySQL, are supported for on-premises. All AWS-managed MySQL databases (Amazon RDS for MySQL, Amazon RDS for MariaDB, Amazon Aurora MySQL) are supported as sources for AWS DMS.

You can use SSL to encrypt connections between your MySQL-compatible endpoint and the replication instance. For more information on using SSL with a MySQL-compatible endpoint, see Using SSL With AWS Database Migration Service.

In the following sections, the term "self-managed" applies to any database that is installed either on-premises or on Amazon EC2. The term "Amazon-managed" applies to any database on Amazon RDS, Amazon Aurora, or Amazon S3.

For additional details on working with MySQL-compatible databases and AWS DMS, see the following sections.

- Using Any MySQL-Compatible Database as a Source for AWS DMS
- Using a Self-Managed MySQL-Compatible Database as a Source for AWS DMS
- Using a Amazon-Managed MySQL-Compatible Database as a Source for AWS DMS
- Limitations on Using a MySQL Database as a Source for AWS DMS
- Extra Connection Attributes When Using MySQL as a Source for AWS DMS
- Source Data Types for MySQL

Using Any MySQL-Compatible Database as a Source for AWS DMS

Before you begin to work with a MySQL database as a source for AWS DMS, make sure that you have the following prerequisites. These prerequisites apply to either self-managed or Amazon-managed sources.

You must have an account for AWS DMS that has the Replication Admin role. The role needs the following privileges:

- **REPLICATION CLIENT** – This privilege is required for change data capture (CDC) tasks only. In other words, full-load-only tasks don't require this privilege.

- **REPLICATION SLAVE** – This privilege is required for change data capture (CDC) tasks only. In other words, full-load-only tasks don't require this privilege.

- **SUPER** – This privilege is required only in MySQL versions before 5.6.6.

The AWS DMS user must also have SELECT privileges for the source tables designated for replication.

Using a Self-Managed MySQL-Compatible Database as a Source for AWS DMS

You can use the following self-managed MySQL-compatible databases as sources for AWS DMS:

- MySQL Community Edition

- MySQL Standard Edition

- MySQL Enterprise Edition

- MySQL Cluster Carrier Grade Edition

- MariaDB Community Edition

- MariaDB Enterprise Edition

- MariaDB Column Store

You must enable binary logging if you plan to use change data capture (CDC). To enable binary logging, the following parameters must be configured in MySQL's my.ini (Windows) or my.cnf (UNIX) file.

Parameter	Value
server_id	Set this parameter to a value of 1 or greater.
log-bin	Set the path to the binary log file, such as log-bin=E:\MySql_Logs\BinLog. Don't include the file extension.
binlog_format	Set this parameter to ROW.
expire_logs_days	Set this parameter to a value of 1 or greater. To prevent overuse of disk space, we recommend that you don't use the default value of 0.
binlog_checksum	Set this parameter to NONE.
binlog_row_image	Set this parameter to FULL.
log_slave_updates	Set this parameter to TRUE if you are using a MySQL or MariaDB read-replica as a source.

If your source uses the NDB (clustered) database engine, the following parameters must be configured to enable CDC on tables that use that storage engine. Add these changes in MySQL's my.ini (Windows) or my.cnf (UNIX) file.

Parameter	Value
ndb_log_bin	Set this parameter to ON. This value ensures that changes in clustered tables are logged to the binary log.
ndb_log_update_as_write	Set this parameter to OFF. This value prevents writing UPDATE statements as INSERT statements in the binary log.
ndb_log_updated_only	Set this parameter to OFF. This value ensures that the binary log contains the entire row and not just the changed columns.

Using a Amazon-Managed MySQL-Compatible Database as a Source for AWS DMS

You can use the following Amazon-managed MySQL-compatible databases as sources for AWS DMS:

- MySQL Community Edition
- MariaDB Community Edition
- Amazon Aurora MySQL

When using an Amazon-managed MySQL-compatible database as a source for AWS DMS, make sure that you have the following prerequisites:

- You must enable automatic backups. For more information on setting up automatic backups, see Working with Automated Backups in the *Amazon Relational Database Service User Guide*.

- You must enable binary logging if you plan to use change data capture (CDC). For more information on setting up binary logging for an Amazon RDS MySQL database, see Working with Automated Backups in the *Amazon Relational Database Service User Guide*.

- You must ensure that the binary logs are available to AWS DMS. Because Amazon-managed MySQL-compatible databases purge the binary logs as soon as possible, you should increase the length of time that the logs remain available. For example, to increase log retention to 24 hours, run the following command.

```
1  call mysql.rds_set_configuration('binlog retention hours', 24);
```

- The `binlog_format` parameter should be set to "ROW."

- The `binlog_checksum` parameter should be set to "NONE". For more information about setting parameters in Amazon RDS MySQL, see Working with Automated Backups in the *Amazon Relational Database Service User Guide.*

- If you are using an Amazon RDS MySQL or Amazon RDS MariaDB read replica as a source, then backups must be enabled on the read replica.

Limitations on Using a MySQL Database as a Source for AWS DMS

When using a MySQL database as a source, AWS DMS doesn't support the following:

- Change data capture (CDC) is not supported for Amazon RDS MySQL 5.5 or lower. For Amazon RDS MySQL, you must use version 5.6 or higher to enable CDC.

- The date definition language (DDL) statements TRUNCATE PARTITION, DROP TABLE, and RENAME TABLE are not supported.

- Using an ALTER TABLE<table_name> ADD COLUMN <column_name> statement to add columns to the beginning (FIRST) or the middle of a table (AFTER) is not supported. Columns are always added to the end of the table.

- CDC is not supported when a table name contains uppercase and lowercase characters, and the source engine is hosted on an operating system with case-insensitive file names. An example is Windows or OS X using HFS+.

- The AR_H_USER header column is not supported.

- The AUTO_INCREMENT attribute on a column is not migrated to a target database column.

- Capturing changes when the binary logs are not stored on standard block storage is not supported. For example, CDC doesn't work when the binary logs are stored on Amazon S3.

- AWS DMS creates target tables with the InnoDB storage engine by default. If you need to use a storage engine other than InnoDB, you must manually create the table and migrate to it using "do nothing" mode.

- You can't use Aurora MySQL read replicas as a source for AWS DMS.

- If the MySQL-compatible source is stopped during full load, the AWS DMS task doesn't stop with an error. The task ends successfully, but the target might be out of sync with the source. If this happens, either restart the task or reload the affected tables.

- Indexes created on a portion of a column value aren't migrated. For example, the index CREATE INDEX first_ten_chars ON customer (name(10)) isn't created on the target.

- In some cases, the task is configured to not replicate LOBs ("SupportLobs" is false in task settings or "Don't include LOB columns" is checked in the task console). In these cases, AWS DMS doesn't migrate any MEDIUMBLOB, LONGBLOB, MEDIUMTEXT, and LONGTEXT columns to the target.

  BLOB, TINYBLOB, TEXT, and TINYTEXT columns are not affected and are migrated to the target.

Extra Connection Attributes When Using MySQL as a Source for AWS DMS

You can use extra connection attributes to configure a MySQL source. You specify these settings when you create the source endpoint. Multiple extra connection attribute settings should be separated from each other by semicolons.

The following table shows the extra connection attributes available when using Amazon RDS MySQL as a source for AWS DMS.

[See the AWS documentation website for more details]

Source Data Types for MySQL

The following table shows the MySQL database source data types that are supported when using AWS DMS and the default mapping from AWS DMS data types.

Note
The UTF-8 4-byte character set (utf8mb4) is not supported and can cause unexpected behavior in a source database. Plan to convert any data using the UTF-8 4-byte character set before migrating.

For information on how to view the data type that is mapped in the target, see the section for the target endpoint you are using.

For additional information about AWS DMS data types, see Data Types for AWS Database Migration Service.

MySQL Data Types	AWS DMS Data Types
INT	INT4
MEDIUMINT	INT4
BIGINT	INT8
TINYINT	INT1
DECIMAL(10)	NUMERIC (10,0)
BINARY	BYTES(1)
BIT	BOOLEAN
BIT(64)	BYTES(8)
BLOB	BYTES(66535)
LONGBLOB	BLOB
MEDIUMBLOB	BLOB
TINYBLOB	BYTES(255)
DATE	DATE
DATETIME	DATETIME
TIME	STRING
TIMESTAMP	DATETIME
YEAR	INT2
DOUBLE	REAL8
FLOAT	REAL(DOUBLE) The supported FLOAT range is -1.79E+308 to -2.23E-308, 0 and 2.23E-308 to 1.79E+308 If FLOAT values aren't in this range, map the FLOAT data type to the STRING data type.
VARCHAR (45)	WSTRING (45)
VARCHAR (2000)	WSTRING (2000)
VARCHAR (4000)	WSTRING (4000)
VARBINARY (4000)	BYTES (4000)
VARBINARY (2000)	BYTES (2000)
CHAR	WSTRING
TEXT	WSTRING (65535)

MySQL Data Types	AWS DMS Data Types
LONGTEXT	NCLOB
MEDIUMTEXT	NCLOB
TINYTEXT	WSTRING (255)
GEOMETRY	BLOB
POINT	BLOB
LINESTRING	BLOB
POLYGON	BLOB
MULTIPOINT	BLOB
MULTILINESTRING	BLOB
MULTIPOLYGON	BLOB
GEOMETRYCOLLECTION	BLOB

Note

If the DATETIME and TIMESTAMP data types are specified with a "zero" value (that is, 0000-00-00), make sure that the target database in the replication task supports "zero" values for the DATETIME and TIMESTAMP data types. Otherwise, these values are recorded as null on the target.

The following MySQL data types are supported in full load only.

MySQL Data Types	AWS DMS Data Types
ENUM	STRING
SET	STRING

Using a SAP ASE Database as a Source for AWS DMS

You can migrate data from a SAP Adaptive Server Enterprise (ASE) database–formerly known as Sybase–using AWS DMS. With a SAP ASE database as a source, you can migrate data to any of the other supported AWS DMS target databases. AWS DMS. supports SAP ASE versions 12.5, 15, 15.5, 15.7, 16 and later as sources.

For additional details on working with SAP ASE databases and AWS DMS, see the following sections.

- Prerequisites for Using a SAP ASE Database as a Source for AWS DMS
- Limitations on Using SAP ASE as a Source for AWS DMS
- User Account Permissions Required for Using SAP ASE as a Source for AWS DMS
- Removing the Truncation Point
- Source Data Types for SAP ASE

Prerequisites for Using a SAP ASE Database as a Source for AWS DMS

For a SAP ASE database to be a source for AWS DMS, you should do the following:

- SAP ASE replication must be enabled for tables by using the `sp_setreptable` command.

- `RepAgent` must be disabled on the SAP ASE database.

- When replicating to SAP ASE version 15.7 installed on a Windows EC2 instance configured with a non-Latin language (for example, Chinese), AWS DMS requires SAP ASE 15.7 SP121 to be installed on the target SAP ASE machine.

Limitations on Using SAP ASE as a Source for AWS DMS

The following limitations apply when using an SAP ASE database as a source for AWS DMS (AWS DMS):

- Only one AWS DMS task can be run per SAP ASE database.

- Renaming a table is not supported, for example: `sp_rename 'Sales.SalesRegion', 'SalesReg;`

- Renaming a column is not supported, for example: `sp_rename 'Sales.Sales.Region', 'RegID', 'COLUMN';`

- Zero values located at the end of binary data type strings are truncated when replicated to the target database. For example, 0x0000000000000000000000000100000100000000 in the source table becomes 0x00000000000000000000000001000001 in the target table.

- If the database default is not to allow NULL values, AWS DMS creates the target table with columns that don't allow NULL values. Consequently, if a full load or CDC replication task contains empty values, errors occur. You can prevent these errors by allowing NULL values in the source database by using the following commands.

```
1 sp_dboption <database name>, 'allow nulls by default', 'true'
2 go
3 use <database name>
4 CHECKPOINT
5 go
```

- The `reorg rebuild` index command isn't supported.

User Account Permissions Required for Using SAP ASE as a Source for AWS DMS

To use an SAP ASE database as a source in an AWS DMS task, the user specified in the AWS DMS SAP ASE database definitions must be granted the following permissions in the SAP ASE database.

- sa_role

- replication_role

- sybase_ts_role

- If you have set the `enableReplication` connection property to Y, then you must also be granted the `sp_setreptable` permission. For more information on connection properties, see Using Extra Connection Attributes with AWS Database Migration Service.

Removing the Truncation Point

When a task starts, AWS DMS establishes a `$replication_truncation_point` entry in the `syslogshold` system view, indicating that a replication process is in progress. While AWS DMS is working, it advances the replication truncation point at regular intervals, according to the amount of data that has already been copied to the target.

Once the `$replication_truncation_point` entry has been established, the AWS DMS task must be kept running at all times to prevent the database log from becoming excessively large. If you want to stop the AWS DMS task permanently, the replication truncation point must be removed by issuing the following command:

```
1 dbcc settrunc('ltm','ignore')
```

After the truncation point has been removed, the AWS DMS task cannot be resumed. The log continues to be truncated automatically at the checkpoints (if automatic truncation is set).

Source Data Types for SAP ASE

Data migration that uses SAP ASE as a source for AWS DMS supports most SAP ASE data types. The following table shows the SAP ASE source data types that are supported when using AWS DMS and the default mapping from AWS DMS data types.

For information on how to view the data type that is mapped in the target, see the section for the target endpoint you are using.

For additional information about AWS DMS data types, see Data Types for AWS Database Migration Service.

SAP ASE Data Types	AWS DMS Data Types
BIGINT	INT8
BINARY	BYTES
BIT	BOOLEAN
CHAR	STRING
DATE	DATE
DATETIME	DATETIME
DECIMAL	NUMERIC
DOUBLE	REAL8
FLOAT	REAL8
IMAGE	BLOB
INT	INT4
MONEY	NUMERIC
NCHAR	WSTRING

SAP ASE Data Types	AWS DMS Data Types
NUMERIC	NUMERIC
NVARCHAR	WSTRING
REAL	REAL4
SMALLDATETIME	DATETIME
SMALLINT	INT2
SMALLMONEY	NUMERIC
TEXT	CLOB
TIME	TIME
TINYINT	UINT1
UNICHAR	UNICODE CHARACTER
UNITEXT	NCLOB
UNIVARCHAR	UNICODE
VARBINARY	BYTES
VARCHAR	STRING

AWS DMS does not support tables that include fields with the following data types:

- User-defined type (UDT)

Using MongoDB as a Source for AWS DMS

AWS DMS supports MongoDB versions 2.6.x and 3.x as a database source. A MongoDB database is a JSON document database where there are multiple MongoDB collections made up of JSON documents. In MongoDB, a collection is somewhat equivalent to a relational database table and a JSON document is somewhat equivalent to a row in that relational database table. Internally, a JSON document is stored as a binary JSON (BSON) file in a compressed format that includes a type for each field in the document. Each document has a unique ID.

AWS DMS supports two migration modes when using MongoDB as a source:

Document mode
In document mode, the MongoDB document is migrated "as is," meaning that its JSON data becomes a single column in a target table named "_doc".
You can optionally set the `extractDocID` parameter to *true* to create a second column named "`_id`" that acts as the primary key. You must set this parameter to *true* if you are going to use change data capture (CDC). Document mode is the default setting when you use MongoDB as a source. To explicitly specify document mode, add `nestingLevel=NONE` to the extra connection attribute on the MongoDB source endpoint.
Following is how AWS DMS manages documents and collections in document mode:

- When adding a new collection, the collection is replication as a CREATE TABLE.

- Renaming a collection is not supported.

Table mode
In table mode, AWS DMS scans a specified number of MongoDB documents and creates a set of all the keys and their types. This set is then used to create the columns of the target table. In this mode, a MongoDB document is transformed into a table data row. Each top-level field is transformed into a column. For each MongoDB document, AWS DMS adds each key and type to the target table's column set. Nested values are flattened into a column containing dot-separated key names. For example, a JSON document consisting of `{"a" : {"b" : {"c": 1}}}` is migrated into a column named `a.b.c`.
You can specify how many documents are scanned by setting the `docsToInvestigate` parameter. The default value is 1000. You can enable table mode by adding `nestingLevel=ONE` to the extra connection attributes of the MongoDB source endpoint.
Following is how AWS DMS manages documents and collections in table mode:

- When you add a document (row) to an existing collection, the document is replicated. If there are fields that don't exist in the collection, those fields are not replicated.

- When you update a document, the updated document is replicated. If there are fields that don't exist in the collection, those fields are not replicated.

- Deleting a document is fully supported.

- Adding a new collection doesn't result in a new table on the target when done during a CDC task.

- Renaming a collection is not supported.

Prerequisites When Using CDC with MongoDB as a Source for AWS DMS

To use change data capture (CDC) with a MongoDB source, you need to do several things. First, you deploy the replica set to create the operations log. Next, you create a user that should have at least READ privileges on the database to be migrated to and those same privileges to the LOCAL database.

You can use CDC with the Primary or Secondary node of a MongoDB replica set as the source endpoint.

Deploying a CDC Replica Set for MongoDB as a Source for AWS DMS

To use MongoDB as an AWS DMS source, you need to deploy a replica set. When you deploy the replica set, you create the operations log that AWS DMS uses for CDC processing. For more information, see the MongoDB documentation.

To convert a standalone instance to a replica set

1. Using the command line, connect to mongo.

```
mongo localhost
```

2. Create a user to be the root account, as shown in the following code. In this example, we call that user root.

```
use admin
db.createUser(
  {
    user: "root",
    pwd: "rootpass",
    roles: [ { role: "root", db: "admin" } ]
  }
)
```

Next, create a user with minimal privileges using the following code. In this example, we call that user root1.

```
use <<database_to_migrate>>
db.createUser(
{
    user: "root1",
    pwd: "rootpass",
    roles: [ { role: "read", db: "local" }, "read"]
})
```

3. Stop the mongod service.

```
service mongod stop
```

4. Restart mongod using the following command:

```
mongod --replSet "rs0" --auth -port <port_number>
```

5. Test the connection to the replica set using the following commands:

```
mongo -u root -p rootpass --host rs0/localhost:<port_number> --authenticationDatabase "
    admin"
```

The final requirement to use CDC with MongoDB is to select the option `_id as a separate column` to create a second column named "`_id`" that acts as the primary key.

Security Requirements When Using MongoDB as a Source for AWS DMS

AWS DMS supports two authentication methods for MongoDB. The two authentication methods are used to encrypt the password, so they are only used when the `Authentication mode` parameter is set to *password*.

The MongoDB authentication methods are:

- **MONOGODB-CR** — the default when using MongoDB 2.x authentication.

- **SCRAM-SHA-1** — the default when using MongoDB version 3.x authentication.

If an authentication method is not specified, AWS DMS uses the default method for the version of the MongoDB source. The two authentication methods are used to encrypt the password.

Limitations When Using MongoDB as a Source for AWS DMS

The following are limitations when using MongoDB as a source for AWS DMS:

- When the `_id as a separate column` parameter is selected, the ID string cannot exceed 200 characters.
- ObjectId and array type keys are converted to columns that are prefixed with `oid` and `array` in table mode.

  Internally these columns are referenced with the prefixed names. When you use transformation rules, you must specify the prefixed column. For example, specify `${oid__id}` and not `${_id}`, or specify `${array__addresses}` and not `${_addresses}`.

- Collection names cannot include the dollar symbol ($).

Configuration Properties When Using MongoDB as a Source for AWS DMS

When you set up your MongoDB source endpoint, you can specify additional configuration settings attributes. Attributes are specified by key-value pairs and separated by semicolons.

The following table describes the configuration properties available when using MongoDB databases as an AWS DMS source database.

Attribute Name	Valid Values	Default Value and Description
authType	NO PASSWORD	PASSWORD – When NO is selected, user name and password parameters are not used and can be empty.
authMechanism	DEFAULT MONGODB_CR SCRAM_SHA_1	DEFAULT – For MongoDB version 2.x, use MONGODB_CR. For MongoDB version 3.x, use SCRAM_SHA_1. This attribute is not used when authType=No.
nestingLevel	NONE ONE	NONE – Specify NONE to use document mode. Specify ONE to use table mode.
extractDocID	true false	false – Use this attribute when `nestingLevel` is set to NONE.
docsToInvestigate	A positive integer greater than 0.	1000 – Use this attribute when `nestingLevel` is set to ONE.
authSource	A valid MongoDB database name.	admin – This attribute is not used when authType=No.

Source Data Types for MongoDB

Data migration that uses MongoDB as a source for AWS DMS supports most MongoDB data types. The following table shows the MongoDB source data types that are supported when using AWS DMS and the default mapping from AWS DMS data types. For more information about MongoDB data types, see https://docs.mongodb.com/manual/reference/bson-types.

For information on how to view the data type that is mapped in the target, see the section for the target endpoint you are using.

For additional information about AWS DMS data types, see Data Types for AWS Database Migration Service.

MongoDB Data Types	AWS DMS Data Types
Boolean	Bool
Binary	BLOB
Date	Date
Timestamp	Date
Int	INT4
Long	INT8
Double	REAL8
String (UTF-8)	CLOB
Array	CLOB
OID	String
REGEX	CLOB
CODE	CLOB

Using Amazon S3 as a Source for AWS DMS

You can migrate data from an Amazon S3 bucket using AWS DMS. To do this, provide access to an S3 bucket containing one or more data files. In that S3 bucket, include a JSON file that describes the mapping between the data and the database tables of the data in those files.

The source data files must be present in the S3 bucket before the full load starts. You specify the bucket name using the `bucketName` parameter.

The source data files must be in comma separated value (CSV) format. Name them using the naming convention shown following. In this convention, *schemaName* is the source schema and *tableName* is the name of a table within that schema.

```
1  /schemaName/tableName/LOAD001.csv
2  /schemaName/tableName/LOAD002.csv
3  /schemaName/tableName/LOAD003.csv
4  ...
```

For example, suppose that your data files are in `mybucket`, at the following S3 path.

```
1  s3://mybucket/hr/employee
```

At load time, AWS DMS assumes that the source schema name is `hr`, and that the source table name is `employee`.

In addition to `bucketName` (which is required), you can optionally provide a `bucketFolder` parameter to specify where AWS DMS should look for data files in the S3 bucket. Continuing the previous example, if you set `bucketFolder` to *sourcedata*, then AWS DMS reads the data files at the following path.

```
1  s3://mybucket/sourcedata/hr/employee
```

You can specify the column delimiter, row delimiter, null value indicator, and other parameters using extra connection attributes. For more information, see Extra Connection Attributes for S3 as a Source for AWS DMS.

Defining External Tables for S3 as a Source for AWS DMS

In addition to the data files, you must also provide an external table definition. An *external table definition* is a JSON document that describes how AWS DMS should interpret the data from S3. The maximum size of this document is 2 MB. If you create a source endpoint using the AWS DMS Management Console, you can enter the JSON directly into the table mapping box. If you use the AWS Command Line Interface (AWS CLI) or AWS DMS API to perform migrations, you can create a JSON file to specify the external table definition.

Suppose that you have a data file that includes the following.

```
1  101,Smith,Bob,4-Jun-14,New York
2  102,Smith,Bob,8-Oct-15,Los Angeles
3  103,Smith,Bob,13-Mar-17,Dallas
4  104,Smith,Bob,13-Mar-17,Dallas
```

Following is an example external table definition for this data.

```
1  {
2      "TableCount": "1",
3      "Tables": [
4          {
5              "TableName": "employee",
6              "TablePath": "hr/employee/",
7              "TableOwner": "hr",
8              "TableColumns": [
```

```
 9              {
10                  "ColumnName": "Id",
11                  "ColumnType": "INT8",
12                  "ColumnNullable": "false",
13                  "ColumnIsPk": "true"
14              },
15              {
16                  "ColumnName": "LastName",
17                  "ColumnType": "STRING",
18                  "ColumnLength": "20"
19              },
20              {
21                  "ColumnName": "FirstName",
22                  "ColumnType": "STRING",
23                  "ColumnLength": "30"
24              },
25              {
26                  "ColumnName": "HireDate",
27                  "ColumnType": "DATETIME"
28              },
29              {
30                  "ColumnName": "OfficeLocation",
31                  "ColumnType": "STRING",
32                  "ColumnLength": "20"
33              }
34          ],
35          "TableColumnsTotal": "5"
36      }
37  ]
38 }
```

The elements in this JSON document are as follows:

TableCount—the number of source tables. In this example, there is only one table.

Tables—an array consisting of one JSON map per source table. In this example, there is only one map. Each map consists of the following elements:

- TableName—the name of the source table.
- TablePath—the path in your S3 bucket where AWS DMS can find the full data load file. If a bucketFolder value is specified, this value is prepended to the path.
- TableOwner—the schema name for this table.
- TableColumns—an array of one or more maps, each of which describes a column in the source table:
  - ColumnName—the name of a column in the source table.
  - ColumnType—the data type for the column. For valid data types, see Source Data Types for Amazon S3.
  - ColumnLength—the number of bytes in this column.
  - ColumnNullable—(optional) a Boolean value that is true if this column can contain NULL values.
  - ColumnIsPk—(optional) a Boolean value that is true if this column is part of the primary key.
- TableColumnsTotal—the total number of columns. This number must match the number of elements in the TableColumns array.

In the example preceding, some of the columns are of type STRING. In this case, use the `ColumnLength` element to specify the maximum number of characters.

`ColumnLength` applies for the following data types:

- BYTE
- STRING

If you don't specify otherwise, AWS DMS assumes that `ColumnLength` is zero.

For a column of the NUMERIC type, you need to specify the precision and scale. *Precision* is the total number of digits in a number, and *scale* is the number of digits to the right of the decimal point. You use the `ColumnPrecision` and `ColumnScale` elements for this, as shown following.

```
1  ...
2      {
3          "ColumnName": "HourlyRate",
4          "ColumnType": "NUMERIC",
5          "ColumnPrecision": "5"
6          "ColumnScale": "2"
7      }
8  ...
```

Using CDC with S3 as a Source for AWS DMS

After AWS DMS performs a full data load, it can optionally replicate data changes to the target endpoint. To do this, you upload change data capture files (CDC files) to your S3 bucket. AWS DMS reads these CDC files when you upload them, and then applies the changes at the target endpoint.

The CDC files are named as follows:

```
1  CDC00001.csv
2  CDC00002.csv
3  CDC00003.csv
4  ...
```

To indicate where AWS DMS can find the files, you must specify the `cdcPath` parameter. Continuing the previous example, if you set `cdcPath` to *changedata*, then AWS DMS reads the CDC files at the following path.

```
1  s3://mybucket/changedata
```

The records in a CDC file are formatted as follows:

- Operation—the change operation to be performed: INSERT, UPDATE, or DELETE. These keywords are case-insensitive.
- Table name—the name of the source table.
- Schema name—the name of the source schema.
- Data—one or more columns that represent the data to be changed.

Following is an example CDC file for a table named `employee`.

```
1  INSERT,employee,hr,101,Smith,Bob,4-Jun-14,New York
2  UPDATE,employee,hr,101,Smith,Bob,8-Oct-15,Los Angeles
3  UPDATE,employee,hr,101,Smith,Bob,13-Mar-17,Dallas
4  DELETE,employee,hr,101,Smith,Bob,13-Mar-17,Dallas
```

Prerequisites When Using S3 as a Source for AWS DMS

When you use S3 as a source for AWS DMS, the source S3 bucket that you use must be in the same AWS Region as the AWS DMS replication instance that you use to migrate your data. In addition, the AWS account you use for the migration must have read access to the source bucket.

The AWS Identity and Access Management (IAM) role assigned to the user account used to create the migration task must have the following set of permissions.

```
1  {
2      "Version": "2012-10-17",
3      "Statement": [
4          {
5              "Effect": "Allow",
6              "Action": [
7                  "s3:GetObject"
8              ],
9              "Resource": [
10                 "arn:aws:s3:::mybucket*"
11             ]
12         },
13         {
14             "Effect": "Allow",
15             "Action": [
16                 "s3:ListBucket"
17             ],
18             "Resource": [
19                 "arn:aws:s3:::mybucket*"
20             ]
21         }
22     ]
23 }
```

Extra Connection Attributes for S3 as a Source for AWS DMS

You can specify the following options as extra connection attributes.

Option	Description
bucketFolder	(Optional) A folder name in the S3 bucket. If this attribute is provided, source data files and CDC files are read from the path bucketFolder/schemaName/tableName/. If this attribute is not specified, then the path used is schemaName/tableName/. An example follows. bucketFolder=testFolder;
bucketName	The name of the S3 bucket. An example follows. bucketName=buckettest;

Option	Description
cdcPath	The location of change data capture (CDC) files. This attribute is required if a task captures change data; otherwise, it's optional. If cdcPath is present, then AWS DMS reads CDC files from this path and replicate the data changes to the target endpoint. For more information, see Using CDC with S3 as a Source for AWS DMS. An example follows.`cdcPath=dataChanges;`
csvRowDelimiter	The delimiter used to separate rows in the source files. The default is a carriage return (`\n`). An example follows. `csvRowDelimiter =\n;`
csvDelimiter	The delimiter used to separate columns in the source files. The default is a comma. An example follows. `csvDelimiter=,;`
externalTableDefinition	A JSON object that describes how AWS DMS should interpret the data in the S3 bucket during the migration. For more information, see Defining External Tables for S3 as a Source for AWS DMS. An example follows. `externalTableDefinition=`*<json_object>*

Source Data Types for Amazon S3

Data migration that uses Amazon S3 as a source for AWS DMS needs to map data from S3 to AWS DMS data types. For more information, see Defining External Tables for S3 as a Source for AWS DMS.

For information on how to view the data type that is mapped in the target, see the section for the target endpoint you are using.

For additional information about AWS DMS data types, see Data Types for AWS Database Migration Service.

AWS DMS Data Types—Amazon S3 as Source
BYTERequires `ColumnLength`. For more information, see Defining External Tables for S3 as a Source for AWS DMS.
DATE
TIME
DATETIME
TIMESTAMP
INT1
INT2
INT4
INT8
NUMERIC Requires `ColumnPrecision` and `ColumnScale`. For more information, see Defining External Tables for S3 as a Source for AWS DMS.
REAL4
REAL8
STRINGRequires `ColumnLength`. For more information, see Defining External Tables for S3 as a Source for AWS DMS.
UINT1
UINT2

AWS DMS Data Types—Amazon S3 as Source
UINT4
UINT8
BLOB
CLOB
BOOLEAN

Targets for Data Migration

AWS Database Migration Service (AWS DMS) can use many of the most popular databases as a target for data replication. The target can be on an Amazon Elastic Compute Cloud (Amazon EC2) instance, an Amazon Relational Database Service (Amazon RDS) instance, or an on-premises database.

Note
Regardless of the source storage engine (MyISAM, MEMORY, and so on), AWS DMS creates a MySQL-compatible target table as an InnoDB table by default. If you need to have a table that uses a storage engine other than InnoDB, you can manually create the table on the MySQL-compatible target and migrate the table using the "do nothing" mode. For more information about the "do nothing" mode, see Full Load Task Settings.

The databases include the following:

On-premises and EC2 instance databases

- Oracle versions 10g, 11g, 12c, for the Enterprise, Standard, Standard One, and Standard Two editions
- Microsoft SQL Server versions 2005, 2008, 2008R2, 2012, 2014, and 2016, for the Enterprise, Standard, Workgroup, and Developer editions. The Web and Express editions are not supported.
- MySQL versions 5.5, 5.6, and 5.7
- MariaDB (supported as a MySQL-compatible data target)
- PostgreSQL versions 9.4 and later
- SAP Adaptive Server Enterprise (ASE) versions 15, 15.5, 15.7, 16 and later

Amazon RDS instance databases, Amazon Redshift, Amazon S3, and Amazon DynamoDB

- Amazon RDS Oracle versions 11g (versions 11.2.0.3.v1 and later) and 12c, for the Enterprise, Standard, Standard One, and Standard Two editions
- Amazon RDS Microsoft SQL Server versions 2008R2, 2012, and 2014, for the Enterprise, Standard, Workgroup, and Developer editions. The Web and Express editions are not supported.
- Amazon RDS MySQL versions 5.5, 5.6, and 5.7
- Amazon RDS MariaDB (supported as a MySQL-compatible data target)
- Amazon RDS PostgreSQL versions 9.4 and later
- Amazon Aurora with MySQL compatibility
- Amazon Aurora with PostgreSQL compatibility
- Amazon Redshift
- Amazon S3
- Amazon DynamoDB
- Using an Oracle Database as a Target for AWS Database Migration Service
- Using a Microsoft SQL Server Database as a Target for AWS Database Migration Service
- Using a PostgreSQL Database as a Target for AWS Database Migration Service
- Using a MySQL-Compatible Database as a Target for AWS Database Migration Service
- Using an Amazon Redshift Database as a Target for AWS Database Migration Service
- Using a SAP ASE Database as a Target for AWS Database Migration Service
- Using Amazon S3 as a Target for AWS Database Migration Service
- Using an Amazon DynamoDB Database as a Target for AWS Database Migration Service

Using an Oracle Database as a Target for AWS Database Migration Service

You can migrate data to Oracle database targets using AWS DMS, either from another Oracle database or from one of the other supported databases. You can use Secure Sockets Layer (SSL) to encrypt connections between your Oracle endpoint and the replication instance. For more information on using SSL with an Oracle endpoint, see Using SSL With AWS Database Migration Service.

AWS DMS supports Oracle versions 10g, 11g, and 12c for on-premises and EC2 instances for the Enterprise, Standard, Standard One, and Standard Two editions as targets. AWS DMS supports Oracle versions 11g (versions 11.2.0.3.v1 and later) and 12c for Amazon RDS instance databases for the Enterprise, Standard, Standard One, and Standard Two editions.

When using Oracle as a target, we assume that the data should be migrated into the schema or user that is used for the target connection. If you want to migrate data to a different schema, you need to use a schema transformation to do so. For example, suppose that your target endpoint connects to the user RDSMASTER and you want to migrate from the user PERFDATA to PERFDATA. In this case, create a transformation as follows.

```
1  {
2      "rule-type": "transformation",
3      "rule-id": "2",
4      "rule-name": "2",
5      "rule-action": "rename",
6      "rule-target": "schema",
7      "object-locator": {
8      "schema-name": "PERFDATA"
9  },
10  "value": "PERFDATA"
11  }
```

For more information about transformations, see Selection and Transformation Table Mapping using JSON.

For additional details on working with Oracle databases as a target for AWS DMS, see the following sections:

- Limitations on Oracle as a Target for AWS Database Migration Service
- User Account Privileges Required for Using Oracle as a Target
- Configuring an Oracle Database as a Target for AWS Database Migration Service
- Extra Connection Attributes When Using Oracle as a Target for AWS DMS
- Target Data Types for Oracle

Limitations on Oracle as a Target for AWS Database Migration Service

Limitations when using Oracle as a target for data migration include the following:

- AWS DMS does not create schema on the target Oracle database. You have to create any schemas you want on the target Oracle database. The schema name must already exist for the Oracle target. Tables from source schema are imported to user/schema, which AWS DMS uses to connect to the target instance. You must create multiple replication tasks if you have to migrate multiple schemas.

- AWS DMS doesn't support the Use direct path full load option for tables with INDEXTYPE CONTEXT. As a workaround, you can use array load.

- In Batch Optimized Apply mode, loading into the net changes table uses Direct Path, which doesn't support XMLType. As a workaround, you can use Transactional Apply mode.

User Account Privileges Required for Using Oracle as a Target

To use an Oracle target in an AWS Database Migration Service task, for the user account specified in the AWS DMS Oracle database definitions you need to grant the following privileges in the Oracle database:

- SELECT ANY TRANSACTION
- SELECT on V$NLS_PARAMETERS
- SELECT on V$TIMEZONE_NAMES
- SELECT on ALL_INDEXES
- SELECT on ALL_OBJECTS
- SELECT on DBA_OBJECTS
- SELECT on ALL_TABLES
- SELECT on ALL_USERS
- SELECT on ALL_CATALOG
- SELECT on ALL_CONSTRAINTS
- SELECT on ALL_CONS_COLUMNS
- SELECT on ALL_TAB_COLS
- SELECT on ALL_IND_COLUMNS
- DROP ANY TABLE
- SELECT ANY TABLE
- INSERT ANY TABLE
- UPDATE ANY TABLE
- CREATE ANY VIEW
- DROP ANY VIEW
- CREATE ANY PROCEDURE
- ALTER ANY PROCEDURE
- DROP ANY PROCEDURE
- CREATE ANY SEQUENCE
- ALTER ANY SEQUENCE
- DROP ANY SEQUENCE

For the requirements specified following, grant the additional privileges named:

- To use a specific table list, grant SELECT on any replicated table and also ALTER on any replicated table.
- To allow a user to create a table in his default tablespace, grant the privilege GRANT UNLIMITED TABLESPACE.
- For logon, grant the privilege CREATE SESSION.
- If you are using a direct path, grant the privilege LOCK ANY TABLE.
- If the "DROP and CREATE table" or "TRUNCATE before loading" option is selected in the full load settings, and the target table schema is different from that for the AWS DMS user, grant the privilege DROP ANY TABLE.

- To store changes in change tables or an audit table when the target table schema is different from that for the AWS DMS user, grant the privileges CREATE ANY TABLE and CREATE ANY INDEX.

Read Privileges Required for AWS Database Migration Service on the Target Database

The AWS DMS user account must be granted read permissions for the following DBA tables:

- SELECT on DBA_USERS
- SELECT on DBA_TAB_PRIVS
- SELECT on DBA_OBJECTS
- SELECT on DBA_SYNONYMS
- SELECT on DBA_SEQUENCES
- SELECT on DBA_TYPES
- SELECT on DBA_INDEXES
- SELECT on DBA_TABLES
- SELECT on DBA_TRIGGERS

If any of the required privileges cannot be granted to V$xxx, then grant them to V_$xxx.

Configuring an Oracle Database as a Target for AWS Database Migration Service

Before using an Oracle database as a data migration target, you must provide an Oracle user account to AWS DMS. The user account must have read/write privileges on the Oracle database, as specified in the section User Account Privileges Required for Using Oracle as a Target.

Extra Connection Attributes When Using Oracle as a Target for AWS DMS

You can use extra connection attributes to configure your Oracle target. You specify these settings when you create the target endpoint. Multiple extra connection attribute settings should be separated by a semicolon.

The following table shows the extra connection attributes available when using Oracle as a target.

[See the AWS documentation website for more details]

Target Data Types for Oracle

A target Oracle database used with AWS DMS supports most Oracle data types. The following table shows the Oracle target data types that are supported when using AWS DMS and the default mapping from AWS DMS data types. For more information about how to view the data type that is mapped from the source, see the section for the source you are using.

AWS DMS Data Type	Oracle Data Type
BOOLEAN	NUMBER (1)
BYTES	RAW (length)
DATE	DATETIME
TIME	TIMESTAMP (0)
DATETIME	TIMESTAMP (scale)
INT1	NUMBER (3)
INT2	NUMBER (5)

AWS DMS Data Type	Oracle Data Type
INT4	NUMBER (10)
INT8	NUMBER (19)
NUMERIC	NUMBER (p,s)
REAL4	FLOAT
REAL8	FLOAT
STRING	With date indication: DATE With time indication: TIMESTAMP With timestamp indication: TIMESTAMP With timestamp_with_timezone indication: TIMESTAMP WITH TIMEZONE With timestamp_with_local_timezone indication: TIMESTAMP WITH LOCAL TIMEZONE With interval_year_to_month indication: INTERVAL YEAR TO MONTH With interval_day_to_second indication: INTERVAL DAY TO SECOND If length > 4000: CLOB In all other cases: VARCHAR2 (length)
UINT1	NUMBER (3)
UINT2	NUMBER (5)
UINT4	NUMBER (10)
UINT8	NUMBER (19)
WSTRING	If length > 2000: NCLOB In all other cases: NVARCHAR2 (length)
BLOB	BLOB To use this data type with AWS DMS, you must enable the use of BLOBs for a specific task. BLOB data types are supported only in tables that include a primary key
CLOB	CLOB To use this data type with AWS DMS, you must enable the use of CLOBs for a specific task. During CDC, CLOB data types are supported only in tables that include a primary key.
NCLOB	NCLOB To use this data type with AWS DMS, you must enable the use of NCLOBs for a specific task. During CDC, NCLOB data types are supported only in tables that include a primary key.
XMLTYPE	The XMLTYPE target data type is only relevant in Oracle-to-Oracle replication tasks. When the source database is Oracle, the source data types are replicated "as is" to the Oracle target. For example, an XMLTYPE data type on the source is created as an XMLTYPE data type on the target.

Using a Microsoft SQL Server Database as a Target for AWS Database Migration Service

You can migrate data to Microsoft SQL Server databases using AWS DMS. With an SQL Server database as a target, you can migrate data from either another SQL Server database or one of the other supported databases.

For on-premises and Amazon EC2 instance databases, AWS DMS supports as a target SQL Server versions 2005, 2008, 2008R2, 2012, 2014, and 2016, for the Enterprise, Standard, Workgroup, and Developer editions. The Web and Express editions are not supported.

For Amazon RDS instance databases, AWS DMS supports as a target SQL Server versions 2008R2, 2012, 2014, and 2016, for the Enterprise, Standard, Workgroup, and Developer editions are supported. The Web and Express editions are not supported.

For additional details on working with AWS DMS and SQL Server target databases, see the following.

- Limitations on Using SQL Server as a Target for AWS Database Migration Service
- Security Requirements When Using SQL Server as a Target for AWS Database Migration Service
- Extra Connection Attributes When Using SQLServer as a Target for AWS DMS
- Target Data Types for Microsoft SQL Server

Limitations on Using SQL Server as a Target for AWS Database Migration Service

The following limitations apply when using a SQL Server database as a target for AWS DMS:

- When you manually create a SQL Server target table with a computed column, full load replication is not supported when using the BCP bulk-copy utility. To use full load replication, disable the **Use BCP for loading tables** option in the console's **Advanced** tab. For more information on working with BCP, see the Microsoft SQL Server documentation.

- When replicating tables with SQL Server spatial data types (GEOMETRY and GEOGRAPHY), AWS DMS replaces any spatial reference identifier (SRID) that you might have inserted with the default SRID. The default SRID is 0 for GEOMETRY and 4326 for GEOGRAPHY.

Security Requirements When Using SQL Server as a Target for AWS Database Migration Service

The following describes the security requirements for using AWS DMS with a Microsoft SQL Server target.

- AWS DMS user account must have at least the `db_owner` user role on the Microsoft SQL Server database you are connecting to.

- A Microsoft SQL Server system administrator must provide this permission to all AWS DMS user accounts.

Extra Connection Attributes When Using SQLServer as a Target for AWS DMS

You can use extra connection attributes to configure your SQL Server target. You specify these settings when you create the target endpoint. Multiple extra connection attribute settings should be separated by a semicolon.

The following table shows the extra connection attributes that you can use when SQL Server is the target.

[See the AWS documentation website for more details]

Target Data Types for Microsoft SQL Server

The following table shows the Microsoft SQL Server target data types that are supported when using AWS DMS and the default mapping from AWS DMS data types. For additional information about AWS DMS data types, see Data Types for AWS Database Migration Service.

AWS DMS Data Type	SQL Server Data Type
BOOLEAN	TINYINT
BYTES	VARBINARY(length)
DATE	For SQL Server 2008 and later, use DATE. For earlier versions, if the scale is 3 or less use DATETIME. In all other cases, use VARCHAR (37).
TIME	For SQL Server 2008 and later, use DATETIME2 (%d). For earlier versions, if the scale is 3 or less use DATETIME. In all other cases, use VARCHAR (37).
DATETIME	For SQL Server 2008 and later, use DATETIME2 (scale). For earlier versions, if the scale is 3 or less use DATETIME. In all other cases, use VARCHAR (37).
INT1	SMALLINT
INT2	SMALLINT
INT4	INT
INT8	BIGINT
NUMERIC	NUMBER (p,s)
REAL4	REAL
REAL8	FLOAT
STRING	If the column is a date or time column, then do the following: [See the AWS documentation website for more details] If the column is not a date or time column, use VARCHAR (length).
UINT1	TINYINT
UINT2	SMALLINT
UINT4	INT
UINT8	BIGINT
WSTRING	NVARCHAR (length)
BLOB	VARBINARY(max) IMAGE To use this data type with AWS DMS, you must enable the use of BLOBs for a specific task. AWS DMS supports BLOB data types only in tables that include a primary key.
CLOB	VARCHAR(max) To use this data type with AWS DMS, you must enable the use of CLOBs for a specific task. During CDC, AWS DMS supports CLOB data types only in tables that include a primary key.
NCLOB	NVARCHAR(max) To use this data type with AWS DMS, you must enable the use of NCLOBs for a specific task. During CDC, AWS DMS supports NCLOB data types only in tables that include a primary key.

Using a PostgreSQL Database as a Target for AWS Database Migration Service

You can migrate data to PostgreSQL databases using AWS DMS, either from another PostgreSQL database or from one of the other supported databases. PostgreSQL versions 9.4 and later are supported for on-premises, Amazon RDS, Amazon Aurora with PostgreSQL compatibility, and EC2 instance databases.

AWS DMS takes a table-by-table approach when migrating data from source to target in the Full Load phase. Table order during the full load phase cannot be guaranteed. Tables are out of sync during the full load phase and while cached transactions for individual tables are being applied. As a result, active referential integrity constraints can result in task failure during the full load phase.

In PostgreSQL, foreign keys (referential integrity constraints) are implemented using triggers. During the full load phase, AWS DMS loads each table one at a time. We strongly recommend that you disable foreign key constraints during a full load, using one of the following methods:

- Temporarily disable all triggers from the instance, and finish the full load.

- Use the `session_replication_role` parameter in PostgreSQL.

At any given time, a trigger can be in one of the following states: `origin`, `replica`, `always`, or `disabled`. When the `session_replication_role` parameter is set to `replica`, only triggers in the `replica` state are active, and they are fired when they are called. Otherwise, the triggers remain inactive.

PostgreSQL has a failsafe mechanism to prevent a table from being truncated, even when `session_replication_role` is set. You can use this as an alternative to disabling triggers, to help the full load run to completion. To do this, set the target table preparation mode to `DO_NOTHING`. Otherwise, DROP and TRUNCATE operations fail when there are foreign key constraints.

In Amazon RDS, you can control set this parameter using a parameter group. For a PostgreSQL instance running on Amazon EC2, you can set the parameter directly.

For additional details on working with a PostgreSQL database as a target for AWS DMS, see the following sections:

- Limitations on Using PostgreSQL as a Target for AWS Database Migration Service
- Security Requirements When Using a PostgreSQL Database as a Target for AWS Database Migration Service
- Extra Connection Attributes When Using PostgreSQL as a Target for AWS DMS
- Target Data Types for PostgreSQL

Limitations on Using PostgreSQL as a Target for AWS Database Migration Service

The following limitations apply when using a PostgreSQL database as a target for AWS DMS:

- The JSON data type is converted to the Native CLOB data type.

Security Requirements When Using a PostgreSQL Database as a Target for AWS Database Migration Service

For security purposes, the user account used for the data migration must be a registered user in any PostgreSQL database that you use as a target.

Extra Connection Attributes When Using PostgreSQL as a Target for AWS DMS

You can use extra connection attributes to configure your PostgreSQL target. You specify these settings when you create the target endpoint. Multiple extra connection attribute settings should be separated by a semicolon.

The following table shows the extra connection attributes you can use to configure PostgreSQL as a target for AWS DMS.

[See the AWS documentation website for more details]

Target Data Types for PostgreSQL

The PostgreSQL database endpoint for AWS DMS supports most PostgreSQL database data types. The following table shows the PostgreSQL database target data types that are supported when using AWS DMS and the default mapping from AWS DMS data types. Unsupported data types are listed following the table.

For additional information about AWS DMS data types, see Data Types for AWS Database Migration Service.

AWS DMS Data Type	PostgreSQL Data Type
BOOL	BOOL
BYTES	BYTEA
DATE	DATE
TIME	TIME
TIMESTAMP	If the scale is from 0 through 6, then use TIMESTAMP. If the scale is from 7 through 9, then use VARCHAR (37).
INT1	SMALLINT
INT2	SMALLINT
INT4	INTEGER
INT8	BIGINT
NUMERIC	DECIMAL (P,S)
REAL4	FLOAT4
REAL8	FLOAT8
STRING	If the length is from 1 through 21,845, then use VARCHAR (length in bytes). If the length is 21,846 through 2,147,483,647, then use VARCHAR (65535).
UINT1	SMALLINT
UINT2	INTEGER
UINT4	BIGINT
UINT8	BIGINT
WSTRING	If the length is from 1 through 21,845, then use VARCHAR (length in bytes). If the length is 21,846 through 2,147,483,647, then use VARCHAR (65535).
BCLOB	BYTEA
NCLOB	TEXT
CLOB	TEXT

Note
When replicating from a PostgreSQL source, AWS DMS creates the target table with the same data types for all columns, apart from columns with user-defined data types. In such cases, the data type is created as "character varying" in the target.

Using a MySQL-Compatible Database as a Target for AWS Database Migration Service

You can migrate data to any MySQL-compatible database using AWS DMS, from any of the source data engines that AWS DMS supports. If you are migrating to an on-premises MySQL-compatible database, then AWS DMS requires that your source engine reside within the AWS ecosystem. The engine can be on an Amazon-managed service such as Amazon RDS, Amazon Aurora, or Amazon S3. Alternatively, the engine can be on a self-managed database on Amazon EC2.

You can use SSL to encrypt connections between your MySQL-compatible endpoint and the replication instance. For more information on using SSL with a MySQL-compatible endpoint, see Using SSL With AWS Database Migration Service.

MySQL versions 5.5, 5.6, and 5.7 are supported, as are MariaDB and Aurora MySQL.

You can use the following MySQL-compatible databases as targets for AWS DMS:

- MySQL Community Edition
- MySQL Standard Edition
- MySQL Enterprise Edition
- MySQL Cluster Carrier Grade Edition
- MariaDB Community Edition
- MariaDB Enterprise Edition
- MariaDB Column Store
- Amazon Aurora MySQL

For additional details on working with a MySQL-compatible database as a target for AWS DMS, see the following sections.

- Using Any MySQL-Compatible Database as a Target for AWS Database Migration Service
- Limitations on Using a MySQL-Compatible Database as a Target for AWS Database Migration Service
- Extra Connection Attributes When Using a MySQL-Compatible Database as a Target for AWS DMS
- Target Data Types for MySQL

Using Any MySQL-Compatible Database as a Target for AWS Database Migration Service

Before you begin to work with a MySQL-compatible database as a target for AWS DMS, make sure that you have the following prerequisites:

- You must provide a user account to AWS DMS that has read/write privileges to the MySQL-compatible database. To create the necessary privileges, run the following commands.

```
1 CREATE USER '<user acct>'@'%' IDENTIFIED BY '<user password>';
2 GRANT ALTER, CREATE, DROP, INDEX, INSERT, UPDATE, DELETE, SELECT ON <schema>.* TO
3 '<user acct>'@'%';
4 GRANT ALL PRIVILEGES ON awsdms_control.* TO '<user acct>'@'%';
```

- During the full-load migration phase, you must disable foreign keys on your target tables. To disable foreign key checks on a MySQL-compatible database during a full load, you can add the following command to the **Extra Connection Attributes** in the **Advanced** section of the target endpoint.

```
1 initstmt=SET FOREIGN_KEY_CHECKS=0
```

Limitations on Using a MySQL-Compatible Database as a Target for AWS Database Migration Service

When using a MySQL database as a target, AWS DMS doesn't support the following:

- The data definition language (DDL) statements TRUNCATE PARTITION, DROP TABLE, and RENAME TABLE.

- Using an `ALTER TABLE <table_name> ADD COLUMN <column_name>` statement to add columns to the beginning or the middle of a table.

- When only the LOB column in a source table is updated, AWS DMS doesn't update the corresponding target column. The target LOB is only updated if at least one other column is updated in the same transaction.

- When loading data to a MySQL-compatible target in a full load task, AWS DMS doesn't report duplicate key errors in the task log.

- When you update a column's value to its existing value, MySQL-compatible databases return a `0 rows affected` warning. Although this behavior isn't technically an error, it is different from how the situation is handled by other database engines. For example, Oracle performs an update of one row. For MySQL-compatible databases, AWS DMS generates an entry in the awsdms_apply_exceptions control table and logs the following warning.

```
1 Some changes from the source database had no impact when applied to
2 the target database. See awsdms_apply_exceptions table for details.
```

Extra Connection Attributes When Using a MySQL-Compatible Database as a Target for AWS DMS

You can use extra connection attributes to configure your MySQL-compatible target. You specify these settings when you create the target endpoint. Multiple extra connection attribute settings should be separated from each other by a semicolon.

The following table shows extra configuration settings that you can use when creating a MySQL-compatible target for AWS DMS.

[See the AWS documentation website for more details]

Target Data Types for MySQL

The following table shows the MySQL database target data types that are supported when using AWS DMS and the default mapping from AWS DMS data types.

For additional information about AWS DMS data types, see Data Types for AWS Database Migration Service.

AWS DMS Data Types	MySQL Data Types
BOOLEAN	BOOLEAN
BYTES	If the length is from 1 through 65,535, then use VARBINARY (length). If the length is from 65,536 through 2,147,483,647, then use LONGLOB.
DATE	DATE
TIME	TIME

AWS DMS Data Types	MySQL Data Types
TIMESTAMP	"If scale is => 0 and =< 6, then: DATE-TIME (Scale) If scale is => 7 and =< 9, then: VARCHAR (37)"
INT1	TINYINT
INT2	SMALLINT
INT4	INTEGER
INT8	BIGINT
NUMERIC	DECIMAL (p,s)
REAL4	FLOAT
REAL8	DOUBLE PRECISION
STRING	If the length is from 1 through 21,845, then use VARCHAR (length). If the length is from 21,846 through 2,147,483,647, then use LONGTEXT.
UINT1	UNSIGNED TINYINT
UINT2	UNSIGNED SMALLINT
UINT4	UNSIGNED INTEGER
UINT8	UNSIGNED BIGINT
WSTRING	If the length is from 1 through 32,767, then use VARCHAR (length). If the length is from 32,768 through 2,147,483,647, then use LONGTEXT.
BLOB	If the length is from 1 through 65,535, then use BLOB. If the length is from 65,536 through 2,147,483,647, then use LONGBLOB. If the length is 0, then use LONGBLOB (full LOB support).
NCLOB	If the length is from 1 through 65,535, then use TEXT. If the length is from 65,536 through 2,147,483,647, then use LONGTEXT with ucs2 for CHARACTER SET. If the length is 0, then use LONGTEXT (full LOB support) with ucs2 for CHARACTER SET.
CLOB	If the length is from 1 through 65,535, then use TEXT. If the length is from 65,536 through 2147483647, then use LONGTEXT. If the length is 0, then use LONGTEXT (full LOB support).

Using an Amazon Redshift Database as a Target for AWS Database Migration Service

You can migrate data to Amazon Redshift databases using AWS Database Migration Service. Amazon Redshift is a fully managed, petabyte-scale data warehouse service in the cloud. With an Amazon Redshift database as a target, you can migrate data from all of the other supported source databases.

The Amazon Redshift cluster must be in the same AWS account and same AWS Region as the replication instance.

During a database migration to Amazon Redshift, AWS DMS first moves data to an S3 bucket. Once the files reside in an S3 bucket, AWS DMS then transfers them to the proper tables in the Amazon Redshift data warehouse. AWS DMS creates the S3 bucket in the same AWS Region as the Amazon Redshift database. The AWS DMS replication instance must be located in that same region.

If you use the AWS Command Line Interface (AWS CLI) or the AWS DMS API to migrate data to Amazon Redshift, you must set up an AWS Identity and Access Management (IAM) role to allow S3 access. For more information about creating this IAM role, see Creating the IAM Roles to Use With the AWS CLI and AWS DMS API.

The Amazon Redshift endpoint provides full automation for the following:

- Schema generation and data type mapping
- Full load of source database tables
- Incremental load of changes made to source tables
- Application of schema changes in data definition language (DDL) made to the source tables
- Synchronization between full load and change data capture (CDC) processes.

AWS Database Migration Service supports both full load and change processing operations. AWS DMS reads the data from the source database and creates a series of comma-separated value (CSV) files. For full-load operations, AWS DMS creates files for each table. AWS DMS then copies the table files for each table to a separate folder in Amazon S3. When the files are uploaded to Amazon S3, AWS DMS sends a copy command and the data in the files are copied into Amazon Redshift. For change-processing operations, AWS DMS copies the net changes to the CSV files. AWS DMS then uploads the net change files to Amazon S3 and copies the data to Amazon Redshift.

For additional details on working with Amazon Redshift as a target for AWS DMS, see the following sections:

- Prerequisites for Using an Amazon Redshift Database as a Target for AWS Database Migration Service
- Limitations on Using Amazon Redshift as a Target for AWS Database Migration Service
- Configuring an Amazon Redshift Database as a Target for AWS Database Migration Service
- Using Enhanced VPC Routing with an Amazon Redshift as a Target for AWS Database Migration Service
- Extra Connection Attributes When Using Amazon Redshift as a Target for AWS DMS
- Target Data Types for Amazon Redshift

Prerequisites for Using an Amazon Redshift Database as a Target for AWS Database Migration Service

The following list describes the prerequisites necessary for working with Amazon Redshift as a target for data migration:

- Use the AWS Management Console to launch an Amazon Redshift cluster. You should note the basic information about your AWS account and your Amazon Redshift cluster, such as your password, user name, and database name. You need these values when creating the Amazon Redshift target endpoint.

- The Amazon Redshift cluster must be in the same AWS account and the same AWS Region as the replication instance.

- The AWS DMS replication instance needs network connectivity to the Amazon Redshift endpoint (hostname and port) that your cluster uses.

- AWS DMS uses an Amazon S3 bucket to transfer data to the Amazon Redshift database. For AWS DMS to create the bucket, the DMS console uses an Amazon IAM role, `dms-access-for-endpoint`. If you use the AWS CLI or DMS API to create a database migration with Amazon Redshift as the target database, you must create this IAM role. For more information about creating this role, see Creating the IAM Roles to Use With the AWS CLI and AWS DMS API.

Limitations on Using Amazon Redshift as a Target for AWS Database Migration Service

When using an Amazon Redshift database as a target, AWS DMS doesn't support the following:

- When migrating from MySQL/Aurora MySQL to Amazon Redshift, you cannot use DDL to alter a column from the BLOB data type to the NVARCHAR data type.

  For example, the following DDL is not supported.

```
1 ALTER TABLE table_name MODIFY column_name NVARCHAR(n);
```

Configuring an Amazon Redshift Database as a Target for AWS Database Migration Service

AWS Database Migration Service must be configured to work with the Amazon Redshift instance. The following table describes the configuration properties available for the Amazon Redshift endpoint.

Property	Description
server	The name of the Amazon Redshift cluster you are using.
port	The port number for Amazon Redshift. The default value is 5439.
username	An Amazon Redshift user name for a registered user.
password	The password for the user named in the username property.
database	The name of the Amazon Redshift data warehouse (service) you are working with.

If you want to add extra connection string attributes to your Amazon Redshift endpoint, you can specify the `maxFileSize` and `fileTransferUploadStreams` attributes. For more information on these attributes, see Extra Connection Attributes When Using Amazon Redshift as a Target for AWS DMS.

Using Enhanced VPC Routing with an Amazon Redshift as a Target for AWS Database Migration Service

If you're using the *Enhanced VPC Routing* feature with your Amazon Redshift target, the feature forces all COPY traffic between your Amazon Redshift cluster and your data repositories through your Amazon VPC. Because

Enhanced VPC Routing affects the way that Amazon Redshift accesses other resources, COPY commands might fail if you haven't configured your VPC correctly.

AWS DMS can be affected by this behavior because it uses the COPY command to move data in S3 to an Amazon Redshift cluster.

Following are the steps AWS DMS takes to load data into an Amazon Redshift target:

1. AWS DMS copies data from the source to CSV files on the replication server.

2. AWS DMS uses the AWS SDK to copy the CSV files into an S3 bucket on your account.

3. AWS DMS then uses the COPY command in Amazon Redshift to copy data from the CSV files in S3 to an appropriate table in Amazon Redshift.

If *Enhanced VPC Routing* is not enabled, Amazon Redshift routes traffic through the Internet, including traffic to other services within the AWS network. If the feature is not enabled, you do not have to configure the network path. If the feature is enabled, you must specifically create a network path between your cluster's VPC and your data resources. For more information on the configuration required, see Enhanced VPC Routing in the Amazon Redshift documentation.

Extra Connection Attributes When Using Amazon Redshift as a Target for AWS DMS

You can use extra connection attributes to configure your Amazon Redshift target. You specify these settings when you create the source endpoint. Multiple extra connection attribute settings should be separated by a semicolon.

The following table shows the extra connection attributes available when Amazon Redshift is the target.

[See the AWS documentation website for more details]

Target Data Types for Amazon Redshift

The Amazon Redshift endpoint for AWS DMS supports most Amazon Redshift data types. The following table shows the Amazon Redshift target data types that are supported when using AWS DMS and the default mapping from AWS DMS data types.

For additional information about AWS DMS data types, see Data Types for AWS Database Migration Service.

AWS DMS Data Types	Amazon Redshift Data Types
BOOLEAN	BOOL
BYTES	VARCHAR (Length)
DATE	DATE
TIME	VARCHAR(20)
DATETIME	If the scale is => 0 and =< 6, then: TIMESTAMP (s) If the scale is => 7 and =< 9, then: VARCHAR (37)
INT1	INT2
INT2	INT2
INT4	INT4
INT8	INT8
NUMERIC	If the scale is => 0 and =< 37, then: NUMERIC (p,s) If the scale is => 38 and =< 127, then: VARCHAR (Length)
REAL4	FLOAT4
REAL8	FLOAT8

AWS DMS Data Types	Amazon Redshift Data Types
STRING	If the length is 1–65,535, then use VARCHAR (length in bytes) If the length is 65,536–2,147,483,647, then use VARCHAR (65535)
UINT1	INT2
UINT2	INT2
UINT4	INT4
UINT8	NUMERIC (20,0)
WSTRING	If the length is 1–65,535, then use NVAR-CHAR (length in bytes) If the length is 65,536–2,147,483,647, then use NVARCHAR (65535)
BLOB	VARCHAR (maximum LOB size *2) The maximum LOB size cannot exceed 31 KB.
NCLOB	NVARCHAR (maximum LOB size) The maximum LOB size cannot exceed 63 KB.
CLOB	VARCHAR (maximum LOB size) The maximum LOB size cannot exceed 63 KB.

Using a SAP ASE Database as a Target for AWS Database Migration Service

You can migrate data to SAP Adaptive Server Enterprise (ASE)–formerly known as Sybase–databases using AWS DMS, either from any of the supported database sources.

SAP ASE versions 15, 15.5, 15.7, 16 and later are supported.

Prerequisites for Using a SAP ASE Database as a Target for AWS Database Migration Service

Before you begin to work with a SAP ASE database as a target for AWS DMS, make sure that you have the following prerequisites:

- You must provide SAP ASE account access to the AWS DMS user. This user must have read/write privileges in the SAP ASE database.

- When replicating to SAP ASE version 15.7 installed on a Windows EC2 instance configured with a non-Latin language (for example, Chinese), AWS DMS requires SAP ASE 15.7 SP121 to be installed on the target SAP ASE machine.

Extra Connection Attributes When Using SAP ASE as a Target for AWS DMS

You can use extra connection attributes to configure your SAP ASE target. You specify these settings when you create the target endpoint. Multiple extra connection attribute settings should be separated by a semicolon.

The following table shows the extra connection attributes available when using SAP ASE as a target:

[See the AWS documentation website for more details]

Note
If the user name or password specified in the connection string contains non-Latin characters (for example, Chinese), the following property is required: `charset=gb18030`

Target Data Types for SAP ASE

The following table shows the SAP ASE database target data types that are supported when using AWS DMS and the default mapping from AWS DMS data types.

For additional information about AWS DMS data types, see Data Types for AWS Database Migration Service.

AWS DMS Data Types	SAP ASE Data Types
BOOLEAN	BIT
BYTES	VARBINARY (Length)
DATE	DATE
TIME	TIME
TIMESTAMP	If scale is => 0 and =< 6, then: BIGDATETIME If scale is => 7 and =< 9, then: VARCHAR (37)
INT1	TINYINT
INT2	SMALLINT
INT4	INTEGER
INT8	BIGINT
NUMERIC	NUMERIC (p,s)

AWS DMS Data Types	SAP ASE Data Types
REAL4	REAL
REAL8	DOUBLE PRECISION
STRING	VARCHAR (Length)
UINT1	TINYINT
UINT2	UNSIGNED SMALLINT
UINT4	UNSIGNED INTEGER
UINT8	UNSIGNED BIGINT
WSTRING	VARCHAR (Length)
BLOB	IMAGE
CLOB	UNITEXT
NCLOB	TEXT

AWS DMS does not support tables that include fields with the following data types. Replicated columns with these data types show as null.

- User-defined type (UDT)

147

Using Amazon S3 as a Target for AWS Database Migration Service

You can migrate data to Amazon S3 using AWS DMS from any of the supported database sources. When using S3 as a target in an AWS DMS task, both full load and change data capture (CDC) data is written to comma-separated-values (CSV) format. AWS DMS names files created during a full load using incremental counters, for example LOAD00001.csv, LOAD00002, and so on. AWS DMS names CDC files using timestamps, for example 20141029-1134010000.csv. For each source table, AWS DMS creates a folder under the specified target folder. AWS DMS writes all full load and CDC files to the specified S3 bucket.

The parameter `bucketFolder` contains the location where the .csv files are stored before being uploaded to the S3 bucket. Table data is stored in the following format in the S3 bucket:

```
1  <schema_name>/<table_name>/LOAD001.csv
2  <schema_name>/<table_name>/LOAD002.csv
3  <schema_name>/<table_name>/<time-stamp>.csv
```

You can specify the column delimiter, row delimiter, and other parameters using the extra connection attributes. For more information on the extra connection attributes, see Extra Connection Attributes at the end of this section.

When you use AWS DMS to replicate data changes, the first column of the CSV output file indicates how the data was changed as shown following:

```
1  I,101,Smith,Bob,4-Jun-14,New York
2  U,101,Smith,Bob,8-Oct-15,Los Angeles
3  U,101,Smith,Bob,13-Mar-17,Dallas
4  D,101,Smith,Bob,13-Mar-17,Dallas
```

For this example, suppose that there is an `EMPLOYEE` table in the source database. AWS DMS writes data to the CSV file, in response to the following events:

- A new employee (Bob Smith, employee ID 101) is hired on 4-Jun-14 at the New York office. In the CSV file, the `I` in the first column indicates that a new row was `INSERT`ed into the EMPLOYEE table at the source database.

- On 8-Oct-15, Bob transfers to the Los Angeles office. In the CSV file, the `U` indicates that the corresponding row in the EMPLOYEE table was `UPDATE`d to reflect Bob's new office location. The rest of the line reflects the row in the EMPLOYEE table as it appears after the `UPDATE`.

- On 13-Mar,17, Bob transfers again to the Dallas office. In the CSV file, the `U` indicates that this row was `UPDATE`d again. The rest of the line reflects the row in the EMPLOYEE table as it appears after the `UPDATE`.

- After some time working in Dallas, Bob leaves the company. In the CSV file, the `D` indicates that the row was `DELETE`d in the source table. The rest of the line reflects how the row in the EMPLOYEE table appeared before it was deleted.

Prerequisites for Using Amazon S3 as a Target

The Amazon S3 bucket you are using as a target must be in the same region as the DMS replication instance you are using to migrate your data.

The AWS account you use for the migration must have write and delete access to the Amazon S3 bucket you are using as a target. The role assigned to the user account used to create the migration task must have the following set of permissions.

```
1  {
2      "Version": "2012-10-17",
```

```
3      "Statement": [
4          {
5              "Effect": "Allow",
6              "Action": [
7                  "s3:PutObject",
8                  "s3:DeleteObject"
9              ],
10             "Resource": [
11                 "arn:aws:s3:::buckettest2*"
12             ]
13         },
14         {
15             "Effect": "Allow",
16             "Action": [
17                 "s3:ListBucket"
18             ],
19             "Resource": [
20                 "arn:aws:s3:::buckettest2*"
21             ]
22         }
23     ]
24 }
```

Limitations to Using Amazon S3 as a Target

The following limitations apply to a file in Amazon S3 that you are using as a target:

- Only the following data definition language (DDL) commands are supported: TRUNCATE TABLE, DROP TABLE, and CREATE TABLE.

- Full LOB mode is not supported.

- Changes to the source table structure during full load are not supported. Changes to the data are supported during full load.

- Multiple tasks that replicate data from the same source table to the same target S3 endpoint bucket result in those tasks writing to the same file. We recommend that you specify different target endpoints (buckets) if your data source is from the same table.

Security

To use Amazon S3 as a target, the account used for the migration must have write and delete access to the Amazon S3 bucket that is used as the target. You must specify the Amazon Resource Name (ARN) of an IAM role that has the permissions required to access Amazon S3.

AWS DMS supports a set of predefined grants for Amazon S3, known as canned ACLs. Each canned ACL has a set of grantees and permissions you can use to set permissions for the Amazon S3 bucket. You can specify a canned ACL using the cannedAclForObjects on the connection string attribute for your S3 target endpoint. For more information about using the extra connection attribute cannedAclForObjects, see Extra Connection Attributes for more information. For more information about Amazon S3 canned ACLs, see Canned ACL.

The IAM role that you use for the migration must be able to perform the s3:PutObjectAcl API action.

Extra Connection Attributes

You can specify the following options as extra connection attributes. Multiple extra connection attribute settings should be separated by a semicolon.

Option	Description
addColumnName	An optional parameter that allows you to add column name information to the .csv output file. The default is false. **Example:** `addColumnName=true;`
bucketFolder	An optional parameter to set a folder name in the S3 bucket. If provided, tables are created in the path /<schema_name>/<table_name>/. If this parameter is not specified, then the path used is <schema_name>/<table_name>/. **Example:** `bucketFolder=testFolder;`
bucketName	The name of the S3 bucket. **Example:** `bucketName=buckettest;`
cannedAclForObjects	Allows AWS DMS to specify a predefined (canned) access control list for objects written to the S3 bucket. For more information about Amazon S3 canned ACLs, see Canned ACL in the Amazon S3 Developer Guide. **Example:** `cannedAclForObjects=PUBLIC_READ;` Valid values for this attribute are: NONE; PRIVATE; PUBLIC_READ; PUBLIC_READ_WRITE; AUTHENTICATED_READ; AWS_EXEC_READ; BUCKET_OWNER_READ; BUCKET_OWNER_FULL_CONTROL. If this attribute isn't specified, it defaults to NONE.
cdcInsertsOnly	An optional parameter to write only `INSERT` operations to the .CSV output files. By default, the first field in a .CSV record contains the letter `I` (insert), `U` (update) or `D` (delete) to indicate whether the row was inserted, updated, or deleted at the source database. If `cdcInsertsOnly` is set to `true`, then only `INSERT`s are recorded in the CSV file, without any `I` annotation. **Example:** `cdcInsertsOnly=true;`
compressionType	An optional parameter to use GZIP to compress the target files. Set to NONE (the default) or do not use to leave the files uncompressed. **Example:** `compressionType=GZIP;`
csvRowDelimiter	The delimiter used to separate rows in the source files. The default is a carriage return (\n). **Example:** `csvRowDelimiter=\n;`
csvDelimiter	The delimiter used to separate columns in the source files. The default is a comma. **Example:** `csvDelimiter=,;`

Option	Description
rfc4180	An optional parameter used to control RFC compliance behavior with data migrated to Amazon S3. When using Amazon S3 as a target, if the data has quotes or a new line character in it then AWS DMS encloses the entire column with an additional ". Every quote mark within the data is repeated twice. This is in compliance with RFC 4180. The default is a true. **Example:** `rfc4180=false ;`

Using an Amazon DynamoDB Database as a Target for AWS Database Migration Service

You can use AWS DMS to migrate data to an Amazon DynamoDB table. Amazon DynamoDB is a fully managed NoSQL database service that provides fast and predictable performance with seamless scalability. AWS DMS supports using a relational database or MongoDB as a source.

In DynamoDB, tables, items, and attributes are the core components that you work with. A table is a collection of items, and each item is a collection of attributes. DynamoDB uses primary keys, called partition keys, to uniquely identify each item in a table. You can also use keys and secondary indexes to provide more querying flexibility.

You use object mapping to migrate your data from a source database to a target DynamoDB table. Object mapping lets you determine where the source data is located in the target.

When AWS DMS creates tables on an Amazon DynamoDB target endpoint, it creates as many tables as in the source database endpoint. AWS DMS also sets several Amazon DynamoDB parameter values. The cost for the table creation depends on the amount of data and the number of tables to be migrated.

When AWS DMS sets Amazon DynamoDB parameter values for a migration task, the default Read Capacity Units (RCU) parameter value is set to 200.

The Write Capacity Units (WCU) parameter value is also set, but its value depends on several other settings:

- The default value for the WCU parameter is 200.
- If the parallelLoadThreads parameter is set greater than 1 (default is 0), then the WCU parameter is set to 200 times the `parallelLoadThreads` value.
- In the US East (N. Virginia) Region (us-east-1), the largest possible WCU parameter value is 40000. If the AWS Region is us-east-1 and the WCU parameter value is greater than 40000, the WCU parameter value is set to 40000.
- In AWS Regions other than us-east-1, the largest possible WCU parameter value is 10000. For any AWS Region other than us-east-1, if the WCU parameter value is set greater than 10000 the WCU parameter value is set to 10000.

Migrating from a Relational Database to a DynamoDB Table

AWS DMS supports migrating data to DynamoDB's scalar data types. When migrating from a relational database like Oracle or MySQL to DynamoDB, you might want to restructure how you store this data.

Currently AWS DMS supports single table to single table restructuring to DynamoDB scalar type attributes. If you are migrating data into DynamoDB from a relational database table, you take data from a table and reformat it into DynamoDB scalar data type attributes. These attributes can accept data from multiple columns, and you can map a column to an attribute directly.

AWS DMS supports the following DynamoDB scalar data types:

- String
- Number
- Boolean

Note
NULL data from the source are ignored on the target.

Prerequisites for Using a DynamoDB as a Target for AWS Database Migration Service

Before you begin to work with a DynamoDB database as a target for AWS DMS, make sure that you create an IAM role that allows AWS DMS to assume and grants access to the DynamoDB tables that are being migrated into. The minimum set of access permissions is shown in the following sample role policy:

```
{
    "Version": "2012-10-17",
    "Statement": [
    {
      "Effect": "Allow",
      "Principal": {
          "Service": "dms.amazonaws.com"
      },
     "Action": "sts:AssumeRole"
    }
  ]
}
```

The user account that you use for the migration to DynamoDB must have the following permissions:

```
{
    "Version": "2012-10-17",
    "Statement": [
      {
        "Effect": "Allow",
        "Action": [
          "dynamodb:PutItem",
          "dynamodb:CreateTable",
          "dynamodb:DescribeTable",
          "dynamodb:DeleteTable",
          "dynamodb:DeleteItem"
        ],
        "Resource": [
          "arn:aws:dynamodb:us-west-2:account-id:table/Name1",
          "arn:aws:dynamodb:us-west-2:account-id:table/OtherName*",
          ]
    },
    {
        "Effect": "Allow",
        "Action": [
          "dynamodb:ListTables"
        ],
        "Resource": "*"
    }
  ]
}
```

Limitations When Using DynamoDB as a Target for AWS Database Migration Service

The following limitations apply when using Amazon DynamoDB as a target:

- DynamoDB limits the precision of the Number data type to 38 places. Store all data types with a higher precision as a String. You need to explicitly specify this using the object mapping feature.

- Because Amazon DynamoDB doesn't have a Date data type, data using the Date data type are converted to strings.

- Amazon DynamoDB doesn't allow updates to the primary key attributes. This restriction is important when using ongoing replication with change data capture (CDC) because it can result in unwanted data in the target. Depending on how you have the object mapping, a CDC operation that updates the primary key can either fail or insert a new item with the updated primary key and incomplete data.

- AWS DMS only supports replication of tables with non-composite primary keys, unless you specify an object mapping for the target table with a custom partition key or sort key, or both.

- AWS DMS doesn't support LOB data unless it is a CLOB. AWS DMS converts CLOB data into a DynamoDB string when migrating data.

Using Object Mapping to Migrate Data to DynamoDB

AWS DMS uses table mapping rules to map data from the source to the target DynamoDB table. To map data to a DynamoDB target, you use a type of table mapping rule called *object-mapping*. Object mapping lets you define the attribute names and the data to be migrated to them. You must have selection rules when you use object mapping,

Amazon DynamoDB doesn't have a preset structure other than having a partition key and an optional sort key. If you have a noncomposite primary key, AWS DMS uses it. If you have a composite primary key or you want to use a sort key, define these keys and the other attributes in your target DynamoDB table.

To create an object mapping rule, you specify the **rule-type** as *object-mapping*. This rule specifies what type of object mapping you want to use.

The structure for the rule is as follows:

```
1  { "rules": [
2      {
3          "rule-type": "object-mapping",
4          "rule-id": "<id>",
5          "rule-name": "<name>",
6          "rule-action": "<valid object-mapping rule action>",
7          "object-locator": {
8          "schema-name": "<case-sensitive schema name>",
9          "table-name": ""
10         },
11         "target-table-name": "<table_name>",
12     }
13     }
14  ]
15 }
```

AWS DMS currently supports *map-record-to-record* and *map-record-to-document* as the only valid values for the **rule-action** parameter. *map-record-to-record* and *map-record-to-document* specify what AWS DMS does by default to records that aren't excluded as part of the **exclude-columns** attribute list; these values don't affect the attribute-mappings in any way.

- *map-record-to-record* can be used when migrating from a relational database to DynamoDB. It uses the primary key from the relational database as the partition key in Amazon DynamoDB and creates an attribute for each column in the source database. When using **map-record-to-record**, for any column in the source table not listed in the **exclude-columns** attribute list, AWS DMS creates a corresponding

154

attribute on the target DynamoDB instance regardless of whether that source column is used in an attribute mapping.

- *map-record-to-document* puts source columns into a single, flat, DynamoDB map on the target using the attribute name "_doc." When using `map-record-to-document`, for any column in the source table not listed in the `exclude-columns` attribute list, AWS DMS places the data into a single, flat, DynamoDB map attribute on the source called "_doc".

One way to understand the difference between the `rule-action` parameters *map-record-to-record* and *map-record-to-document* is to see the two parameters in action. For this example, assume that you are starting with a relational database table row with the following structure and data:

FirstName	LastName	NickName	WorkAddress	WorkPhone	HomeAddress	HomePhone	income
Daniel	Sheridan	Dan	101 Main St Cambridge, MA	800-867-5309	100 Secret St. Unknownville, MA	123-456-7890	12345678

To migrate this information to DynamoDB, you create rules to map the data into a DynamoDB table item. Note the columns listed for the `exclude-columns` parameter. These columns are not directly mapped over to the target. Instead, attribute mapping is used to combine the data into new items, such as where *FirstName* and *LastName* are grouped together to become *CustomerName* on the DynamoDB target. *NickName* and *income* are not excluded.

```
1  {
2    "rules": [
3      {
4        "rule-type": "selection",
5        "rule-id": "1",
6        "rule-name": "1",
7        "object-locator": {
8          "schema-name": "test",
9          "table-name": "%"
10       },
11       "rule-action": "include"
12     },
13     {
14       "rule-type": "object-mapping",
15       "rule-id": "1",
16       "rule-name": "TransformToDDB",
17       "rule-action": "map-record-to-record",
18       "object-locator": {
19         "schema-name": "test",
20         "table-name": "customer",
21
22       },
23       "target-table-name": "customer_t",
24       "mapping-parameters": {
25         "partition-key-name": "CustomerName",
26         "exclude-columns": [
27           "FirstName",
28           "LastName",
29           "HomeAddress",
30           "HomePhone",
31           "WorkAddress",
32           "WorkPhone"
33         ],
34         "attribute-mappings": [
35           {
36             "target-attribute-name": "CustomerName",
```

```
37        "attribute-type": "scalar",
38        "attribute-sub-type": "string",
39        "value": "${FirstName},${LastName}"
40      },
41      {
42        "target-attribute-name": "ContactDetails",
43        "attribute-type": "document",
44        "attribute-sub-type": "dynamodb-map",
45        "value": {
46          "M": {
47            "Home": {
48              "M": {
49                "Address": {
50                  "S": "${HomeAddress}"
51                },
52                "Phone": {
53                  "S": "${HomePhone}"
54                }
55              }
56            },
57            "Work": {
58              "M": {
59                "Address": {
60                  "S": "${WorkAddress}"
61                },
62                "Phone": {
63                  "S": "${WorkPhone}"
64                }
65              }
66            }
67          }
68        }
69      }
70    ]
71  }
72  }
73 ]
74 }
```

By using the **rule-action** parameter *map-record-to-record*, the data for *NickName* and *income* are mapped to items of the same name in the DynamoDB target.

```
▼ Item {4}
    ⊕        CustomerName String : Daniel,Sheridan
    ⊕     ▼ ContactDetails Map {2}
    ⊕        ▼ Home Map {2}
    ⊕              Address String : 100 Secret St, Unknownville, MA
    ⊕              Phone String : 123-456-7890
    ⊕        ▼ Work Map {2}
    ⊕              Address String : 101 Main St Cambridge, MA
    ⊕              Phone String : 800-867-5309
    ⊕        NickName String : Dan
    ⊕        income Number : 12345678
```

However, suppose that you use the same rules but change the **rule-action** parameter to *map-record-to-document*. In this case, the columns not listed in the **exclude-columns** parameter, *NickName* and *income*, are mapped to a *__doc* item.

```
▼ Item {3}
    ⊕        CustomerName String : Daniel,Sheridan
    ⊕     ▼ ContactDetails Map {2}
    ⊕        ▼ Home Map {2}
    ⊕              Address String : 100 Secret St, Unknownville, MA
    ⊕              Phone String : 123-456-7890
    ⊕        ▼ Work Map {2}
    ⊕              Address String : 101 Main St Cambridge, MA
    ⊕              Phone String : 800-867-5309
    ⊕     ▼ _doc Map {2}
    ⊕           NickName String : Dan
    ⊕           income Number : 12345678
```

Using Custom Condition Expressions with Object Mapping

You can use a feature of Amazon DynamoDB called conditional expressions to manipulate data that is being written to a DynamoDB table. For more information about condition expressions in DynamoDB, see Condition Expressions.

A condition expression member consists of:

- an expression (required)

- expression attribute values (optional) . Specifies a DynamoDB json structure of the attribute value

- expression attribute names (optional)

- options for when to use the condition expression (optional). The default is apply-during-cdc = false and apply-during-full-load = true

The structure for the rule is as follows:

```
 1  "target-table-name": "customer_t",
 2      "mapping-parameters": {
 3          "partition-key-name": "CustomerName",
 4          "condition-expression": {
 5              "expression":"<conditional expression>",
 6              "expression-attribute-values": [
 7                  {
 8                      "name":"<attribute name>",
 9                      "value":<attribute value>
10                  }
11              ],
12              "apply-during-cdc":<optional Boolean value>,
13              "apply-during-full-load": <optional Boolean value>
14          }
```

The following sample highlights the sections used for condition expression.

```
{
  "rules": [
    {
      "rule-type": "object-mapping",
      "rule-id": "1",
      "rule-name": "TransformToDDB",
      "rule-action": "map-record-to-record",
      "object-locator": {
        "schema-name": "test",
        "table-name": "customer",
      },
      "target-table-name": "customer_t",
      "mapping-parameters": {
        "partition-key-name": "CustomerName",
        "condition-expression": [
          "expression":"attribute_not_exists(version) or version <= :record_version",
          "expression-attribute-values": [
            {
              "name":":record_version",
              "value":{"N":"${version}"}
            }
          ],
          "apply-during-cdc":true,
          "apply-during-full-load": true
        }
        "attribute-mappings": {
          {
            "target-attribute-name": "CustomerName",
            "attribute-type": "scalar",
            "attribute-sub-type": "string",
            "value": "${FirstName},${LastName}"
          }
        }
      }
    }
  ]
}
```

Object mapping section defines name, rule-action, and object locator information

Condition expression

Options

Using Attribute Mapping with Object Mapping

Attribute mapping lets you specify a template string using source column names to restructure data on the target. There is no formatting done other than what the user specifies in the template.

The following example shows the structure of the source database and the desired structure of the DynamoDB target. First is shown the structure of the source, in this case an Oracle database, and then the desired structure of the data in DynamoDB. The example concludes with the JSON used to create the desired target structure.

The structure of the Oracle data is as follows:

FirstName	LastName	StoreId	HomeAd-dress	Home-Phone	WorkAd-dress	Work-Phone	DateOf-Birth
Primary Key	N/A						
Randy	Marsh	5	221B Baker Street	1234567890	31 Spooner Street, Quahog	9876543210	02/29/1988

The structure of the DynamoDB data is as follows:

CustomerName	StoreId	ContactDetails	DateOfBirth
Partition Key	Sort Key	N/A	

```
 |
1 Randy,Marsh
2 ``` |

5

{ "Name": "Randy", "Home": { "Address": "221B Baker Street", "Phone": 1234567890 }, "Work": { "Address": "31 Spooner Street, Quahog", "Phone": 9876541230 } }

02/29/1988

1
2 The following JSON shows the object mapping and column mapping used to achieve the DynamoDB
        structure:
```

{ "rules": [{ "rule-type": "selection", "rule-id": "1", "rule-name": "1", "object-locator": { "schema-name": "test", "table-name": "%" }, "rule-action": "include" }, { "rule-type": "object-mapping", "rule-id": "2", "rule-name": "TransformToDDB", "rule-action": "map-record-to-record", "object-locator": { "schema-name": "test", "table-name": "customer" }, "target-table-name": "customer_t", "mapping-parameters": { "partition-key-name": "CustomerName", "sort-key-name": "StoreId", "exclude-columns": ["FirstName", "LastName", "HomeAd-dress", "HomePhone", "WorkAddress", "WorkPhone"], "attribute-mappings": [{ "target-attribute-name": "CustomerName", "attribute-type": "scalar", "attribute-sub-type": "string", "value": "${FirstName},${Last-Name}" }, { "target-attribute-name": "StoreId", "attribute-type": "scalar", "attribute-sub-type": "string", "value": "${StoreId}" }, { "target-attribute-name": "ContactDetails", "attribute-type": "scalar", "attribute-sub-type": "string", "value": "{"Name":"${FirstName}","Home":{"Address":"${HomeAddress}","Phone":"${Home-Phone}"}, "Work":{"Address":"${WorkAddress}","Phone":"${WorkPhone}"}}" }] } }] }

Another way to use column mapping is to use DynamoDB format as your document type\. The following code example uses *dynamodb\-map* as the `attribute-sub-type` for attribute mapping\.

```
{ "rules": [ { "rule-type": "object-mapping", "rule-id": "1", "rule-name": "TransformToDDB", "rule-action":
"map-record-to-record", "object-locator": { "schema-name": "test", "table-name": "customer",
},
"target-table-name": "customer_t",
"mapping-parameters": {
  "partition-key-name": "CustomerName",
  "sort-key-name": "StoreId",
  "exclude-columns": [
    "FirstName",
    "LastName",
    "HomeAddress",
    "HomePhone",
    "WorkAddress",
    "WorkPhone"
  ],
  "attribute-mappings": [
    {
      "target-attribute-name": "CustomerName",
      "attribute-type": "scalar",
      "attribute-sub-type": "string",
      "value": "${FirstName},${LastName}"
    },
    {
      "target-attribute-name": "StoreId",
      "attribute-type": "scalar",
      "attribute-sub-type": "string",
      "value": "${StoreId}"
    },
    {
      "target-attribute-name": "ContactDetails",
      "attribute-type": "document",
      "attribute-sub-type": "dynamodb-map",
      "value": {
        "M": {
          "Name": {
            "S": "${FirstName}"
          }"Home": {
            "M": {
              "Address": {
                "S": "${HomeAddress}"
              },
              "Phone": {
                "S": "${HomePhone}"
              }
            }
          },
          "Work": {
            "M": {
              "Address": {
```

```
48              "S": "${WorkAddress}"
49            },
50            "Phone": {
51              "S": "${WorkPhone}"
52            }
53          }
54        }
55      }
56    }
57  }
58  ]
59  }
60 }

] }
```

Example 1: Using Attribute Mapping with Object Mapping

The following example migrates data from two MySQL database tables, *nfl_data* and *sport_team*, to two DynamoDB table called *NFLTeams* and *SportTeams*\. The structure of the tables and the JSON used to map the data from the MySQL database tables to the DynamoDB tables are shown following\.

The structure of the MySQL database table *nfl_data* is shown below:

mysql> desc nfl_data; +---------------+-------------+------+-----+---------+-------+ | Field | Type | Null | Key | Default | Extra | +---------------+-------------+------+-----+---------+-------+ | Position | varchar(5) | YES | | NULL | | | player_number | smallint(6) | YES | | NULL | | | Name | varchar(40) | YES | | NULL | | | status | varchar(10) | YES | | NULL | | | stat1 | varchar(10) | YES | | NULL | | | stat1_val | varchar(10) | YES | | NULL | | | stat2 | varchar(10) | YES | | NULL | | | stat2_val | varchar(10) | YES | | NULL | | | stat3 | varchar(10) | YES | | NULL | | | stat3_val | varchar(10) | YES | | NULL | | | stat4 | varchar(10) | YES | | NULL | | | stat4_val | varchar(10) | YES | | NULL | | | team | varchar(10) | YES | | NULL | | +---------------+-------------+------+-----+---------+-------+

The structure of the MySQL database table *sport_team* is shown below:

mysql> desc sport_team; +---------------------------+--------------+------+-----+---------+----------------+ | Field | Type | Null | Key | Default | Extra | +---------------------------+--------------+------+-----+---------+----------------+ | id | mediumint(9) | NO | PRI | NULL | auto_increment | | name | varchar(30) | NO | | NULL | | | abbreviated_name | varchar(10) | YES | | NULL | | | home_field_id | smallint(6) | YES | MUL | NULL | | | sport_type_name | varchar(15) | NO | MUL | NULL | | | sport_league_short_name | varchar(10) | NO | | NULL | | | sport_division_short_name | varchar(10) | YES | | NULL | |

The table mapping rules used to map the two tables to the two DynamoDB tables is shown below:

{ "rules":[{ "rule-type": "selection", "rule-id": "1", "rule-name": "1", "object-locator": { "schema-name": "dms_sample", "table-name": "nfl_data" }, "rule-action": "include" }, { "rule-type": "selection", "rule-id": "2", "rule-name": "2", "object-locator": { "schema-name": "dms_sample", "table-name": "sport_team" }, "rule-action": "include" }, { "rule-type":"object-mapping", "rule-id":"3", "rule-name":"MapNFLData", "rule-action":"map-record-to-record", "object-locator":{ "schema-name":"dms_sample", "table-name":"nfl_data" }, "target-table-name":"NFLTeams", "mapping-parameters":{ "partition-key-name":"Team", "sort-key-name":"PlayerName", "exclude-columns": ["player_number", "team", "Name"], "attribute-mappings":[{ "target-attribute-name":"Team", "attribute-type":"scalar", "attribute-sub-type":"string", "value":"${team}" }, { "target-attribute-name":"PlayerName", "attribute-type":"scalar", "attribute-sub-type":"string", "value":"${Name}" }, { "target-attribute-name":"PlayerInfo", "attribute-type":"scalar", "attribute-sub-type":"string", "value":"{"Number": "${player_number}","Position": "${Position}","Status": "${status}","Stats": {"Stat1": "${stat1}:${stat1_val}","Stat2": "${stat2}:${stat2_val}","Stat3": "${stat3}:${stat3_val}","Stat4": "${stat4}:${stat4_val}"}" }] } }, { "rule-type":"object-mapping", "rule-id":"4", "rule-name":"MapSportTeam", "rule-action":"map-record-to-record", "object-locator":{ "schema-name":"dms_sample", "table-name":"sport_team" }, "target-table-name":"SportTeams", "mapping-parameters":{ "partition-key-name":"TeamName", "exclude-columns": ["name", "id"], "attribute-mappings":[{ "target-attribute-name":"TeamName", "attribute-type":"scalar", "attribute-sub-type":"string", "value":"${name}" }, { "target-attribute-name":"TeamInfo", "attribute-type":"scalar", "attribute-sub-type":"string", "value":"{"League": "${sport_league_short_name}","Division": "${sport_division_short_name}"}" }] } }] }

The sample output for the *NFLTeams* DynamoDB table is shown below:

"PlayerInfo": "{"Number": "6","Position": "P","Status": "ACT","Stats": {"Stat1": "PUNTS:73","Stat2": "AVG:46","Stat3": "LNG:67","Stat4": "IN 20:31"}", "PlayerName": "Allen, Ryan", "Position": "P", "stat1": "PUNTS", "stat1_val": "73", "stat2": "AVG", "stat2_val": "46", "stat3": "LNG", "stat3_val": "67", "stat4": "IN 20", "stat4_val": "31", "status": "ACT", "Team": "NE" }

The sample output for the SportsTeams *DynamoDB* table is shown below:

{ "abbreviated_name": "IND", "home_field_id": 53, "sport_division_short_name": "AFC South", "sport_league_short_name": "NFL", "sport_type_name": "football", "TeamInfo": "{"League": "NFL","Division": "AFC South"}", "TeamName": "Indianapolis Colts" }

Target Data Types for Amazon DynamoDB

The Amazon DynamoDB endpoint for Amazon AWS DMS supports most Amazon DynamoDB data types\. The following table shows the Amazon AWS DMS target data types that are supported when using AWS DMS and the default mapping from AWS DMS data types\.

For additional information about AWS DMS data types, see [Data Types for AWS Database Migration Service](CHAP_Reference.DataTypes.md)\.

When AWS DMS migrates data from heterogeneous databases, we map data types from the source database to intermediate data types called AWS DMS data types\. We then map the intermediate data types to the target data types\. The following table shows each AWS DMS data type and the data type it maps to in DynamoDB:

AWS DMS Data Type	DynamoDB Data Type
String	String
WString	String
Boolean	Boolean
Date	String
DateTime	String
INT1	Number
INT2	Number
INT4	Number
INT8	Number
Numeric	Number
Real4	Number

```
24 |  Real8  |  Number  |
25 |  UINT1  |  Number  |
26 |  UINT2  |  Number  |
27 |  UINT4  |  Number  |
28 |  UINT8 |  Number  |
29 |  CLOB |  String  |
30
31
32
33
34 # Working with AWS DMS Tasks<a name="CHAP_Tasks"></a>
35
36 An AWS Database Migration Service \(AWS DMS\) task is where all the work happens\. You use tasks
      to migrate data from the source endpoint to the target endpoint, and the task processing is
      done on the replication instance\. You specify what tables and schemas to use for your
      migration and any special processing, such as logging requirements, control table data, and
      error handling\.
37
38 There are several things you need to know when creating a migration task:
39
40 + You must create a source endpoint, a target endpoint, and a replication instance before you
      can create a migration task\.
41
42 + There are a significant number of migration setting you can specify to tailor your migration
      task when using the AWS CLI or DMS APIs\. These include setting how migration errors are
      handled, logging, and control table information\.
43
44 + Once you create a task, you can run it immediately\. The target tables with the necessary
      metadata definitions are automatically created and loaded, and you can specify that the CDC
      replication process be started\.
45
46 + You can monitor, stop, or restart replication tasks using the AWS DMS console, AWS CLI, or AWS
      DMS API\.
47
48 The following are actions you can do when working with an AWS DMS task
49
50
51 | Task | Relevant Documentation |
52 | --- | --- |
53 |    **Creating a Task Assessment Report**  You can create a task assessment report that shows
      any unsupported data types that could cause problems during migration\. You can run this
      report on your task before running the task to find out potential issues\.  |  [Creating a
      Task Assessment Report](CHAP_Tasks.AssessmentReport.md)  |
54 |    **Creating a Migration Task**  When you create a task, you specify the source, target, and
      replication instance, along with any migration settings\.  |  [Creating a Task](CHAP_Tasks.
      Creating.md)  |
55 |    **Applying Task Settings**  Each task has settings that you can configure according to the
      needs of your database migration\. You create these settings in a JSON file or, with some
      settings, you can specify the settings using the AWS DMS console\.  |  [Specifying Task
      Settings for AWS Database Migration Service Tasks](CHAP_Tasks.CustomizingTasks.TaskSettings.
      md)  |
56 |    **Data Validation**  Data validation is a task setting you can use to have AWS DMS compare
      the data on your target data store with the data from your source data store\.  |  [
      Validating AWS Database Migration Service Tasks](CHAP_Validating.md)\.  |
```

57 | **Modifying a Task** When a task is stopped, you can modify the settings for the task\. | [Modifying a Task](CHAP_Tasks.Modifying.md) |

58 | **Reloading Tables During a Task** You can reload a table during a task if an error occurs during the task\. | [Reloading Tables During a Task](CHAP_Tasks.ReloadTables.md) |

59 | **Using Table Mapping** Table mapping uses several types of rules to specify the data source, source schema, data, and any transformations that should occur during the task\. | Selection Rules [Selection Rules and Actions](CHAP_Tasks.CustomizingTasks.TableMapping.md #CHAP_Tasks.CustomizingTasks.TableMapping.SelectionTransformation.Selections) Transformation Rules [Transformation Rules and Actions](CHAP_Tasks.CustomizingTasks.TableMapping.md# CHAP_Tasks.CustomizingTasks.TableMapping.SelectionTransformation.Transformations) |

60 | **Applying Filters** You can use source filters to limit the number and type of records transferred from your source to your target\. For example, you can specify that only employees with a location of headquarters are moved to the target database\. You apply filters on a column of data\. | [Using Source Filters](CHAP_Tasks.CustomizingTasks. TableMapping.md#CHAP_Tasks.CustomizingTasks.Filters) |

61 | Monitoring a Task | There are several ways to get information on the performance of a task and the tables used by the task\. [Monitoring AWS Database Migration Service Tasks](CHAP_Monitoring.md) |

62 | Managing Task Logs | You can view and delete task logs using the AWS DMS API or AWS CLI\. [Managing AWS DMS Task Logs](CHAP_Monitoring.md#CHAP_Monitoring.ManagingLogs) |

Creating a Task

There are several things you must do to create an AWS DMS migration task:

+ Create a source endpoint, a target endpoint, and a replication instance before you create a migration task\.

+ Select a migration method:

  + **Migrating Data to the Target Database** - This process creates files or tables in the target database, automatically defines the metadata that is required at the target, and populates the tables with data from the source\. The data from the tables is loaded in parallel for improved efficiency\. This process is the **Migrate existing data** option in the AWS console and is called `Full Load` in the API\.

  + **Capturing Changes During Migration** - This process captures changes to the source database that occur while the data is being migrated from the source to the target\. When the migration of the originally requested data has completed, the change data capture \(CDC\) process then applies the captured changes to the target database\. Changes are captured and applied as units of single committed transactions, and several different target tables can be updated as a single source commit\. This approach guarantees transactional integrity in the target database\. This process is the **Migrate existing data and replicate ongoing changes** option in the AWS console and is called `full-load-and-cdc` in the API\.

  + **Replicating Only Data Changes on the Source Database** - This process reads the recovery log file of the source database management system \(DBMS\) and groups together the entries for each transaction\. If AWS DMS can't apply changes to the target within a reasonable time \(for example, if the target is not accessible\), AWS DMS buffers the changes on the replication server for as long as necessary\. It doesn't reread the source DBMS logs,

which can take a large amount of time\. This process is the **Replicate data changes only
** option in the AWS DMS console\.

80

81 + Determine how the task should handle large binary objects \(LOBs\) on the source\. For more
information, see [Setting LOB Support for Source Databases in the AWS DMS task](CHAP_Tasks.
LOBSupport.md)\.

82

83 + Specify migration task settings\. These include setting up logging, specifying what data is
written to the migration control table, how errors are handled, and other settings\. For
more information about task settings, see [Specifying Task Settings for AWS Database
Migration Service Tasks](CHAP_Tasks.CustomizingTasks.TaskSettings.md)\.

84

85 + Set up table mapping to define rules to select and filter data that you are migrating\. For
more information about table mapping, see [Using Table Mapping with a Task to Select and
Filter Data](CHAP_Tasks.CustomizingTasks.TableMapping.md)\. Before you specify your mapping,
make sure you review the documentation section on data type mapping for your source and
your target database\.

86

87 You can choose to start a task as soon as you finish specifying information for that task on the
Create task page, or you can start the task from the Dashboard page once you finish
specifying task information\.

88

89 The procedure following assumes that you have chosen the AWS DMS console wizard and specified
replication instance information and endpoints using the console wizard\. Note that you can
also do this step by selecting **Tasks** from the AWS DMS console's navigation pane and then
selecting **Create task**\.

90

91 **To create a migration task**

92

93 1. On the **Create Task** page, specify the task options\. The following table describes the
settings\.

94 ![\[Create task\]](http://docs.aws.amazon.com/dms/latest/userguide/images/datarep-gs-wizard4.png
)

95 [\[See the AWS documentation website for more details\]](http://docs.aws.amazon.com/dms/latest/
userguide/CHAP_Tasks.Creating.html)

96

97 1. Choose the **Task Settings** tab, shown following, and specify values for your target table,
LOB support, and to enable logging\. The task settings shown depend on the **Migration type
** value you select\. For example, when you select **Migrate existing data**, the following
options are shown:

98 ![\[Task settings\]](http://docs.aws.amazon.com/dms/latest/userguide/images/datarep-gs-wizard4-
settings.png)

99 [\[See the AWS documentation website for more details\]](http://docs.aws.amazon.com/dms/latest/
userguide/CHAP_Tasks.Creating.html)

100

101 When you select **Migrate existing data and replicate** for **Migration type**, the following
options are shown:

102 ![\[Task settings\]](http://docs.aws.amazon.com/dms/latest/userguide/images/datarep-gs-wizard4a-
settings.png)

103 [\[See the AWS documentation website for more details\]](http://docs.aws.amazon.com/dms/latest/
userguide/CHAP_Tasks.Creating.html)

104

105 1. Choose the **Table mappings** tab, shown following, to set values for schema mapping and the
mapping method\. If you choose **Custom**, you can specify the target schema and table

values\. For more information about table mapping, see [Using Table Mapping with a Task to Select and Filter Data](CHAP_Tasks.CustomizingTasks.TableMapping.md)\.

106 ![\[Table mapping\]](http://docs.aws.amazon.com/dms/latest/userguide/images/datarep-gs-wizard4-tablemapping.png)

107

108 1. Once you have finished with the task settings, choose **Create task**\.

109

110

111

112

113 # Specifying Task Settings for AWS Database Migration Service Tasks

114

115 Each task has settings that you can configure according to the needs of your database migration \. You create these settings in a JSON file or, with some settings, you can specify the settings using the AWS DMS console\.

116

117 There are several main types of task settings:

118

119

120 + [Target Metadata Task Settings](CHAP_Tasks.CustomizingTasks.TaskSettings.TargetMetadata.md)
121 + [Full Load Task Settings](CHAP_Tasks.CustomizingTasks.TaskSettings.FullLoad.md)
122 + [Logging Task Settings](CHAP_Tasks.CustomizingTasks.TaskSettings.Logging.md)
123 + [Control Table Task Settings](CHAP_Tasks.CustomizingTasks.TaskSettings.ControlTable.md)
124 + [Stream Buffer Task Settings](CHAP_Tasks.CustomizingTasks.TaskSettings.StreamBuffer.md)
125 + [Change Processing Tuning Settings](CHAP_Tasks.CustomizingTasks.TaskSettings.ChangeProcessingTuning.md)
126 + [Data Validation Task Settings](CHAP_Tasks.CustomizingTasks.TaskSettings.DataValidation.md)
127 + [Change Processing DDL Handling Policy Task Settings](CHAP_Tasks.CustomizingTasks.TaskSettings.DDLHandling.md)
128 + [Error Handling Task Settings](CHAP_Tasks.CustomizingTasks.TaskSettings.ErrorHandling.md)
129 + [Saving Task Settings](CHAP_Tasks.CustomizingTasks.TaskSettings.Saving.md)

130

131 A task settings JSON file can look like this:

{ "TargetMetadata": { "TargetSchema": "", "SupportLobs": true, "FullLobMode": false, "LobChunkSize": 64, "LimitedSizeLobMode": true, "LobMaxSize": 32, "BatchApplyEnabled": true }, "FullLoadSettings": { "TargetTablePrepMode": "DO_NOTHING", "CreatePkAfterFullLoad": false, "StopTaskCachedChangesApplied": false, "StopTaskCachedChangesNotApplied": false, "MaxFullLoadSubTasks": 8, "TransactionConsistencyTimeout": 600, "CommitRate": 10000 }, "Logging": { "EnableLogging": false }, "ControlTablesSettings": { "ControlSchema":"", "HistoryTimeslotInMinutes":5, "HistoryTableEnabled": false, "SuspendedTablesTableEnabled": false, "StatusTableEnabled": false }, "StreamBufferSettings": { "StreamBufferCount": 3, "StreamBufferSizeInMB": 8 }, "ChangeProcessingTuning": { "BatchApplyPreserveTransaction": true, "BatchApplyTimeoutMin": 1, "BatchApplyTimeoutMax": 30, "BatchApplyMemoryLimit": 500, "BatchSplitSize": 0, "MinTransactionSize": 1000, "CommitTimeout": 1, "MemoryLimitTotal": 1024, "MemoryKeepTime": 60, "StatementCacheSize": 50 }, "ChangeProcessingDdlHandlingPolicy": { "HandleSourceTableDropped": true, "HandleSourceTableTruncated": true, "HandleSourceTableAltered": true }, "ValidationSettings": { "EnableValidation": false, "ThreadCount": 5 }, "ErrorBehavior": { "DataErrorPolicy": "LOG_ERROR", "DataTruncationErrorPolicy":"LOG_ERROR", "DataErrorEscalationPolicy":"SUSPEND_TABLE", "DataErrorEscalationCount": 50, "TableErrorPolicy":"SUSPEND_TABLE", "TableErrorEscalationPolicy":"STOP_TASK", "TableErrorEscalationCount": 50, "RecoverableErrorCount": 0, "RecoverableErrorInterval": 5, "RecoverableErrorThrottling": true, "RecoverableErrorThrottlingMax": 1800, "ApplyErrorDeletePolicy":"IGNORE_RECORD", "ApplyErrorInsertPolicy":"LOG_ERROR", "ApplyErrorUpdatePolicy":"LOG_ERROR", "ApplyErrorEscalationPolicy":"LOG_ERROR", "ApplyErrorEscalationCount": 0, "FullLoadIgnoreConflicts": true } }

Target Metadata Task Settings

Target metadata settings include the following:

+ `TargetSchema` - The target table schema name\. If this metadata option is empty, the schema from the source table is used\. AWS DMS automatically adds the owner prefix for the target database to all tables if no source schema is defined\. This option should be left empty for MySQL\-type target endpoints\.

+ `LOB settings` - Settings that determine how large objects \(LOBs\) are managed\. If you set `SupportLobs=true`, you must set one of the following to `true`:

  + `FullLobMode` - If you set this option to `true`, then you must enter a value for the `LobChunkSize` option\. Enter the size, in kilobytes, of the LOB chunks to use when replicating the data to the target\. The `FullLobMode` option works best for very large LOB sizes but tends to cause slower loading\.

  + `LimitedSizeLobMode` - If you set this option to `true`, then you must enter a value for the `LobMaxSize` option\. Enter the maximum size, in kilobytes, for an individual LOB\.

+ `LoadMaxFileSize` - An option for PostgreSQL and MySQL target endpoints that defines the maximum size on disk of stored, unloaded data, such as \.csv files\. This option overrides the connection attribute\. You can provide values from 0, which indicates that this option doesn't override the connection attribute, to 100,000 KB\.

+ `BatchApplyEnabled` - Determines if each transaction is applied individually or if changes are committed in batches\. The default value is `false`\.

If set to `true`, AWS DMS commits changes in batches by a pre\-processing action that groups the transactions into batches in the most efficient way\. Setting this value to `true` can affect transactional integrity, so you must select `BatchApplyPreserveTransaction` in the `ChangeProcessingTuning` section to specify how the system handles referential integrity issues\.

If set to `false`, AWS DMS applies each transaction individually, in the order it is committed \. In this case, strict referential integrity is ensured for all tables\.

When LOB columns are included in the replication, `BatchApplyEnabled`can only be used in **Limited\-size LOB mode**\.

+ `ParallelLoadThreads` - Specifies the number of threads AWS DMS uses to load each table into the target database\. The maximum value for a MySQL target is 16; the maximum value for a DynamoDB target is 32\. The maximum limit can be increased upon request\.

+ `ParallelLoadBufferSize` - Specifies the maximum number of records to store in the buffer used by the parallel load threads to load data to the target\. The default value is 50\. Maximum value is 1000\. This field is currently only valid when DynamoDB is the target\. This parameter should be used in conjunction with `ParallelLoadThreads` and is valid only when ParallelLoadThreads > 1\.

30

31

32

33

34 # Full Load Task Settings

35

36 Full load settings include the following:

37

38 + To indicate how to handle loading the target at full\-load startup, specify one of the following values for the `TargetTablePrepMode` option:

39

40   + `DO_NOTHING` - Data and metadata of the existing target table are not affected\.

41

42   + `DROP_AND_CREATE` - The existing table is dropped and a new table is created in its place\.

43

44   + `TRUNCATE_BEFORE_LOAD` - Data is truncated without affecting the table metadata\.

45

46 + To delay primary key or unique index creation until after full load completes, set the `CreatePkAfterFullLoad` option\. When this option is selected, you cannot resume incomplete full load tasks\.

47

48 + For full load and CDC\-enabled tasks, you can set the following `Stop task after full load completes` options:

49

50   + `StopTaskCachedChangesApplied` - Set this option to `true` to stop a task after a full load completes and cached changes are applied\.

51

52   + `StopTaskCachedChangesNotApplied` - Set this option to `true` to stop a task before cached changes are applied\.

53

54 + `MaxFullLoadSubTasks` - Set this option to indicate the maximum number of tables to load in parallel\. The default is 8; the maximum value is 50\.

55

56 + To set the number of seconds that AWS DMS waits for transactions to close before beginning a full\-load operation, if transactions are open when the task starts, set the `TransactionConsistencyTimeout` option\. The default value is 600 \(10 minutes\)\. AWS DMS begins the full load after the timeout value is reached, even if there are open transactions \. Note that a full\-load only task does not wait for 10 minutes and will start immediately \.

57

58 + To indicate the maximum number of events that can be transferred together, set the `CommitRate` option\.

59

60

61

62

63 # Logging Task Settings

64

65 Logging task settings are written to a JSON file and they let you specify which component activities are logged and what amount of information is written to the log\. The logging feature uses Amazon CloudWatch to log information during the migration process\.

66

67 There are several ways to enable Amazon CloudWatch logging\. You can select the `EnableLogging` option on the AWS Management Console when you create a migration task or set the `

EnableLogging` option to `true` when creating a task using the AWS DMS API\. You can also specify `"EnableLogging": true` in the JSON of the logging section of task settings\.

To delete the task logs, you can specify `"DeleteTaskLogs": true` in the JSON of the logging section of task settings\.

You can specify logging for the following component activities:

+ SOURCE_UNLOAD - Data is unloaded from the source database\.

+ SOURCE_CAPTURE - Data is captured from the source database\.

+ TARGET_LOAD - Data is loaded into the target database\.

+ TARGET_APPLY - Data and DDL are applied to the target database\.

+ TASK_MANAGER - The task manager triggers an event\.

Once you specify a component activity, you can then specify the amount of information that is logged\. The following list is in order from the lowest level of information to the highest level of information\. The higher levels always include information from the lower levels\. These severity values include:

+ LOGGER_SEVERITY_ERROR - Error messages are written to the log\.

+ LOGGER_SEVERITY_WARNING - Warnings and error messages are written to the log\.

+ LOGGER_SEVERITY_INFO - Informational messages, warnings, and error messages are written to the log\.

+ LOGGER_SEVERITY_DEFAULT - Debug messages, informational messages, warnings, and error messages are written to the log\.

+ LOGGER_SEVERITY_DEBUG - Debug messages, informational messages, warnings, and error messages are written to the log\.

+ LOGGER_SEVERITY_DETAILED_DEBUG - All information is written to the log\.

For example, the following JSON section gives task settings for logging for all component activities:

... "Logging": { "EnableLogging": true, "LogComponents": [{ "Id": "SOURCE_UNLOAD", "Severity": "LOGGER_SEVERITY_DEFAULT" },{ "Id": "SOURCE_CAPTURE", "Severity": "LOGGER_SEVERITY_DEFAULT" },{ "Id": "TARGET_LOAD", "Severity": "LOGGER_SEVERITY_DEFAULT" },{ "Id": "TARGET_APPLY", "Severity": "LOGGER_SEVERITY_INFO" },{ "Id": "TASK_MANAGER", "Severity": "LOGGER_SEVERITY_DEBUG" }] }, ...

Control Table Task Settings

Control tables provide information about the AWS DMS task, as well as useful statistics that you

can use to plan and manage both the current migration task and future tasks\. You can apply
these task settings in a JSON file or using the **Advanced Settings** link on the **Create
task** page in the AWS DMS console\. In addition to the **Apply Exceptions \(dmslogs\.awsdms
_apply_exceptions\)** table, which is always created, you can choose to create additional
tables including the following:

+ **Replication Status \(dmslogs\.awsdms_status\)** - This table provides details about the
current task including task status, amount of memory consumed by the task, number of changes
not yet applied to the target, and the position in the source database from which AWS DMS
is currently reading\. It also indicates if the task is a full load or change data capture
\(CDC\)\.

+ **Suspended Tables \(dmslogs\.awsdms_suspended_tables\)** - This table provides a list of
suspended tables as well as the reason they were suspended\.

+ **Replication History \(dmslogs\.awsdms_history\)** - This table provides information about
the replication history including the number and volume of records processed during the task
, latency at the end of a CDC task, and other statistics\.

The **Apply Exceptions \(dmslogs\.awsdms_apply_exceptions\)** table contains the following
parameters:

Column	Type	Description
TASK_NAME	nvchar	The name of the AWS DMS task\.
TABLE_OWNER	nvchar	The table owner\.
TABLE_NAME	nvchar	The table name\.
ERROR_TIME	timestamp	The time the exception \(error\) occurred\.
STATEMENT	nvchar	The statement that was being run when the error occurred\.
ERROR	nvchar	The error name and description\.

The **Replication History \(dmslogs\.awsdms_history\)** table contains the following parameters
:

Column	Type	Description
SERVER_NAME	nvchar	The name of the machine where the replication task is running\.
TASK_NAME	nvchar	The name of the AWS DMS task\.
TIMESLOT_TYPE	varchar	One of the following values: [\[See the AWS documentation website for more details\]](http://docs.aws.amazon.com/dms/latest/userguide/CHAP_Tasks.CustomizingTasks.TaskSettings.ControlTable.html) If the task is running both full load and CDC, two history records are written to the time slot\.
TIMESLOT	timestamp	The ending timestamp of the time slot\.
TIMESLOT_DURATION	int	The duration of the time slot\.
TIMESLOT_LATENCY	int	The target latency at the end of the time slot\. This value is only applicable to CDC time slots\.
RECORDS	int	The number of records processed during the time slot\.
TIMESLOT_VOLUME	int	The volume of data processed in MB\.

The **Replication Status \(dmslogs\.awsdms_status\)** table contains the current status of the
task and the target database\. It has the following settings:

170

Column	Type	Description
SERVER_NAME	nvchar	The name of the machine where the replication task is running\.
TASK_NAME	nvchar	The name of the AWS DMS task\.
TASK_STATUS	varchar	One of the following values: [\[See the AWS documentation website for more details\]] (http://docs.aws.amazon.com/dms/latest/userguide/CHAP_Tasks.CustomizingTasks.TaskSettings.ControlTable.html) Task status is set to FULL LOAD as long as there is at least one table in full load\. After all tables have been loaded, the task status changes to CHANGE PROCESSING if CDC is enabled\.
STATUS_TIME	timestamp	The timestamp of the task status\.
PENDING_CHANGES	int	The number of change records that were not applied to the target\.
DISK_SWAP_SIZE	int	The amount of disk space used by old or offloaded transactions\.
TASK_MEMORY	int	Current memory used, in MB\.
SOURCE_CURRENT _POSITION	varchar	The position in the source database that AWS DMS is currently reading from\.
SOURCE_CURRENT _TIMESTAMP	timestamp	The timestamp in the source database that AWS DMS is currently reading from\.
SOURCE_TAIL _POSITION	varchar	The position of the oldest start transaction that is not committed\. This value is the newest position that you can revert to without losing any changes\.
SOURCE_TAIL _TIMESTAMP	timestamp	The timestamp of the oldest start transaction that is not committed\. This value is the newest timestamp that you can revert to without losing any changes\.\.
SOURCE_TIMESTAMP _APPLIED	timestamp	The timestamp of the last transaction commit\. In a bulk apply process, this value is the timestamp for the commit of the last transaction in the batch\.

Additional control table settings include the following:

+ `ControlSchema` - Use this option to indicate the database schema name for the AWS DMS target Control Tables\. If you do not enter any information in this field, then the tables are copied to the default location in the database\.

+ `HistoryTimeslotInMinutes` - Use this option to indicate the length of each time slot in the Replication History table\. The default is 5 minutes\.

Stream Buffer Task Settings

You can set stream buffer settings using the AWS CLI, include the following:

+ `StreamBufferCount` - Use this option to specify the number of data stream buffers for the migration task\. The default stream buffer number is 3\. Increasing the value of this setting may increase the speed of data extraction\. However, this performance increase is highly dependent on the migration environment, including the source system and instance class of the replication server\. The default is sufficient for most situations\.

73

74 + `StreamBufferSizeInMB` - Use this option to indicate the maximum size of each data stream
buffer\. The default size is 8 MB\. You might need to increase the value for this option
when you work with very large LOBs or if you receive a message in the log files stating that
the stream buffer size is insufficient\. When calculating the size of this option you can
use the following equation: \[Max LOB size \(or LOB chunk size\)\]*\[number of LOB columns
\]*\[number of stream buffers\]*\[number of tables loading in parallel per task\(
MaxFullLoadSubTasks\)\]*3

75

76 + `CtrlStreamBufferSizeInMB` - Use this option to set the size of the control stream buffer\.
Value is in MB, and can be from 1 to 8\. The default value is 5\. You may need to increase
this when working with a very large number of tables, such as tens of thousands of tables\.

77

78

79

80

81 # Change Processing Tuning Settings<a name="CHAP_Tasks.CustomizingTasks.TaskSettings.
ChangeProcessingTuning"></a>

82

83 The following settings determine how AWS DMS handles changes for target tables during change
data capture \(CDC\)\. Several of these settings depend on the value of the target metadata
parameter `BatchApplyEnabled`\. For more information on the `BatchApplyEnabled` parameter,
see [Target Metadata Task Settings](CHAP_Tasks.CustomizingTasks.TaskSettings.TargetMetadata.
md)\.

84

85 Change processing tuning settings include the following:

86

87 The following settings apply only when the target metadata parameter `BatchApplyEnabled` is set
to `true`\.

88

89 + `BatchApplyPreserveTransaction` - If set to `true`, transactional integrity is preserved and a
batch is guaranteed to contain all the changes within a transaction from the source\. The
default value is `true`\. This setting applies only to Oracle target endpoints\.

90

91   If set to `false`, there can be temporary lapses in transactional integrity to improve
performance\. There is no guarantee that all the changes within a transaction from the
source will be applied to the target in a single batch\.

92

93 + `BatchApplyTimeoutMin` - Sets the minimum amount of time in seconds that AWS DMS waits between
each application of batch changes\. The default value is 1\.

94

95 + `BatchApplyTimeoutMax` - Sets the maximum amount of time in seconds that AWS DMS waits between
each application of batch changes before timing out\. The default value is 30\.

96

97 + `BatchApplyMemoryLimit` - Sets the maximum amount of memory in \(MB\) to use for pre\-
processing in **Batch optimized apply mode**\. The default value is 500\.

98

99 + `BatchSplitSize` - Sets the number of changes applied in a single change processing statement
\. Select the check box and then optionally change the default value\. The default value is
10,000\. A value of 0 means there is no limit applied\.

100

101 The following settings apply only when the target metadata parameter `BatchApplyEnabled` is set
to `false`\.

102

172

103 + `MinTransactionSize` - Sets the minimum number of changes to include in each transaction\. The default value is 1000\.

104

105 + `CommitTimeout` - Sets the maximum time in seconds for AWS DMS to collect transactions in batches before declaring a timeout\. The default value is 1\.

106

107 + `HandleSourceTableAltered` - Set this option to `true` to alter the target table when the source table is altered\.

108

109 AWS DMS attempts to keep transaction data in memory until the transaction is fully committed to the source and/or the target\. However, transactions that are larger than the allocated memory or that are not committed within the specified time limit are written to disk\.

110

111 The following settings apply to change processing tuning regardless of the change processing mode\.

112

113 + `MemoryLimitTotal` - Sets the maximum size \(in MB\) that all transactions can occupy in memory before being written to disk\. The default value is 1024\.

114

115 + `MemoryKeepTime` - Sets the maximum time in seconds that each transaction can stay in memory before being written to disk\. The duration is calculated from the time that AWS DMS started capturing the transaction\. The default value is 60\.

116

117 + `StatementCacheSize` - Sets the maximum number of prepared statements to store on the server for later execution when applying changes to the target\. The default value is 50\. The maximum value is 200\.

118

119

120

121

122 # Data Validation Task Settings

123

124 You can ensure that your data was migrated accurately from the source to the target\. If you enable it for a task, then AWS DMS begins comparing the source and target data immediately after a full load is performed for a table\. For more information on data validation, see [Validating AWS Database Migration Service Tasks](CHAP_Validating.md)\.

125

126 Data validation settings include the following:

127

128 + To enable data validation, set the `EnableValidation` setting to `true`\.

129

130 + To adjust the number of execution threads that AWS DMS uses during validation, set the `ThreadCount` value\. The default value for `ThreadCount` is 5\. If you set `ThreadCount` to a higher number, AWS DMS will be able to complete the validation -fasterhowever, it will also execute more simultaneous queries, consuming more resources on the source and the target\.

131

132 For example, the following JSON enables data validation:

"ValidationSettings": { "EnableValidation": true, "ThreadCount": 5 }

1

2 For an Oracle endpoint, AWS DMS uses DBMS_CRYPTO to validate BLOBs\. If your Oracle endpoint uses BLOBs, then you must grant the execute permission on dbms_crypto to the user account

that is used to access the Oracle endpoint\. You can do this by running the following statement:

grant execute on sys.dbms_crypto to <dms_endpoint_user>;

1
2
3
4
5 # Change Processing DDL Handling Policy Task Settings
6
7 The following settings determine how AWS DMS handles DDL changes for target tables during change data capture \(CDC\)\. Change processing DDL handling policy settings include the following:
8
9 + `HandleSourceTableDropped ` - Set this option to `true` to drop the target table when the source table is dropped
10
11 + `HandleSourceTableTruncated` - Set this option to `true` to truncate the target table when the source table is truncated
12
13 + `HandleSourceTableAltered` - Set this option to `true` to alter the target table when the source table is altered\.
14
15
16
17
18 # Error Handling Task Settings
19
20 You can set the error handling behavior of your replication task during change data capture \(CDC\) using the following settings:
21
22 + `DataErrorPolicy` - Determines the action AWS DMS takes when there is an error related to data processing at the record level\. Some examples of data processing errors include conversion errors, errors in transformation, and bad data\. The default is `LOG_ERROR`\.
23
24   + `IGNORE_RECORD` - The task continues and the data for that record is ignored\. The error counter for the `DataErrorEscalationCount` property is incremented so that if you set a limit on errors for a table, this error will count toward that limit\.
25
26   + `LOG_ERROR` - The task continues and the error is written to the task log\.
27
28   + `SUSPEND_TABLE` - The task continues but data from the table with the error record is moved into an error state and the data is not replicated\.
29
30   + `STOP_TASK` - The task stops and manual intervention is required\.
31
32 + `DataTruncationErrorPolicy` - Determines the action AWS DMS takes when data is truncated\. The default is `LOG_ERROR`\.
33
34   + `IGNORE_RECORD` - The task continues and the data for that record is ignored\. The error counter for the `DataErrorEscalationCount` property is incremented so that if you set a limit on errors for a table, this error will count toward that limit\.

35

36   + `LOG_ERROR` - The task continues and the error is written to the task log\.

37

38   + `SUSPEND_TABLE` - The task continues but data from the table with the error record is moved into an error state and the data is not replicated\.

39

40   + `STOP_TASK` - The task stops and manual intervention is required\.

41

42 + `DataErrorEscalationPolicy` - Determines the action AWS DMS takes when the maximum number of errors \(set in the `DataErrorsEscalationCount` parameter\) is reached\. The default is `SUSPEND_TABLE`\.

43

44   + `LOG_ERROR` - The task continues and the error is written to the task log\.

45

46   + `SUSPEND_TABLE` - The task continues but data from the table with the error record is moved into an error state and the data is not replicated\.

47

48   + `STOP_TASK` - The task stops and manual intervention is required\.

49

50 + `DataErrorEscalationCount` - Sets the maximum number of errors that can occur to the data for a specific record\. When this number is reached, the data for the table that contains the error record is handled according to the policy set in the `DataErrorEscalationCount`\. The default is 0\.

51

52 + `TableErrorPolicy` - Determines the action AWS DMS takes when an error occurs when processing data or metadata for a specific table\. This error only applies to general table data and is not an error that relates to a specific record\. The default is `SUSPEND_TABLE`\.

53

54   + `SUSPEND_TABLE` - The task continues but data from the table with the error record is moved into an error state and the data is not replicated\.

55

56   + `STOP_TASK` - The task stops and manual intervention is required\.

57

58 + `TableErrorEscalationPolicy` - Determines the action AWS DMS takes when the maximum number of errors \(set using the `TableErrorEscalationCount` parameter\)\. The default and only user setting is `STOP_TASK`, where the task is stopped and manual intervention is required\.

59

60 + `TableErrorEscalationCount` - The maximum number of errors that can occur to the general data or metadata for a specific table\. When this number is reached, the data for the table is handled according to the policy set in the `TableErrorEscalationPolicy`\. The default is 0\.

61

62 + `RecoverableErrorCount` - The maximum number of attempts made to restart a task when an environmental error occurs\. After the system attempts to restart the task the designated number of times, the task is stopped and manual intervention is required\. Set this value to \-1 to attempt a restart six times\. Set this value to 0 to never attempt to restart a task \. The default is 1\.

63

64 + `RecoverableErrorInterval` - The number of seconds that AWS DMS waits between attempts to restart a task\. The default is 5\.

65

66 + `RecoverableErrorThrottling` - When enabled, the interval between attempts to restart a task is increased each time a restart is attempted\. The default is `true`\.

67

68 + `RecoverableErrorThrottlingMax` - The maximum number of seconds that AWS DMS waits between

attempts to restart a task if `RecoverableErrorThrottling` is enabled\. The default is 1800\.

69

70 + `ApplyErrorDeletePolicy` - Determines what action AWS DMS takes when there is a conflict with a DELETE operation\. The default is `IGNORE_RECORD`\.

71

72   + `IGNORE_RECORD` - The task continues and the data for that record is ignored\. The error counter for the `ApplyErrorEscalationCount` property is incremented so that if you set a limit on errors for a table, this error will count toward that limit\.

73

74   + `LOG_ERROR` - The task continues and the error is written to the task log\.

75

76   + `SUSPEND_TABLE` - The task continues but data from the table with the error record is moved into an error state and the data is not replicated\.

77

78   + `STOP_TASK` - The task stops and manual intervention is required\.

79

80 + `ApplyErrorInsertPolicy` - Determines what action AWS DMS takes when there is a conflict with an INSERT operation\. The default is `LOG_ERROR`\.

81

82   + `IGNORE_RECORD` - The task continues and the data for that record is ignored\. The error counter for the `ApplyErrorEscalationCount` property is incremented so that if you set a limit on errors for a table, this error will count toward that limit\.

83

84   + `LOG_ERROR` - The task continues and the error is written to the task log\.

85

86   + `SUSPEND_TABLE` - The task continues but data from the table with the error record is moved into an error state and the data is not replicated\.

87

88   + `STOP_TASK` - The task stops and manual intervention is required\.

89

90   + `UPDATE_RECORD` - If there is an existing target record with the same primary key as the inserted source record, the target record is updated\.

91

92 + `ApplyErrorUpdatePolicy` - Determines what action AWS DMS takes when there is a conflict with an UPDATE operation\. The default is `LOG_ERROR`\.

93

94   + `IGNORE_RECORD` - The task continues and the data for that record is ignored\. The error counter for the `ApplyErrorEscalationCount` property is incremented so that if you set a limit on errors for a table, this error will count toward that limit\.

95

96   + `LOG_ERROR` - The task continues and the error is written to the task log\.

97

98   + `SUSPEND_TABLE` - The task continues but data from the table with the error record is moved into an error state and the data is not replicated\.

99

100   + `STOP_TASK` - The task stops and manual intervention is required\.

101

102   + `UPDATE_RECORD` - If the target record is missing, the missing target record will be inserted into the target table\. Selecting this option requires full supplemental logging to be enabled for all the source table columns when Oracle is the source database\.

103

104 + `ApplyErrorEscalationPolicy` - Determines what action AWS DMS takes when the maximum number of errors \(set using the `ApplyErrorsEscalationCount` parameter\) is reached\.

176

105

106 + `LOG_ERROR` - The task continues and the error is written to the task log\.

107

108 + `SUSPEND_TABLE` - The task continues but data from the table with the error record is moved into an error state and the data is not replicated\.

109

110 + `STOP_TASK` - The task stops and manual intervention is required\.

111

112 + `ApplyErrorEscalationCount` - Sets the maximum number of APPLY conflicts that can occur for a specific table during a change process operation\. When this number is reached, the data for the table is handled according to the policy set in the `ApplyErrorEscalationPolicy` parameter\. The default is 0\.

113

114 + `ApplyErrorFailOnTruncationDdl` - Set this to `true` to cause the task to fail when a truncation is performed on any of the tracked tables during CDC\. The failure message will be: "Truncation DDL detected"\. The default is `false`\.

115

116 This does not work with PostgreSQL or any other source endpoint the does not replicate DDL table truncation\.

117

118 + `FailOnNoTablesCaptured` - Set this to `true` to cause a task to fail when the transformation rules defined for a task find no tables when the task starts\. The default is `false`\.

119

120 + `FailOnTransactionConsistencyBreached` - This option applies to tasks using Oracle as a source with CDC\. Set this to `true` to cause a task to fail when a transaction is open for more time than the specified timeout and could be dropped\.

121

122 When a CDC task starts with Oracle AWS DMS waits for a limited time for the oldest open transaction to close before starting CDC\. If the oldest open transaction doesn't close until the timeout is reached, then we normally start CDC anyway, ignoring that transaction \. if this setting is set to `true`, the task fails\.

123

124 + `FulloadIgnoreConflicts` - Set this to `false` to have AWS DMS ignore "zero rows affected" and "duplicates" errors when applying cached events\. If set to `true`, AWS DMS reports all errors instead of ignoring them\. The default is `false`\.

125

126

127

128

129 # Saving Task Settings

130

131 You can save the settings for a task as a JSON file, in case you want to reuse the settings for another task\.

132

133 For example, the following JSON file contains settings saved for a task:

{ "TargetMetadata": { "TargetSchema": "", "SupportLobs": true, "FullLobMode": false, "LobChunkSize": 64, "LimitedSizeLobMode": true, "LobMaxSize": 32, "BatchApplyEnabled": true }, "FullLoadSettings": { "TargetTablePrepMode": "DO_NOTHING", "CreatePkAfterFullLoad": false, "StopTaskCachedChangesApplied": false, "StopTaskCachedChangesNotApplied": false, "MaxFullLoadSubTasks": 8, "TransactionConsistencyTimeout": 600, "CommitRate": 10000 }, "Logging": { "EnableLogging": false }, "ControlTablesSettings": { "ControlSchema":"", "HistoryTimeslotInMinutes":5, "HistoryTableEnabled": false, "SuspendedTablesTableEnabled": false, "StatusTableEnabled": false }, "StreamBufferSettings": { "StreamBufferCount": 3, "StreamBufferSizeInMB": 8 }, "ChangeProcessingTuning": { "BatchApplyPreserveTransaction": true, "BatchApplyTimeoutMin": 1, "BatchApplyTimeoutMax": 30, "BatchApplyMemoryLimit": 500, "Batch-

SplitSize": 0, "MinTransactionSize": 1000, "CommitTimeout": 1, "MemoryLimitTotal": 1024, "Memory-
KeepTime": 60, "StatementCacheSize": 50 }, "ChangeProcessingDdlHandlingPolicy": { "HandleSourceTable-
Dropped": true, "HandleSourceTableTruncated": true, "HandleSourceTableAltered": true }, "ErrorBehavior": {
"DataErrorPolicy": "LOG_ERROR", "DataTruncationErrorPolicy":"LOG_ERROR", "DataErrorEscalation-
Policy":"SUSPEND_TABLE", "DataErrorEscalationCount": 50, "TableErrorPolicy":"SUSPEND_TABLE",
"TableErrorEscalationPolicy":"STOP_TASK", "TableErrorEscalationCount": 50, "RecoverableErrorCount": 0,
"RecoverableErrorInterval": 5, "RecoverableErrorThrottling": true, "RecoverableErrorThrottlingMax": 1800,
"ApplyErrorDeletePolicy":"IGNORE_RECORD", "ApplyErrorInsertPolicy":"LOG_ERROR", "ApplyErrorUp-
datePolicy":"LOG_ERROR", "ApplyErrorEscalationPolicy":"LOG_ERROR", "ApplyErrorEscalationCount":
0, "FullLoadIgnoreConflicts": true } }

Setting LOB Support for Source Databases in the AWS DMS task

Large objects, \(LOBs\) can sometimes be difficult to migrate between systems\. AWS DMS offers a number of options to help with the tuning of LOB columns\. To see which and when datatypes are considered LOBS by AWS DMS, see the AWS DMS documentation\.

When you migrate data from one database to another, you might take the opportunity to rethink how your LOBs are stored, especially for heterogeneous migrations\. If you want to do so, 'theres no need to migrate the LOB data\.

If you decide to include LOBs, you can then decide the other LOB settings:

+ The LOB mode determines how LOBs are handled:

  + **Full LOB mode** \- In **full LOB mode** AWS DMS migrates all LOBs from source to target regardless of size\. In this configuration, AWS DMS has no information about the maximum size of LOBs to expect\. Thus, LOBs are migrated one at a time, piece by piece\. Full LOB mode can be quite slow\.

  + **Limited LOB mode** \- In **limited LOB mode**, you set a maximum size LOB that AWS DMS should accept\. Doing so allows AWS DMS to pre\-allocate memory and load the LOB data in bulk\. LOBs that exceed the maximum LOB size are truncated and a warning is issued to the log file\. In** limited LOB mode** you get significant performance gains over **full LOB mode**\. We recommend that you use **limited LOB mode** whenever possible\.

Note

With Oracle, LOBs are treated as VARCHAR data types whenever possible\. This approach means AWS DMS fetches them from the database in bulk, which is significantly faster than other methods \. The maximum size of a VARCHAR in Oracle is 64K, therefore a limited LOB size of less than 64K is optimal when Oracle is your source database\.

+ When a task is configured to run in **limited LOB mode**, the **Max LOB size \(K\)** option sets the maximum size LOB that AWS DMS accepts\. Any LOBs that are larger than this value will be truncated to this value\.

+ When a task is configured to use **full LOB mode**, AWS DMS retrieves LOBs in pieces\. The ** LOB chunk size \(K\)** option determines the size of each piece\. When setting this option, pay particular attention to the maximum packet size allowed by your network configuration\. If the LOB chunk size exceeds your maximum allowed packet size, you might see disconnect errors\.

24
25
26
27
28 # Creating Multiple Tasks
29
30 In some migration scenarios, you might have to create several migration tasks\. Note that tasks
    work independently and can run concurrently; each task has its own initial load, CDC, and
    log reading process\. Tables that are related through data manipulation language \(DML\)
    must be part of the same task\.
31
32 Some reasons to create multiple tasks for a migration include the following:
33
34 + The target tables for the tasks reside on different databases, such as when you are fanning
    out or breaking a system into multiple systems\.
35
36 + You want to break the migration of a large table into multiple tasks by using filtering\.
37
38 **Note**
39 Because each task has its own change capture and log reading process, changes are *not*
    coordinated across tasks\. Therefore, when using multiple tasks to perform a migration, make
    sure that source transactions are wholly contained within a single task\.
40
41
42
43
44 # Creating a Task Assessment Report
45
46 The task assessment feature identifies data types that might not get migrated correctly\. During
    a task assessment, AWS DMS reads the source database schema and creates a list of data
    types\. It then compares this list to a pre\-defined list of data types supported by AWS DMS
    \. AWS DMS creates a report you can look at to see if your migration task has unsupported
    data types\. For more information about the data types that AWS DMS supports, see [Data
    Types for AWS Database Migration Service](CHAP_Reference.DataTypes.md)\. For more
    information about supported source data types and how they are converted, see [Source Data
    Types](CHAP_Reference.Source.md)\. For more information about supported target data types
    and how they are converted, see [Target Data Types](CHAP_Reference.Target.md)\.
47
48 The task assessment report includes a summary that lists the unsupported data types and the
    column count for each one\. It includes a list of data structures in JSON for each
    unsupported data type\. You can use the report to modify the source data types and improve
    the migration success\.
49
50 There are two levels of unsupported data types\. Data types that are shown on the report as "not
    "supported 'cant be migrated\. Data types that are shown on the report as "partially
    "supported might be converted to another data type and not migrate as you expect\.
51
52 For example, the following is a sample task assessment report\.

{ "summary":{ "task-name":"test15", "not-supported":{ "data-type": ["sql-variant"], "column-count":3 },
"partially-supported":{ "data-type":["float8", "jsonb"], "column-count":2 } }, "types":[
{
"data-type":"float8", "support-level":"partially-supported", "schemas":[
{
"schema-name":"schema1", "tables":[

{
"table-name":"table1", "columns":[
"column1", "column2"] }, {
"table-name":"table2", "columns":[
"column3", "column4"] }] }, {
"schema-name":"schema2", "tables":[
{
"table-name":"table3", "columns":[
"column5", "column6"] }, {
"table-name":"table4", "columns":[
"column7", "column8"] }] }] }, {
"datatype":"int8", "support-level":"partially-supported", "schemas":[
{
"schema-name":"schema1", "tables":[
{
"table-name":"table1", "columns":[
"column9", "column10"] }, {
"table-name":"table2", "columns":[
"column11", "column12"] }] }] }] }

1
2 The latest task assessment report can be viewed from the **Assessment** tab on the **Tasks page ** on the AWS console\. AWS DMS stores previous task assessment reports in an Amazon S3 bucket\. The Amazon S3 bucket name is in the following format\.

dms–

1
2 The report is stored in the bucket in a folder named with the task name\. The 'reports file name is the date of the assessment in the format yyyy\-mm\-dd\-hh\-mm\. You can view and compare previous task assessment reports from the Amazon S3 console\.

3
4 AWS DMS also creates an AWS Identity and Access Management \(IAM\) role to allow access to the S3 bucket; the role name is dms\-access\-for\-tasks\. The role uses the ` AmazonDMSCustomerS3Role` policy\.

5
6 You can enable the task assessment feature using the AWS console, the AWS CLI, or the DMS API:
7
8 + On the console, choose **Task Assessment** when creating or modifying a task\. To view the task assessment report using the console, choose the task on the **Tasks** page and choose the **Assessment results** tab in the details section\.
9
10 + The CLI commands are `start-replication-task-assessment` to begin a task assessment and ` describe-replication-task-assessment-results` to receive the task assessment report in JSON format\.
11
12 + The AWS DMS API uses the `StartReplicationTaskAssessment` action to begin a task assessment and the `DescribeReplicationTaskAssessment` action to receive the task assessment report in JSON format\.
13
14
15
16
17 # Modifying a Task
18
19 You can modify a task if you need to change the task settings, table mapping, or other settings

\. You modify a task in the DMS console by selecting the task and choosing **Modify**\. You can also use the AWS CLI or AWS DMS API command `ModifyReplicationTask`\.

There are a few limitations to modifying a task\. These include:

+ You cannot modify the source or target endpoint of a task\.

+ You cannot change the migration type of a task\.

+ A task that have been run must have a status of **Stopped** or **Failed** to be modified\.

Reloading Tables During a Task

While a task is running, you can reload a target database table using data from the source\. You may want to reload a table if, during the task, an error occurs or data changes due to partition operations \(for example, when using Oracle\)\. You can reload up to 10 tables from a task\.

To reload a table, the following conditions must apply:

+ The task must be running\.

+ The migration method for the task must be either Full Load or Full Load with CDC\.

+ Duplicate tables are not allowed\.

AWS Management Console

To reload a table using the AWS DMS console

1. Sign in to the AWS Management Console and choose AWS DMS\. Note that if you are signed in as an AWS Identity and Access Management \(IAM\) user, you must have the appropriate permissions to access AWS DMS\. For more information on the permissions required, see [IAM Permissions Needed to Use AWS DMS](CHAP_Security.IAMPermissions.md)\.

1. Select **Tasks** from the navigation pane\.

1. Select the running task that has the table you want to reload\.

1. Click the **Table Statistics** tab\.
![\[AWS DMS monitoring\]](http://docs.aws.amazon.com/dms/latest/userguide/images/datarep-reloading1.png)

1. Select the table you want to reload\. Note that if the task is no longer running, you will not be able to reload the table\.

1. Choose **Drop and reload table data**\.

When AWS DMS is preparing to reload a table, the console changes the table status to **The table is being reloaded**\.

63 ![\[AWS DMS monitoring\]](http://docs.aws.amazon.com/dms/latest/userguide/images/datarep-reloading2.png)

64

65

66

67

68 # Using Table Mapping with a Task to Select and Filter Data

69

70 Table mapping uses several types of rules to specify the data source, source schema, data, and any transformations that should occur during the task\. You can use table mapping to specify individual tables in a database to migrate and the schema to use for the migration\. In addition, you can use filters to specify what data from a given table column you want replicated and you can use transformations to modify the data written to the target database \.

71

72 ## Selection and Transformation Table Mapping using the AWS Console

73

74 You can use the AWS console to perform table mapping, including specifying table selection and transformations\. In the AWS Console user interface, you use the **Where** section to specify the schema, table, and action \(include or exclude\)\. You use the **Filter** section to specify the column name in a table and the conditions you want to apply to the replication task\. Together these two actions create a selection rule\.

75

76 Transformations can be included in a table mapping after you have specified at least one selection rule\. Transformations can be used to rename a schema or table, add a prefix or suffix to a schema or table, or remove a table column\.

77

78 The following example shows how to set up selection rules for a table called Customers in a schema called EntertainmentAgencySample\. Note that the **Guided** tab, where you create selection rules and transformations, only appears when you have a source endpoint that has schema and table information\.

79

80 **To specify a table selection, filter criteria, and transformations using the AWS console**

81

82 1. Sign in to the AWS Management Console and choose AWS DMS\. Note that if you are signed in as an AWS Identity and Access Management \(IAM\) user, you must have the appropriate permissions to access AWS DMS\. For more information on the permissions required, see [IAM Permissions Needed to Use AWS DMS](CHAP_Security.IAMPermissions.md)\.

83

84 1. On the **Dashboard** page, choose **Tasks**\.

85

86 1. Select **Create Task**\.

87

88 1. Enter the task information, including **Task name**, **Replication instance**, **Source endpoint**, **Target endpoint**, and **Migration type**\. Select **Guided** from the **Table mappings** section\.

89 ![\[Schema and table selection\]](http://docs.aws.amazon.com/dms/latest/userguide/images/datarep-Tasks-selecttransfrm0.png)

90

91 1. In the **Table mapping** section, select the schema name and table name\. You can use the "%" as a wildcard value when specifying the table name\. Specify the action to be taken, to include or exclude data defined by the filter\.

92 ![\[Schema and table selection\]](http://docs.aws.amazon.com/dms/latest/userguide/images/datarep
   -Tasks-selecttransfrm.png)

93

94 1. You specify filter information using the **Add column filter** and the **Add condition **
   links\. First, select **Add column filter** to specify a column and conditions\. Select **
   Add condition ** to add additional conditions\. The following example shows a filter for the
   Customers table that includes **AgencyIDs** between **01** and **85**\.

95 ![\[Schema and table selection\]](http://docs.aws.amazon.com/dms/latest/userguide/images/datarep
   -Tasks-filter.png)

96

97 1. When you have created the selections you want, select **Add selection rule**\.

98

99 1. After you have created at least one selection rule, you can add a transformation to the task
   \. Select **add transformation rule**\.

100 ![\[transformation rule\]](http://docs.aws.amazon.com/dms/latest/userguide/images/datarep-Tasks-
   transform1.png)

101

102 1. Select the target you want to transform and enter the additional information requested\. The
   following example shows a transformation that deletes the **AgencyStatus** column from the
   Customer table\.

103 ![\[transformation rule\]](http://docs.aws.amazon.com/dms/latest/userguide/images/datarep-Tasks-
   transform2.png)

104

105 1. Choose **Add transformation rule**\.

106

107 1. You can add additional selection rules or transformations by selecting the **add selection
   rule** or **add transformation rule**\. When you are finished, choose **Create task**\.

108 ![\[transformation rule\]](http://docs.aws.amazon.com/dms/latest/userguide/images/datarep-Tasks-
   transform3.png)

109

110 ## Selection and Transformation Table Mapping using JSON<a name="CHAP_Tasks.CustomizingTasks.
   TableMapping.SelectionTransformation"></a>

111

112 Table mappings can be created in the JSON format\. If you create a migration task using the AWS
   DMS Management Console, you can enter the JSON directly into the table mapping box\. If
   you use the AWS Command Line Interface \(AWS CLI\) or AWS Database Migration Service API to
   perform migrations, you can create a JSON file to specify the table mappings that you want
   to occur during migration\.

113

114 You can specify what tables or schemas you want to work with, and you can perform schema and
   table transformations\. You create table mapping rules using the `selection` and `
   transformation` rule types\.

115

116 ### Selection Rules and Actions<a name="CHAP_Tasks.CustomizingTasks.TableMapping.
   SelectionTransformation.Selections"></a>

117

118 Using table mapping, you can specify what tables or schemas you want to work with by using
   selection rules and actions\. For table mapping rules that use the selection rule type, the
   following values can be applied:

119

120 [\[See the AWS documentation website for more details\]](http://docs.aws.amazon.com/dms/latest/
   userguide/CHAP_Tasks.CustomizingTasks.TableMapping.html)

121

122 **Example Migrate All Tables in a Schema**

123 The following example migrates all tables from a schema named **Test** in your source to your target endpoint:

{ "rules": [{ "rule-type": "selection", "rule-id": "1", "rule-name": "1", "object-locator": { "schema-name": "Test", "table-name": "%" }, "rule-action": "include" }] }

1

2 **Example Migrate Some Tables in a Schema**

3 The following example migrates all tables except those starting with **DMS** from a schema named **Test** in your source to your target endpoint:

{ "rules": [{ "rule-type": "selection", "rule-id": "1", "rule-name": "1", "object-locator": { "schema-name": "Test", "table-name": "%" }, "rule-action": "include" }, { "rule-type": "selection", "rule-id": "2", "rule-name": "2", "object-locator": { "schema-name": "Test", "table-name": "DMS%" }, "rule-action": "exclude" }] }

1

2 ### Transformation Rules and Actions

3

4 You use the transformation actions to specify any transformations you want to apply to the selected schema or table\. Transformation rules are optional\.

5

6 For table mapping rules that use the transformation rule type, the following values can be applied:

7

8 [\[See the AWS documentation website for more details\]](http://docs.aws.amazon.com/dms/latest/userguide/CHAP_Tasks.CustomizingTasks.TableMapping.html)

9

10 **Example Rename a Schema**

11 The following example renames a schema from **Test** in your source to **Test1** in your target endpoint:

{ "rules": [{ "rule-type": "selection", "rule-id": "1", "rule-name": "1", "object-locator": { "schema-name": "Test", "table-name": "%" }, "rule-action": "include" }, { "rule-type": "transformation", "rule-id": "2", "rule-name": "2", "rule-action": "rename", "rule-target": "schema", "object-locator": { "schema-name": "Test" }, "value": "Test1" }] }

1

2 **Example Rename a Table**

3 The following example renames a table from **Actor** in your source to **Actor1** in your target endpoint:

{ "rules": [{ "rule-type": "selection", "rule-id": "1", "rule-name": "1", "object-locator": { "schema-name": "Test", "table-name": "%" }, "rule-action": "include" }, { "rule-type": "transformation", "rule-id": "2", "rule-name": "2", "rule-action": "rename", "rule-target": "table", "object-locator": { "schema-name": "Test", "table-name": "Actor" }, "value": "Actor1" }] }

1

2 **Example Rename a Column**

3 The following example renames a column in table **Actor** from **first_name** in your source to **fname** in your target endpoint:

{ "rules": [{ "rule-type": "selection", "rule-id": "1", "rule-name": "1", "object-locator": { "schema-name": "test", "table-name": "%" }, "rule-action": "include" }, { "rule-type": "transformation", "rule-id": "4", "rule-name": "4", "rule-action": "rename", "rule-target": "column", "object-locator": { "schema-name": "test", "table-name": "Actor", "column-name" : "first_name" }, "value": "fname" }] }

Example Remove a Column

The following example transforms the table named **Actor** in your source to remove all columns starting with the characters **col** from it in your target endpoint:

{ "rules": [{ "rule-type": "selection", "rule-id": "1", "rule-name": "1", "object-locator": { "schema-name": "test", "table-name": "%" }, "rule-action": "include" }, { "rule-type": "transformation", "rule-id": "2", "rule-name": "2", "rule-action": "remove-column", "rule-target": "column", "object-locator": { "schema-name": "test", "table-name": "Actor", "column-name": "col%" } }] }

Example Convert to Lowercase

The following example converts a table name from **ACTOR** in your source to **actor** in your target endpoint:

{ "rules": [{ "rule-type": "selection", "rule-id": "1", "rule-name": "1", "object-locator": { "schema-name": "test", "table-name": "%" }, "rule-action": "include" }, { "rule-type": "transformation", "rule-id": "2", "rule-name": "2", "rule-action": "convert-lowercase", "rule-target": "table", "object-locator": { "schema-name": "test", "table-name": "ACTOR" } }] }

Example Convert to Uppercase

The following example converts all columns in all tables and all schemas from lowercase in your source to uppercase in your target endpoint:

{ "rules": [{ "rule-type": "selection", "rule-id": "1", "rule-name": "1", "object-locator": { "schema-name": "test", "table-name": "%" }, "rule-action": "include" }, { "rule-type": "transformation", "rule-id": "2", "rule-name": "2", "rule-action": "convert-uppercase", "rule-target": "column", "object-locator": { "schema-name": "%", "table-name": "%", "column-name": "%" } }] }

Example Add a Prefix

The following example transforms all tables in your source to add the prefix **DMS_** to them in your target endpoint:

{ "rules": [{ "rule-type": "selection", "rule-id": "1", "rule-name": "1", "object-locator": { "schema-name": "test", "table-name": "%" }, "rule-action": "include" }, { "rule-type": "transformation", "rule-id": "2", "rule-name": "2", "rule-action": "add-prefix", "rule-target": "table", "object-locator": { "schema-name": "test", "table-name": "%" }, "value": "DMS_" }]
}

Example Replace a Prefix

The following example transforms all columns containing the prefix **Pre_** in your source to replace the prefix with **NewPre_** in your target endpoint:

{ "rules": [{ "rule-type": "selection", "rule-id": "1", "rule-name": "1", "object-locator": { "schema-name": "test", "table-name": "%" }, "rule-action": "include" }, { "rule-type": "transformation", "rule-id": "2", "rule-name": "2", "rule-action": "replace-prefix", "rule-target": "column", "object-locator": { "schema-name": "%", "table-name": "%", "column-name": "%" }, "value": "NewPre_", "old-value": "Pre_" }] }

Example Remove a Suffix

The following example transforms all tables in your source to remove the suffix **_DMS** from them in your target endpoint:

{ ”rules”: [{ ”rule-type”: ”selection”, ”rule-id”: ”1”, ”rule-name”: ”1”, ”object-locator”: { ”schema-name”: ”test”, ”table-name”: ”%” }, ”rule-action”: ”include” }, { ”rule-type”: ”transformation”, ”rule-id”: ”2”, ”rule-name”: ”2”, ”rule-action”: ”remove-suffix”, ”rule-target”: ”table”, ”object-locator”: { ”schema-name”: ”test”, ”table-name”: ”%” }, ”value”: ”_DMS” }] }

Using Source Filters

You can use source filters to limit the number and type of records transferred from your source to your target\. For example, you can specify that only employees with a location of headquarters are moved to the target database\. Filters are part of a selection rule\. You apply filters on a column of data\.

Source filters must follow these constraints:

+ A selection rule can have no filters or one or more filters\.

+ Every filter can have one or more filter conditions\.

+ If more than one filter is used, the list of filters will be combined as if using an AND operator between the filters\.

+ If more than one filter condition is used within a single filter, the list of filter conditions will be combined as if using an OR operator between the filter conditions\.

+ Filters are only applied when `rule-action = 'include'`\.

+ Filters require a column name and a list of filter conditions\. Filter conditions must have a filter operator and a value\.

+ Column names, table names, and schema names are case sensitive\.

Filtering by Time and Date

When selecting data to import, you can specify a date or time as part of your filter criteria\. AWS DMS uses the date format YYYY\-MM-DD and the time format YYYY\-MM\-DD HH:MM:SS for filtering\. The AWS DMS comparison functions follow the SQLite conventions\. For more information about SQLite data types and date comparisons, see [Datatypes In SQLite Version 3](https://sqlite.org/datatype3.html)\.

The following example shows how to filter on a date\.

Example Single Date Filter
The following filter replicates all employees where `empstartdate >= January 1, 2002` to the target database\.

{ ”rules”: [{ ”rule-type”: ”selection”, ”rule-id”: ”1”, ”rule-name”: ”1”, ”object-locator”: { ”schema-name”: ”test”, ”table-name”: ”employee” }, ”rule-action”: ”include”, ”filters”: [{ ”filter-type”: ”source”, ”column-name”: ”empstartdate”, ”filter-conditions”: [{ ”filter-operator”: ”gte”, ”value”: ”2002-01-01” }] }] }] }

Creating Source Filter Rules in JSON

You can create source filters by specifying a column name, filter condition, filter operator, and a filter value\.

The following table shows the parameters used for source filtering\.

Parameter	Value
filter\-type	source
column\-name	The name of the source column you want the filter applied to\. The name is case sensitive\.
filter\-conditions	
filter\-operator	This parameter can be one of the following: [\[See the AWS documentation website for more details\]](http://docs.aws.amazon.com/dms/latest/userguide/CHAP_Tasks.CustomizingTasks.TableMapping.html)
value	The value of the filter\-operator parameter\. If the filter\-operator is `between`, provide two values, one for start\-value and one for end\-value\.

The following examples show some common ways to use source filters\.

Example Single Filter
The following filter replicates all employees where `empid >= 100` to the target database\.

```
{ "rules": [{ "rule-type": "selection", "rule-id": "1", "rule-name": "1", "object-locator": { "schema-name": "test", "table-name": "employee" }, "rule-action": "include", "filters": [{ "filter-type": "source", "column-name": "empid", "filter-conditions": [{ "filter-operator": "gte", "value": "100" }] }] }] }
```

Example Multiple Filter Operators
The following filter applies multiple filter operators to a single column of data\. The filter replicates all employees where `(empid <=10)` OR `(empid is between 50 and 75)` OR `(empid >= 100)` to the target database\.

```
{ "rules": [{ "rule-type": "selection", "rule-id": "1", "rule-name": "1", "object-locator": { "schema-name": "test", "table-name": "employee" }, "rule-action": "include", "filters": [{ "filter-type": "source", "column-name": "empid", "filter-conditions": [{ "filter-operator": "ste", "value": "10" }, { "filter-operator": "between", "start-value": "50", "end-value": "75" }, { "filter-operator": "gte", "value": "100" }] }] }] }
```

Example Multiple Filters
The following filter applies multiple filters to two columns in a table\. The filter replicates all employees where `(empid <= 100)` AND `(dept= tech)` to the target database\.

```
{ "rules": [{ "rule-type": "selection", "rule-id": "1", "rule-name": "1", "object-locator": { "schema-name": "test", "table-name": "employee" }, "rule-action": "include", "filters": [{ "filter-type": "source", "column-name": "empid", "filter-conditions": [{ "filter-operator": "ste", "value": "100" }] }, { "filter-type": "source", "column-name": "dept", "filter-conditions": [{ "filter-operator": "eq", "value": "tech" }] }] }] }
```

Migrating Large Data Stores Using AWS Database Migration Service and AWS Snowball

Large\-scale data migrations can include many terabytes of information, and can be slowed by network performance and by the sheer amount of data that has to be moved\. AWS DMS can load data onto an AWS Snowball device, transfer that data to AWS, and then load the data to the target AWS data store\.

Using AWS DMS and the AWS Schema Conversion Tool \(AWS SCT\), you migrate your data in two stages\. First, you use the AWS SCT to process the data locally and then move that data to the AWS Snowball Edge appliance\. AWS Snowball then automatically loads the data into an Amazon S3 bucket\. Next, when the data is available on Amazon S3, AWS DMS takes the files and migrates the data to the target data store\. If you are using change data capture \(CDC \), those updates are written to the Amazon S3 bucket and the target data store is constantly updated\.

AWS Snowball is an AWS service you can use to transfer data to the cloud at faster\-than\-network speeds using an AWS\-owned appliance\. An AWS Snowball Edge device can hold up to 100 TB of data\. It uses 256\-bit encryption and an industry\-standard Trusted Platform Module \(TPM\) to ensure both security and full chain\-of\-custody for your data\.

Amazon S3 is a storage and retrieval service\. To store an object in Amazon S3, you upload the file you want to store to a bucket\. When you upload a file, you can set permissions on the object and also on any metadata\.

AWS DMS supports the following scenarios:

+ Migration from an on\-premises data warehouse to Amazon Redshift\. This approach involves a client\-side software installation of the AWS Schema Conversion Tool\. The tool reads information from the warehouse \(the extractor\), and then moves data to S3 or Snowball\. Then in the AWS Cloud, information is either read from S3 or Snowball and injected into Amazon Redshift\.

+ Migration from an on\-premises relational database to an Amazon RDS database\. This approach again involves a client\-side software installation of the AWS Schema Conversion Tool\. The tool reads information from a local database that AWS supports\. The tool then moves data to S3 or Snowball\. When the data is in the AWS Cloud, AWS DMS writes it to a supported database in either Amazon EC2 or Amazon RDS\.

Process Overview

The process of using AWS DMS and AWS Snowball involves several steps, and it uses not only AWS DMS and AWS Snowball but also the AWS Schema Conversion Tool \(AWS SCT\)\. The sections following this overview provide a step\-by\-step guide to each of these tasks\.

Note

We recommend that you test your migration before you use the AWS Snowball device\. To do so, you can set up a task to send data, such as a single table, to an Amazon S3 bucket instead of the AWS Snowball device\.

![\[AWS Database Migration Service and AWS Snowball process\]](http://docs.aws.amazon.com/dms/latest/userguide/images/Snowball-flow.png)

The migration involves a local task, where AWS SCT moves the data to the AWS Snowball Edge device, an intermediate action where the data is copied from the AWS Snowball Edge device to an S3 bucket\. The process then involves a remote task where AWS DMS loads the data from the Amazon S3 bucket to the target data store on AWS\.

The following steps need to occur to migrate data from a local data store to an AWS data store using AWS Snowball\.

34 1. Create an AWS Snowball job using the AWS Snowball console\. For more information, see [Create an Import Job](https://docs.aws.amazon.com/snowball/latest/ug/create-import-job.html) in the AWS Snowball documentation\.

35

36 1. Download and install the AWS SCT application on a local machine\. The machine must have network access and be able to access the AWS account to be used for the migration\. For more information about the operating systems AWS SCT can be installed on, see [Installing and Updating the AWS Schema Conversion Tool](http://docs.aws.amazon.com/SchemaConversionTool/latest/userguide/CHAP_SchemaConversionTool.Installing.html)\.

37

38 1. Install the AWS SCT DMS Agent \(DMS Agent\) on a local, dedicated Linux machine\. We recommend that you do not install the DMS Agent on the same machine that you install the AWS SCT application\.

39

40 1. Unlock the AWS Snowball Edge device using the local, dedicated Linux machine where you installed the DMS Agent\.

41

42 1. Create a new project in AWS SCT\.

43

44 1. Configure the AWS SCT to use the DMS Agent\.

45

46 1. Register the DMS Agent with the AWS SCT\.

47

48 1. Install the database driver for your source database on the dedicated machine where you installed the DMS Agent\.

49

50 1. Create and set permissions for the Amazon S3 bucket to use\.

51

52 1. Edit the **AWS Service Profile** in AWS SCT\.

53

54 1. Create **Local & DMS Task** in SCT\.

55

56 1. Run and monitor the **Local & DMS Task** in SCT\.

57

58 1. Run the AWS SCT task and monitor progress in SCT\.

59

60 ## Step\-by\-Step Procedures for Migrating Data Using AWS DMS and AWS Snowball

61

62 The following sections provide detailed information on the migration steps\.

63

64 ### Step 1: Create an AWS Snowball Job

65

66 Create an AWS Snowball job by following the steps outlined in the section [Getting Started with AWS Snowball Edge: Your First Job](http://docs.aws.amazon.com/snowball/latest/developer-guide/common-get-start.html) in the AWS Snowball documentation\.

67

68 ### Step 2: Download and Install the AWS Schema Conversion Tool \(AWS SCT\)

69

70 Download and install the AWS Schema Conversion Tool using the instructions at [Installing and Updating the AWS Schema Conversion Tool](http://docs.aws.amazon.com/SchemaConversionTool/latest/userguide/CHAP_SchemaConversionTool.Installing.html) in the AWS SCT documentation\. Install the AWS SCT on a local machine that has access to AWS\. This machine should be a

different one than that the one where you plan to install the DMS Agent\.

71

72 ### Step 3: Install and Configure the AWS SCT DMS Agent

73

74 In this step, you install the DMS Agent on a dedicated machine that has access to AWS and to the machine where AWS SCT was installed\.

75

76 You can install the DMS Agent on the following Linux platforms:

77

78 + Red Hat Enterprise Linux versions 6\.2 through 6\.8, 7\.0 and 7\.1 \(64\-bit\)

79

80 + SUSE Linux version 11\.1 \(64\-bit\)

81

82 **To install the DMS Agent**

83

84 1. Copy the RPM file called `aws-schema-conversion-tool-dms-agent-2.4.0-R2.x86_64.rpm` from the AWS SCT installation directory to a dedicated Linux machine\.

85

86 1. Run the following command as root to install the DMS Agent\. If you install or upgrade the DMS Agent on SUSE Linux, you must add the `--nodeps` parameter to the command\.

```
sudo rpm -i amazonrdsmigrationtool-2.2.1-R1.x86_64.rpm
```

1

2 The default installation location is /opt/amazon/aws\-schema\-conversion\-tool\-dms\-agent\. To install the DMS Agent in a non\-default directory, use `--prefix` `<path to new product dir>`\.

3

4 1. To verify that the Amazon RDS Migration Server is running, issue the following command\.

```
ps -ef | grep repctl
```

1

2 The output of this command should show two processes running\.

3

4 To configure the DMS Agent, you must provide a password and port number\. You use the password in AWS SCT, so keep it handy\. The port is the one that the DMS Agent should listen on for AWS SCT connections\. You might have to configure your firewall to allow connectivity\.

5

6 Run the following script to configure the DMS Agent\.

```
sudo /opt/amazon/rdsmigrationtool/configure.sh
```

1

2 ### Step 4: Unlock the AWS Snowball Edge Device

3

4 You should run the commands that unlock and provide credentials to the Snowball Edge device from the machine where you installed the DMS Agent\. This way you can be sure that the DMS Agent call connect to the AWS Snowball Edge device\. For more information about unlocking the AWS Snowball Edge device, see [Unlock the Snowball Edge](http://docs.aws.amazon.com/snowball/latest/developer-guide/unlockappliance.html)\.

5

6 For example, the following command lists the Amazon S3 bucket used by the device\.

```
aws s3 ls s3:// --profile --endpoint http://:8080 --recursive
```

Step 5: Create a New AWS SCT Project

Next, you create a new AWS SCT project\.

To create a new project in AWS SCT

1. Start AWS SCT, and choose **New Project** for **File**\. The **New Project** dialog box appears\.

1. Add the following project information\.
[\[See the AWS documentation website for more details\]](http://docs.aws.amazon.com/dms/latest/userguide/CHAP_LargeDBs.html)

1. Choose **OK** to create your AWS SCT project\.

1. \(Optional\) Test your connection\.

Step 6: Configure the AWS SCT Profile to Work with the DMS Agent

The AWS SCT Profile must be updated to use the DMS Agent\.

To update the AWS SCT profile to work with the DMS Agent

1. Start AWS SCT\.

1. Choose **Settings**, and then choose **Global Settings**\. Choose **AWS Service Profiles**\.

1. Choose **Add New AWS Service Profile**\.
![\[AWS Database Migration Service and AWS Snowball process\]](http://docs.aws.amazon.com/dms/latest/userguide/images/snowball-AWSserviceprofile.png)

1. Add the following profile information\.
[\[See the AWS documentation website for more details\]](http://docs.aws.amazon.com/dms/latest/userguide/CHAP_LargeDBs.html)

1. After you have entered the information, choose **Test Connection** to verify that AWS SCT can connect to the Amazon S3 bucket\.

   The **OLTP Local & DMS Data Migration** section in the pop\-up window should show all entries with a status of **Pass**\. If the test fails, the failure is probably because the account you are using does not have the correct privileges to access the Amazon S3 bucket\.

1. If the test passes, choose **OK** and then **OK** again to close the window and dialog box\.

Step 7: Register the DMS Agent in AWS SCT

Next, you register the DMS Agent in AWS SCT\. SCT then tries to connect to the agent, showing status\. When the agent is available, the status turns to active\.

To register the DMS Agent

45 1. Start AWS SCT, choose **View**, and then choose **Database Migration View \(DMS\)**\.

46 ![\[View dropdown menu\]](http://docs.aws.amazon.com/dms/latest/userguide/images/snowball-view-
   databasemigview.png)

47

48 1. Choose the **Agent** tab, and then choose **Register**\. The **New Agent Registration**
   dialog box appears\.

49 ![\[New Agent Registration dialog box\]](http://docs.aws.amazon.com/dms/latest/userguide/images
   /snowball-newagentregistration.png)

50

51 1. Type your information in the **New Agent Registration** dialog box\.

52 [\[See the AWS documentation website for more details\]](http://docs.aws.amazon.com/dms/latest/
   userguide/CHAP_LargeDBs.html)

53

54 1. Choose **Register** to register the agent with your AWS SCT project\.

55

56 ### Step 8: Install the Source Database Driver for the DMS Agent on the Linux Computer<a name="
   CHAP_LargeDBs.SBS.SourceDriver"></a>

57

58 For the migration to succeed, the DMS Agent must be able to connect to the source database\. To
   make this possible, you install the database driver for your source database\. The required
   driver varies by database\.

59

60 To restart the DMS Agent after database driver installation, change the working directory to `<
   product_dir>/bin` and use the steps listed following for each source database\.

cd <product_dir>/bin ./arep.ctl stop ./arep.ctl start

1

2 **To install on Oracle**

3 Install Oracle Instant Client for Linux \(x86\-64\) version 11\.2\.0\.3\.0 or later\.

4 In addition, if not already included in your system, you need to create a symbolic link in the
   $ORACLE_HOME\\lib directory\. This link should be called libclntsh\.so, and should point to
   a specific version of this file\. For example, on an Oracle 12c client:

lrwxrwxrwx 1 oracle oracle 63 Oct 2 14:16 libclntsh.so -> /u01/app/oracle/home/lib/libclntsh.so.12.1

1 In addition, the LD_LIBRARY_PATH environment variable should be appended with the Oracle lib
   directory and added to the site_arep_login\.sh script under the lib folder of the
   installation\. Add this script if it doesn't exist\.

vi cat /bin/site_arep_login.sh

export   ORACLE_HOME=/usr/lib/oracle/12.2/client64;   export   LD_LIBRARY_PATH=$LD_LI-
BRARY_PATH:$ORACLE_HOME/lib

1

2 **To install on Microsoft SQL Server **

3 Install the Microsoft ODBC Driver

4 Update the site_arep_login\.sh with the following code\.

export LD_LIBRARY_PATH=$LD_LIBRARY_PATH:/opt/microsoft/msodbcsql/lib64/

1 **Simba ODBC Driver **

2 Install the Microsoft ODBC Driver

3 Edit the simba\.sqlserverodbc\.ini file as follows

DriverManagerEncoding=UTF-16 ODBCInstLib=libodbcinst.so

To install on SAP Sybase

The SAP Sybase ASE ODBC 64\-bit client should be installed

If the installation dir is /opt/sap, update the site_arep_login\.sh with

export SYBASE_HOME=/opt/sap export
LD_LIBRARY_PATH=$LD_LIBRARY_PATH:$SYBASE_HOME/   DataAccess64/OD-
BC/lib:$SYBASE_HOME/DataAccess/ODBC/ lib:$SYBASE_HOME/OCS-16_0/lib:$SYBASE_HOME/OCS-
16_0/ lib3p64:$SYBASE_HOME/OCS-16_0/lib3p

The /etc/odbcinst\.ini should include these entries

[Sybase] Driver=/opt/sap/DataAccess64/ODBC/lib/libsybdrvodb.so Description=Sybase ODBC driver

To install on MySQL

Install MySQL Connector/ODBC for Linux, version 5\.2\.6 or later

Make sure that the /etc/odbcinst\.ini file contains an entry for MySQL, as in the following example

[MySQL ODBC 5.2.6 Unicode Driver] Driver = /usr/lib64/libmyodbc5w.so UsageCount = 1

To install on PostgreSQL

Install postgresql94\-9\.4\.4\-1PGDG\.<OS Version>\.x86_64\.rpm\. This is the package that contains the psql executable\.

For example, postgresql94\-9\.4\.4\-1PGDG\.rhel7\.x86_64\.rpm is the package required for Red Hat 7\.

Install the ODBC driver postgresql94\-odbc\-09\.03\.0400\-1PGDG\.<OS version>\.x86_64 or above for Linux, where <OS version> is the OS of the agent machine\.

For example, postgresql94\-odbc\-09\.03\.0400\-1PGDG\.rhel7\.x86_64 is the client required for Red Hat 7\.

Make sure that the /etc/odbcinst\.ini file contains an entry for PostgreSQL, as in the following example

[PostgreSQL] Description = PostgreSQL ODBC driver Driver = /usr/pgsql-9.4/lib/psqlodbc.so Setup = /usr/pgsql-9.4/lib/psqlodbcw.so Debug = 0 CommLog = 1 UsageCount = 2

Step 9: Configure AWS SCT to Access the Amazon S3 Bucket

For information on configuring an Amazon S3 bucket, see [Working with Amazon S3 Buckets](http://docs.aws.amazon.com/AmazonS3/latest/dev/UsingBucket.html) in the Amazon S3 documentation\.

Note

To use the resulting Amazon S3 bucket in migration, you must have an AWS DMS replication instance created in the same AWS Region as the S3 bucket\. If you haven't already created one, do so by using the AWS DMS Management Console, as described in [Step 2: Create a Replication Instance](CHAP_GettingStarted.md#CHAP_GettingStarted.ReplicationInstance)\.

Step 10: Creating a Local & DMS Task

Next, you create the task that is the end\-to\-end migration task\. The task includes two subtasks\. One subtask migrates data from the source database to the AWS Snowball appliance \. The other subtask takes the data that the appliance loads into an Amazon S3 bucket and migrates it to the target database\.

To create the end\-to\-end migration task

1. Start AWS SCT, choose **View**, and then choose **Database Migration View \(Local & DMS\)**\.
![\[View > Database Migration View (Local & DMS) \]](http://docs.aws.amazon.com/dms/latest/userguide/images/snowball-view-databasemigview.png)

1. In the left panel that displays the schema from your source database, choose a schema object to migrate\. Open the context \(right\-click\) menu for the object, and then choose **Create Local & DMS Task**\.
![\[AWS Database Migration Service and AWS Snowball process\]](http://docs.aws.amazon.com/dms/latest/userguide/images/snowball-contextmenucreatelocal.png)

1. Add your task information\.
[\[See the AWS documentation website for more details\]](http://docs.aws.amazon.com/dms/latest/userguide/CHAP_LargeDBs.html)

1. Choose **Create** to create the task\.

Step 11: Running and Monitoring the Local & DMS Task in SCT

You can start the Local & DMS Task when all connections to endpoints are successful\. This means all connections for the Local task, which includes connections from the DMS Agent to the source database, the staging Amazon S3 bucket, and the AWS Snowball device, as well as the connections for the DMS task, which includes connections from the staging Amazon S3 bucket to the target database on AWS\.

You can monitor the DMS Agent logs by choosing **Show Log**\. The log details include agent server \(**Agent Log**\) and local running task \(**Task Log**\) logs\. Because the endpoint connectivity is done by the server \(since the local task is not running and there are no task logs\), connection issues are listed under the **Agent Log** tab\.

![\[Local task completed, waiting for the second task\]](http://docs.aws.amazon.com/dms/latest/userguide/images/snowball-tasklog.png)

Step 12: Manage the AWS Snowball Appliance

Once the Snowball appliance is fully loaded, AWS SCT updates the status of the task to show it is 50% complete\. Remember that the other part of the task involves AWS DMS taking the data from Amazon S3 to the target data store\.

To do so, disconnect the AWS Snowball appliance and ship back to AWS\. For more information about returning the AWS Snowball appliance to AWS, see the steps outlined in [Getting Started with AWS Snowball Edge: Your First Job](http://docs.aws.amazon.com/snowball/latest/developer-guide/common-get-start.html) in the AWS Snowball documentation\. You can use the AWS Snowball console or AWS SCT \(show details of the DMS task\) to check the status of the appliance and find out when AWS DMS begins to load data to the Amazon S3 bucket\.

![\[Local task completed, waiting for the second task\]](http://docs.aws.amazon.com/dms/latest/userguide/images/snowball-twotasksonedone.png)

After the AWS Snowball appliance arrives at AWS and unloads data to S3 bucket, you can see that the remote \(DMS\) task starts to run\. If the migration type you selected for the task was

Migrate existing data, the status for the DMS task will show 100% complete when the data has been transferred from Amazon S3 to the target data store\. If you set the a task mode to include ongoing replication, then after full load is complete the task status shows that the task continues to run, while AWS DMS applies ongoing changes\.

Limitations When Working with AWS Snowball and AWS Database Migration Service \(AWS DMS\)

There are some limitations you should be aware of when working with AWS Snowball\.

+ The LOB mode limits LOB file size to 32K\.

+ If an error occurs during the data migration during the load from the local database to the AWS Snowball Edge device or when AWS DMS loads data from Amazon S3 to the target database, the task will restart if the error is recoverable\. If AWS DMS cannot recover from the error, the migration will stop\.

+ Every AWS SCT task creates two endpoint connections on AWS DMS\. If you create multiple tasks, you could reach a resource limit for the number of endpoints that can be created\.

Monitoring AWS Database Migration Service Tasks

You can monitor the progress of your task by checking the task status and by monitoring the task's control table\. For more information about control tables, see [Control Table Task Settings](CHAP_Tasks.CustomizingTasks.TaskSettings.ControlTable.md)\.

You can also monitor the progress of your tasks using Amazon CloudWatch\. By using the AWS Management Console, the AWS Command Line Interface \(CLI\), or AWS DMS API, you can monitor the progress of your task and also the resources and network connectivity used\.

Finally, you can monitor the status of your source tables in a task by viewing the table state\.

Note that the "last updated" column the DMS console only indicates the time that AWS DMS last updated the table statistics record for a table\. It does not indicate the time of the last update to the table\.

For more information, see the following topics\.

+ [Task Status](#CHAP_Tasks.Status)
+ [Table State During Tasks](#CHAP_Tasks.CustomizingTasks.TableState)
+ [Monitoring Replication Tasks Using Amazon CloudWatch](#CHAP_Monitoring.CloudWatch)
+ [Data Migration Service Metrics](#CHAP_Monitoring.Metrics)
+ [Managing AWS DMS Task Logs](#CHAP_Monitoring.ManagingLogs)
+ [Logging AWS DMS API Calls Using AWS CloudTrail](#CHAP_Monitoring.CloudTrail)

Task Status

The task status indicated the condition of the task\. The following table shows the possible statuses a task can have:

```
81
82 | Task Status | Description |
83 | --- | --- |
84 |    **Creating**    |    AWS DMS is creating the task\.    |
85 |    **Running**    |    The task is performing the migration duties specified\.    |
86 |    **Stopped**    |    The task is stopped\.    |
87 |    **Stopping**    |    The task is being stopped\. This is usually an indication of user
        intervention in the task\.    |
88 |    **Deleting**    |    The task is being deleted, usually from a request for user intervention\.
        |
89 |    **Failed**    |    The task has failed\. See the task log files for more information\.    |
90 |    **Starting**    |    The task is connecting to the replication instance and to the source and
        target endpoints\. Any filters and transformations are being applied\.    |
91 |    **Ready**    |    The task is ready to run\. This status usually follows the "creating" status
        \.    |
92 |    **Modifying**    |    The task is being modified, usually due to a user action that modified
        the task settings\.    |
93
94 The task status bar gives an estimation of the task's progress\. The quality of this estimate
        depends on the quality of the source 'databases table statistics; the better the table
        statistics, the more accurate the estimation\. For tasks with only one table that has no
        estimated rows statistic, we are unable to provide any kind of percentage complete estimate
        \. In this case, the task state and the indication of rows loaded can be used to confirm
        that the task is indeed running and making progress\.
95
96 ## Table State During Tasks<a name="CHAP_Tasks.CustomizingTasks.TableState"></a>
97
98 The AWS DMS console updates information regarding the state of your tables during migration\.
        The following table shows the possible state values:
99
100 ![\[ AWS Database Migration Service replication instance\]](http://docs.aws.amazon.com/dms/
        latest/userguide/images/datarep-TableState.png)
101
102
103 | State | Description |
104 | --- | --- |
105 |    **Table does not exist**    |    AWS DMS cannot find the table on the source endpoint\.    |
106 |    **Before load**    |    The full load process has been enabled, but it hasn't started yet\.    |
107 |    **Full load**    |    The full load process is in progress\.    |
108 |    **Table completed**    |    Full load has completed\.    |
109 |    **Table cancelled**    |    Loading of the table has been cancelled\.    |
110 |    **Table error**    |    An error occurred when loading the table\.    |
111
112 ## Monitoring Replication Tasks Using Amazon CloudWatch<a name="CHAP_Monitoring.CloudWatch"></a>
113
114 You can use Amazon CloudWatch alarms or events to more closely track your migration\. For more
        information about Amazon CloudWatch, see [What Are Amazon CloudWatch, Amazon CloudWatch
        Events, and Amazon CloudWatch Logs?](http://docs.aws.amazon.com/AmazonCloudWatch/latest/
        DeveloperGuide/WhatIsCloudWatch.html) in the Amazon CloudWatch User Guide\. Note that there
        is a charge for using Amazon CloudWatch\.
115
116 The AWS DMS console shows basic CloudWatch statistics for each task, including the task status,
        percent complete, elapsed time, and table statistics, as shown following\. Select the
        replication task and then select the **Task monitoring** tab\.
```

117

118 ![\[AWS DMS monitoring\]](http://docs.aws.amazon.com/dms/latest/userguide/images/datarep-monitoring1.png)

119

120 The AWS DMS console shows performance statistics for each table, including the number of inserts, deletions, and updates, when you select the **Table statistics** tab\.

121

122 ![\[AWS DMS monitoring\]](http://docs.aws.amazon.com/dms/latest/userguide/images/datarep-monitoring3.png)

123

124 In addition, if you select a replication instance from the **Replication Instance** page, you can view performance metrics for the instance by selecting the **Monitoring** tab\.

125

126 ![\[AWS DMS monitoring\]](http://docs.aws.amazon.com/dms/latest/userguide/images/datarep-monitoring4.png)

127

128 ## Data Migration Service Metrics

129

130 AWS DMS provides statistics for the following:

131

132 + **Host Metrics** - Performance and utilization statistics for the replication host, provided by Amazon CloudWatch\. For a complete list of the available metrics, see [Replication Instance Metrics](#CHAP_Monitoring.Metrics.CloudWatch)\.

133

134 + **Replication Task Metrics** - Statistics for replication tasks including incoming and committed changes, and latency between the replication host and both the source and target databases\. For a complete list of the available metrics, see [Replication Task Metrics](#CHAP_Monitoring.Metrics.Task)\.

135

136 + **Table Metrics** - Statistics for tables that are in the process of being migrated, including the number of insert, update, delete, and DDL statements completed\.

137

138 Task metrics are divided into statistics between the replication host and the source endpoint, and statistics between the replication host and the target endpoint\. You can determine the total statistic for a task by adding two related statistics together\. For example, you can determine the total latency, or replica lag, for a task by combining the **CDCLatencySource** and **CDCLatencyTarget** values\.

139

140 Task metric values can be influenced by current activity on your source database\. For example, if a transaction has begun, but has not been committed, then the **CDCLatencySource** metric continues to grow until that transaction has been committed\.

141

142 For the replication instance, the **FreeableMemory** metric requires clarification\. Freeable memory is not a indication of the actual free memory available\. It is the memory that is currently in use that can be freed and used for other uses; it's is a combination of buffers and cache in use on the replication instance\.

143

144 While the **FreeableMemory** metric does not reflect actual free memory available, the combination of the **FreeableMemory** and **SwapUsage** metrics can indicate if the replication instance is overloaded\.

145

146 Monitor these two metrics for the following conditions\.•

147

148   The **FreeableMemory** metric approaching zero\.•

149

The **SwapUsage** metric increases or fluctuates\.

151

If you see either of these two conditions, they indicate that you should consider moving to a larger replication instance\. You should also consider reducing the number and type of tasks running on the replication instance\. Full Load tasks require more memory than tasks that just replicate changes\.

153

Replication Instance Metrics

155

Replication instance monitoring include Amazon CloudWatch metrics for the following statistics:

157

CPUUtilization
The amount of CPU used\.
Units: Bytes

161

FreeStorageSpace
The amount of available storage space\.
Units: Bytes

165

FreeableMemory
The amount of available random access memory\.
Units: Bytes

169

WriteIOPS
The average number of disk I/O operations per second\.
Units: Count/Second

173

ReadIOPS
The average number of disk I/O operations per second\.
Units: Count/Second

177

WriteThroughput
The average number of bytes written to disk per second\.
Units: Bytes/Second

181

ReadThroughput
The average number of bytes read from disk per second\.
Units: Bytes/Second

185

WriteLatency
The average amount of time taken per disk I/O operation\.
Units: Seconds

189

ReadLatency
The average amount of time taken per disk I/O operation\.
Units: Seconds

193

SwapUsage
The amount of swap space used on the replication instance\.
Units: Bytes

197

NetworkTransmitThroughput
The outgoing \(Transmit\) network traffic on the replication instance, including both customer

database traffic and AWS DMS traffic used for monitoring and replication\.

200 Units: Bytes/second

201

202 **NetworkReceiveThroughput**

203 The incoming \(Receive\) network traffic on the replication instance, including both customer database traffic and AWS DMS traffic used for monitoring and replication\.

204 Units: Bytes/second

205

206 ### Replication Task Metrics

207

208 Replication task monitoring includes metrics for the following statistics:

209

210 **FullLoadThroughputBandwidthSource**

211 Incoming network bandwidth from a full load from the source in kilobytes \(KB\) per second\.

212

213 **FullLoadThroughputBandwidthTarget**

214 Outgoing network bandwidth from a full load for the target in KB per second\.

215

216 **FullLoadThroughputRowsSource**

217 Incoming changes from a full load from the source in rows per second\.

218

219 **FullLoadThroughputRowsTarget**

220 Outgoing changes from a full load for the target in rows per second\.

221

222 **CDCIncomingChanges**

223 The total number of change events at a point\-in\-time that are waiting to be applied to the target\. Note that this is not the same as a measure of the transaction change rate of the source endpoint\. A large number for this metric usually indicates AWS DMS is unable to apply captured changes in a timely manner, thus causing high target latency\.

224

225 **CDCChangesMemorySource**

226 Amount of rows accumulating in a memory and waiting to be committed from the source\.

227

228 **CDCChangesMemoryTarget**

229 Amount of rows accumulating in a memory and waiting to be committed to the target\.

230

231 **CDCChangesDiskSource**

232 Amount of rows accumulating on disk and waiting to be committed from the source\.

233

234 **CDCChangesDiskTarget**

235 Amount of rows accumulating on disk and waiting to be committed to the target\.

236

237 **CDCThroughputBandwidthTarget**

238 Outgoing task network bandwidth for the target in KB per second\.

239

240 **CDCThroughputRowsSource**

241 Incoming task changes from the source in rows per second\.

242

243 **CDCThroughputRowsTarget**

244 Outgoing task changes for the target in rows per second\.

245

246 **CDCLatencySource**

247 The gap, in seconds, between the last event captured from the source endpoint and current system time stamp of the AWS DMS instance\. If no changes have been captured from the source due

248   to task scoping, AWS DMS sets this value to zero\.

249 **CDCLatencyTarget**

250 The gap, in seconds, between the last event applied on the target and the current system
    timestamp of the AWS DMS instance\. Target latency should never be smaller than the source
    latency\.

251

252 ## Managing AWS DMS Task Logs

253

254 AWS DMS uses Amazon CloudWatch to log task information during the migration process\. You can
    use the AWS CLI or the AWS DMS API to view information about the task logs\. To do this, use
    the `describe-replication-instance-task-logs` AWS CLI command or the AWS DMS API action `
    DescribeReplicationInstanceTaskLogs`\.

255

256 For example, the following AWS CLI command shows the task log metadata in JSON format\.

    $ aws dms describe-replication-instance-task-logs
    --replication-instance-arn arn:aws:dms:us-east-1:237565436:rep:CDSFSFSFFFSSUFCAY

1

2 A sample response from the command is as follows\.

{   "ReplicationInstanceTaskLogs":   [{   "ReplicationTaskArn":   "arn:aws:dms:us-east-1:237565436:task:MY34U6Z4MSY52GRTIX3O4AY", "ReplicationTaskName": "mysql-to-ddb", "ReplicationInstanceTaskLogSize": 3726134 }], "ReplicationInstanceArn": "arn:aws:dms:us-east-1:237565436:rep:CDS-FSFSFFFSSUFCAY" }

1

2 In this response, there is a single task log \(`mysql-to-ddb`\) associated with the replication
    instance\. The size of this log is 3,726,124 bytes\.

3

4 You can use the information returned by `describe-replication-instance-task-logs` to diagnose
    and troubleshoot problems with task logs\. For example, if you enable detailed debug logging
    for a task, the task log will grow -quicklypotentially consuming all of the available
    storage on the replication instance, and causing the instance status to change to `storage-
    full`\. By describing the task logs, you can determine which ones you no longer need; then
    you can delete them, freeing up storage space\.

5

6 To delete the task logs for a task, set the task setting `DeleteTaskLogs` to true\. For example,
    the following JSON deletes the task logs when modifying a task using the AWS CLI `modify-
    replication-task` command or the AWS DMS API `ModifyReplicationTask` action\.

    { "Logging": { "DeleteTaskLogs":true } }

1

2 ## Logging AWS DMS API Calls Using AWS CloudTrail

3

4 The AWS CloudTrail service logs all AWS Database Migration Service \(AWS DMS\) API calls made by
    or on behalf of your AWS account\. AWS CloudTrail stores this logging information in an S3
    bucket\. You can use the information collected by CloudTrail to monitor AWS DMS activity,
    such as creating or deleting a replication instance or an endpoint\. For example, you can
    determine whether a request completed successfully and which user made the request\. To
    learn more about CloudTrail, see the [AWS CloudTrail User Guide](http://docs.aws.amazon.com/
    awscloudtrail/latest/userguide/)\.

5

6 If an action is taken on behalf of your AWS account using the AWS DMS console or the AWS DMS command line interface, then AWS CloudTrail logs the action as calls made to the AWS DMS API \. For example, if you use the AWS DMS console to describe connections, or call the AWS CLI [describe\-connections](http://docs.aws.amazon.com//cli/latest/reference/dms/describe-connections.html) command, then the AWS CloudTrail log shows a call to the AWS DMS API [DescribeConnections](http://docs.aws.amazon.com/dms/latest/APIReference//API_DescribeConnections.html) action\. For a list of the AWS DMS API actions that are logged by AWS CloudTrail, see the [AWS DMS API Reference](http://docs.aws.amazon.com/dms/latest/APIReference//Welcome.html)\.

7

8 ### Configuring CloudTrail Event Logging

9

10 CloudTrail creates audit trails in each region separately and stores them in an S3 bucket\. You can configure CloudTrail to use Amazon Simple Notification Service \(Amazon SNS\) to notify you when a log file is created, but that is optional\. CloudTrail will notify you frequently, so we recommend that you use Amazon SNS with an Amazon Simple Queue Service \(Amazon SQS\) queue and handle notifications programmatically\.

11

12 You can enable CloudTrail using the AWS Management Console, CLI, or API\. When you enable CloudTrail logging, you can have the CloudTrail service create an S3 bucket for you to store your log files\. For details, see [Creating and Updating Your Trail](http://docs.aws.amazon.com/awscloudtrail/latest/userguide/setupyourtrail.html) in the *AWS CloudTrail User Guide*\. The *AWS CloudTrail User Guide* also contains information on how to [aggregate CloudTrail logs from multiple regions into a single S3 bucket](http://docs.aws.amazon.com/awscloudtrail/latest/userguide/aggregatinglogs.html)\.

13

14 There is no cost to use the CloudTrail service\. However, standard rates for S3 usage apply, and also rates for Amazon SNS usage should you include that option\. For pricing details, see the [S3](http://aws.amazon.com/s3/pricing/) and [Amazon SNS](http://aws.amazon.com/sns/pricing/) pricing pages\.

15

16 ### AWS Database Migration Service Event Entries in CloudTrail Log Files

17

18 CloudTrail log files contain event information formatted using JSON\. An event record represents a single AWS API call and includes information about the requested action, the user that requested the action, the date and time of the request, and so on\.

19

20 CloudTrail log files include events for all AWS API calls for your AWS account, not just calls to the AWS DMS API\. However, you can read the log files and scan for calls to the AWS DMS API using the `eventName` element\.

21

22 For more information about the different elements and values in CloudTrail log files, see [CloudTrail Event Reference](http://docs.aws.amazon.com/awscloudtrail/latest/userguide/eventreference.html) in the *AWS CloudTrail User Guide*\.

23

24 You might also want to make use of one of the Amazon partner solutions that integrate with CloudTrail to read and analyze your CloudTrail log files\. For options, see the [AWS partners](http://aws.amazon.com/cloudtrail/partners/) page\.

25

26

27

28

29 # Validating AWS Database Migration Service Tasks

30
31 AWS DMS provides support for data validation, to ensure that your data was migrated accurately from the source to the target\. If you enable it for a task, then AWS DMS begins comparing the source and target data immediately after a full load is performed for a table\.

32
33 Data validation is optional\. AWS DMS compares the source and target records, and reports any mismatches\. In addition, for a CDC\-enabled task, AWS DMS compares the incremental changes and reports any mismatches\.

34
35 During data validation, AWS DMS compares each row in the source with its corresponding row at the target, and verifies that those rows contain the same data\. To accomplish this, AWS DMS issues appropriate queries to retrieve the data\. Note that these queries will consume additional resources at the source and the target, as well as additional network resources\.

36
37 Data validation works with the following databases:

38
39 + Oracle

40
41 + PostgreSQL

42
43 + MySQL

44
45 + MariaDB

46
47 + Microsoft SQL Server

48
49 + Amazon Aurora \(MySQL\)

50
51 + Amazon Aurora \(PostgreSQL\)

52
53 Data validation requires additional time, beyond the amount required for the migration itself\. The extra time required depends on how much data was migrated\.

54
55 Data validation settings include the following:

56
57 + To enable data validation, set the `EnableValidation` setting to `true`\.

58
59 + To adjust the number of execution threads that AWS DMS uses during validation, set the `ThreadCount` value\. The default value for `ThreadCount` is 5\. If you set `ThreadCount` to a higher number, AWS DMS will be able to complete the validation -fasterhowever, it will also execute more simultaneous queries, consuming more resources on the source and the target\.

60
61 For example, the following JSON turns on validation and increases the number of threads from the default setting of 5 to 8\.

ValidationSettings": { "EnableValidation":true, "ThreadCount":8 }

1
2 ## Replication Task Statistics

3
4 When data validation is enabled, AWS DMS provides the following statistics at the table level:

5
6 + **ValidationState-**The validation state of the table\. The parameter can have the following values:

7

8 + **Not enabled-**Validation is not enabled for the table in the migration task\.

9

10 + **Pending records-**Some records in the table are waiting for validation\.

11

12 + **Mismatched records-**Some records in the table do not match between the source and target
\.

13

14 + **Suspended records-**Some records in the table could not be validated\.

15

16 + **No primary key-**The table could not be validated because it had no primary key\.

17

18 + **Table error-**The table was not validated because it was in an error state and some data
was not migrated\.

19

20 + **Validated-**All rows in the table were validated\. If the table is updated, the status can
change from Validated\.

21

22 + **Error-**The table could not be validated because of an unexpected error\.

23

24 + **ValidationPending-**The number of records that have been migrated to the target, but that
have not yet been validated\.

25

26 **ValidationSuspended-**The number of records that AWS DMS can't compare\. For example, if a
record at the source is constantly being updated, AWS DMS will not be able to compare the
source and the target\. For more information, see [Error Handling Task Settings](
CHAP_Tasks.CustomizingTasks.TaskSettings.ErrorHandling.md)

27

28 + **ValidationFailed-**The number of records that did not pass the data validation phase\. For
more information, see [Error Handling Task Settings](CHAP_Tasks.CustomizingTasks.
TaskSettings.ErrorHandling.md)\.

29

30 You can view the data validation information using the AWS console, the AWS CLI, or the AWS DMS
API\.

31

32 + On the console, you can choose to validate a task when you create or modify the task\. To view
the data validation report using the console, choose the task on the **Tasks** page and
choose the **Table statistics** tab in the details section\.

33

34 + Using the CLI, set the `EnableValidation` parameter to **true** when creating or modifying a
task to begin data validation\. The following example creates a task and enables data
validation\.

```
create-replication-task
--replication-task-settings    '{"ValidationSettings":{"EnableValidation":true}}'    --replication-instance-arn
arn:aws:dms:us-east-1:5731014: rep:36KWVMB7Q
--source-endpoint-arn arn:aws:dms:us-east-1:5731014: endpoint:CSZAEFQURFYMM
--target-endpoint-arn arn:aws:dms:us-east-1:5731014: endpoint:CGPP7MF6WT4JQ --migration-type full-load-
and-cdc --table-mappings '{"rules": [{"rule-type": "selection", "rule-id": "1", "rule-name": "1", "object-locator":
{"schema-name": "data_types", "table-name": "%"}, "rule-action": "include"}]}'
```

1

2 Use the `describe-table-statistics` command to receive the data validation report in JSON format
\. The following command shows the data validation report\.

aws dms describe-table-statistics --replication-task-arn arn:aws:dms:us-east-1:5731014: rep:36KWVMB7Q

1

2 The report would be similar to the following\.

{ "ReplicationTaskArn": "arn:aws:dms:us-west-2:5731014:task:VFPFTYKK2RYSI", "TableStatistics": [{ "ValidationPendingRecords": 2, "Inserts": 25, "ValidationState": "Pending records", "ValidationSuspendedRecords": 0, "LastUpdateTime": 1510181065.349, "FullLoadErrorRows": 0, "FullLoadCondtnlChkFailedRows": 0, "Ddls": 0, "TableName": "t_binary", "ValidationFailedRecords": 0, "Updates": 0, "FullLoadRows": 10, "TableState": "Table completed", "SchemaName": "d_types_s_sqlserver", "Deletes": 0 }] }

1

2 + Using the AWS DMS API, create a task using the **CreateReplicationTask** action and set the `EnableValidation` parameter to **true** to validate the data migrated by the task\. Use the **DescribeTableStatistics** action to receive the data validation report in JSON format\.

3

4 ## Troubleshooting

5

6 During validation, AWS DMS creates a new table at the target endpoint: `awsdms_validation_failures`\. If any record enters the *ValidationSuspended* or the *ValidationFailed* state, AWS DMS writes diagnostic information to `awsdms_validation_failures`\. You can query this table to help troubleshoot validation errors\.

7

8 Following is a description of the `awsdms_validation_failures` table:

9

10

11 | Colum Name | Data Type | Description |
12 | --- | --- | --- |
13 | `TASK_NAME` | `VARCHAR(128) NOT NULL` | AWS DMS task identifier\. |
14 | TABLE_OWNER | VARCHAR\(128\) NOT NULL | Schema \(owner\) of the table\. |
15 | `TABLE_NAME` | VARCHAR\(128\) NOT NULL | Table name\. |
16 | FAILURE_TIME | DATETIME\(3\) NOT NULL | Time when the failure occurred\. |
17 | KEY | TEXT NOT NULL | This is the primary key for row record type\. |
18 | FAILURE_TYPE | VARCHAR\(128\) NOT NULL | Severity of validation error\. Can be either `Failed` or `Suspended`\. |

19

20 The following query will show you all the failures for a task by querying the `awsdms_validation_failures` table\. The task name should be the external resource ID of the task\. The external resource ID of the task is the last value in the task ARN\. For example, for a task with an ARN value of arn:aws:dms:us\-west\-2:5599:task: VFPFKH4FJR3FTYKK2RYSI, the external resource ID of the task would be VFPFKH4FJR3FTYKK2RYSI\.

select * from awsdms_validation_failures where TASK_NAME = 'VFPFKH4FJR3FTYKK2RYSI'

1

2 Once you have the primary key of the failed record, you can query the source and target endpoints to see what part of the record does not match\.

3

4 ## Limitations

5

6 + Data validation requires that the table has a primary key or unique index\.

7

8 + Primary key column\(s\) cannot be of type `CLOB`, `BLOB`, or `BYTE`\.

9

10 + For primary key column\(s\) of type `VARCHAR` or `CHAR`, the length must be less than 1024\.

11

12 + Data validation will generate additional queries against the source and target databases\. You must ensure that both databases have enough resources to handle this additional load\.

13

14 + Data validation is not supported if a migration uses customized filtering or when consolidating several databases into one\.

15

16 + For an Oracle endpoint, AWS DMS uses DBMS_CRYPTO to validate BLOBs\. If your Oracle endpoint uses BLOBs, then you must grant the execute permission on dbms_crypto to the user account that is used to access the Oracle endpoint\. You can do this by running the following statement:

grant execute on sys.dbms_crypto to <dms_endpoint_user>;

1

2 + If the target database is modified outside of AWS DMS during validation, then discrepancies might not be reported accurately\. This can occur if one of your applications writes data to the target table, while AWS DMS is performing validation on that same table\.

3

4 + If one or more rows are being continuously modified during the validation, then AWS DMS will not be able to validate those rows\. However, you can validate those "busy" rows manually, after the task completes\.

5

6 + If AWS DMS detects more than 10,000 failed or suspended records, it will stop the validation\. You will need to resolve any underlying problems with the data before you proceed further\.

7

8

9

10

11 # Tagging AWS Database Migration Service Resources

12

13 You can use AWS Database Migration Service tags to add metadata to your AWS DMS resources\. In addition, these tags can be used with IAM policies to manage access to AWS DMS resources and to control what actions can be applied to the AWS DMS resources\. Finally, these tags can be used to track costs by grouping expenses for similarly tagged resources\.

14

15 All AWS DMS resources can be tagged:

16

17 + Replication instances

18

19 + Endpoints

20

21 + Replication tasks

22

23 + Certificates

24

25 An AWS DMS tag is a name\-value pair that you define and associate with an AWS DMS resource\. The name is referred to as the key\. Supplying a value for the key is optional\. You can use tags to assign arbitrary information to an AWS DMS resource\. A tag key could be used, for example, to define a category, and the tag value could be a item in that category\. For example, you could define a tag key of "project" and a tag value of "Salix", indicating that the AWS DMS resource is assigned to the Salix project\. You could also use tags to designate AWS DMS resources as being used for test or production by using a key such as environment=test or environment =production\. We recommend that you use a consistent set of tag keys to make it easier to track metadata associated with AWS DMS resources\.

26

27 Use tags to organize your AWS bill to reflect your own cost structure\. To do this, sign up to
    get your AWS account bill with tag key values included\. Then, to see the cost of combined
    resources, organize your billing information according to resources with the same tag key
    values\. For example, you can tag several resources with a specific application name, and
    then organize your billing information to see the total cost of that application across
    several services\. For more information, see [Cost Allocation and Tagging](http://docs.aws.
    amazon.com/awsaccountbilling/latest/aboutv2/cost-alloc-tags.html) in *About AWS Billing and
    Cost Management*\.

28

29 Each AWS DMS resource has a tag set, which contains all the tags that are assigned to that AWS
    DMS resource\. A tag set can contain as many as ten tags, or it can be empty\. If you add a
    tag to an AWS DMS resource that has the same key as an existing tag on resource, the new
    value overwrites the old value\.

30

31 AWS does not apply any semantic meaning to your tags; tags are interpreted strictly as character
    strings\. AWS DMS might set tags on an AWS DMS resource, depending on the settings that you
    use when you create the resource\.

32

33 The following list describes the characteristics of an AWS DMS tag\.

34

35 + The tag key is the required name of the tag\. The string value can be from 1 to 128 Unicode
    characters in length and cannot be prefixed with "aws:" or "dms:"\. The string might contain
    only the set of Unicode letters, digits, white\-space, '_', '\.', '/', '=', '\+', '\-' \(
    Java regex: "^\(\[\\\\p\{L\}\\\\p\{Z\}\\\\p\{N\}_\.:/=\+\\\\\-\]*\)$"\)\.

36

37 + The tag value is an optional string value of the tag\. The string value can be from 1 to 256
    Unicode characters in length and cannot be prefixed with "aws:" or "dms:"\. The string might
    contain only the set of Unicode letters, digits, white\-space, '_', '\.', '/', '=', '\+',
    '\-' \(Java regex: "^\(\[\\\\p\{L\}\\\\p\{Z\}\\\\p\{N\}_\.:/=\+\\\\\-\]*\)$"\)\.

38

39 Values do not have to be unique in a tag set and can be null\. For example, you can have a key\-
    value pair in a tag set of project/Trinity and cost\-center/Trinity\.

40

41 You can use the AWS CLI or the AWS DMS API to add, list, and delete tags on AWS DMS resources\.
    When using the AWS CLI or the AWS DMS API, you must provide the Amazon Resource Name \(ARN\)
    for the AWS DMS resource you want to work with\. For more information about constructing an
    ARN, see [Constructing an Amazon Resource Name \(ARN\) for AWS DMS](CHAP_Introduction.ARN.
    md)\.

42

43 Note that tags are cached for authorization purposes\. Because of this, additions and updates to
    tags on AWS DMS resources might take several minutes before they are available\.

44

45 ## API

46

47 You can add, list, or remove tags for a AWS DMS resource using the AWS DMS API\.

48

49 + To add a tag to an AWS DMS resource, use the [http://docs.aws.amazon.com/dms/latest/
    APIReference//API_AddTagsToResource.html](http://docs.aws.amazon.com/dms/latest/APIReference
    //API_AddTagsToResource.html) operation\.

50

51 + To list tags that are assigned to an AWS DMS resource, use the [http://docs.aws.amazon.com/dms
    /latest/APIReference//API_ListTagsForResource.html](http://docs.aws.amazon.com/dms/latest/
    APIReference//API_ListTagsForResource.html) operation\.

52

53 + To remove tags from an AWS DMS resource, use the [http://docs.aws.amazon.com/dms/latest/
   APIReference//API_RemoveTagsFromResource.html](http://docs.aws.amazon.com/dms/latest/
   APIReference//API_RemoveTagsFromResource.html) operation\.

54

55 To learn more about how to construct the required ARN, see [Constructing an Amazon Resource Name
   \(ARN\) for AWS DMS](CHAP_Introduction.ARN.md)\.

56

57 When working with XML using the AWS DMS API, tags use the following schema:

The following table provides a list of the allowed XML tags and their characteristics. Note that values for Key
and Value are case dependent. For example, project=Trinity and PROJECT=Trinity are two distinct tags.

[See the AWS documentation website for more details]

Working with Events and Notifications

AWS Database Migration Service (AWS DMS) uses Amazon Simple Notification Service (Amazon SNS) to provide notifications when an AWS DMS event occurs, for example the creation or deletion of a replication instance. You can work with these notifications in any form supported by Amazon SNS for an AWS Region, such as an email message, a text message, or a call to an HTTP endpoint.

AWS DMS groups events into categories that you can subscribe to, so you can be notified when an event in that category occurs. For example, if you subscribe to the Creation category for a given replication instance, you are notified whenever a creation-related event occurs that affects your replication instance. If you subscribe to a Configuration Change category for a replication instance, you are notified when the replication instance's configuration is changed. You also receive notification when an event notification subscription changes. For a list of the event categories provided by AWS DMS, see AWS DMS Event Categories and Event Messages, following.

AWS DMS sends event notifications to the addresses you provide when you create an event subscription. You might want to create several different subscriptions, such as one subscription receiving all event notifications and another subscription that includes only critical events for your production DMS resources. You can easily turn off notification without deleting a subscription by setting the **Enabled** option to **No** in the AWS DMS console or by setting the `Enabled` parameter to *false* using the AWS DMS API.

Note
AWS DMS event notifications using SMS text messages are currently available for AWS DMS resources in all regions where AWS DMS is supported. For more information on using text messages with SNS, see Sending and Receiving SMS Notifications Using Amazon SNS.

AWS DMS uses a subscription identifier to identify each subscription. You can have multiple AWS DMS event subscriptions published to the same Amazon SNS topic. When you use event notification, Amazon SNS fees apply; for more information on Amazon SNS billing, see Amazon SNS Pricing.

To subscribe to AWS DMS events, you use the following process:

1. Create an Amazon SNS topic. In the topic, you specify what type of notification you want to receive and to what address or number the notification will go to.

2. Create an AWS DMS event notification subscription by using the AWS Management Console, AWS CLI, or AWS DMS API.

3. AWS DMS sends an approval email or SMS message to the addresses you submitted with your subscription. To confirm your subscription, click the link in the approval email or SMS message.

4. When you have confirmed the subscription, the status of your subscription is updated in the AWS DMS console's **Event Subscriptions** section.

5. You then begin to receive event notifications.

For the list of categories and events that you can be notified of, see the following section. For more details about subscribing to and working with AWS DMS event subscriptions, see Subscribing to AWS DMS Event Notification.

AWS DMS Event Categories and Event Messages

AWS DMS generates a significant number of events in categories that you can subscribe to using the AWS DMS console or the AWS DMS API. Each category applies to a source type; currently AWS DMS supports the replication instance and replication task source types.

The following table shows the possible categories and events for the replication instance source type.

Category	DMS Event ID	Description
Configuration Change	DMS-EVENT-0012	REP_IN-STANCE_CLASS_CHANGING – The replication instance class for this replication instance is being changed.
Configuration Change	DMS-EVENT-0014	REP_IN-STANCE_CLASS_CHANGE_COM-PLETE – The replication instance class for this replication instance has changed.
Configuration Change	DMS-EVENT-0018	BEGIN_SCALE_STOR-AGE – The storage for the replication instance is being increased.
Configuration Change	DMS-EVENT-0017	FINISH_SCALE_STOR-AGE – The storage for the replication instance has been increased.
Configuration Change	DMS-EVENT-0024	BEGIN_CONVER-SION_TO_HIGH_AVAIL-ABILITY – The replication instance is transitioning to a Multi-AZ configuration.
Configuration Change	DMS-EVENT-0025	FINISH_CONVER-SION_TO_HIGH_AVAIL-ABILITY – The replication instance has finished transitioning to a Multi-AZ configuration.
Configuration Change	DMS-EVENT-0030	BEGIN_CONVER-SION_TO_NON_HIGH_AVAIL-ABILITY – The replication instance is transitioning to a Single-AZ configuration.
Configuration Change	DMS-EVENT-0029	FINISH_CONVER-SION_TO_NON_HIGH_AVAIL-ABILITY – The replication instance has finished transitioning to a Single-AZ configuration.
Creation	DMS-EVENT-0067	CREATING_REPLICA-TION_INSTANCE – A replication instance is being created.
Creation	DMS-EVENT-0005	CREATED_REPLICA-TION_INSTANCE – A replication instance has been created.
Deletion	DMS-EVENT-0066	DELETING_REPLICA-TION_INSTANCE – The replication instance is being deleted.

Category	DMS Event ID	Description
Deletion	DMS-EVENT-0003	DELETED_REPLICA-TION_INSTANCE – The replication instance has been deleted.
Maintenance	DMS-EVENT-0047	FINISH_PATCH_IN-STANCE – Management software on the replication instance has been updated.
Maintenance	DMS-EVENT-0026	BEGIN_PATCH_OFFLINE – Offline maintenance of the replication instance is taking place. The replication instance is currently unavailable.
Maintenance	DMS-EVENT-0027	FINISH_PATCH_OFFLINE – Offline maintenance of the replication instance is complete. The replication instance is now available.
LowStorage	DMS-EVENT-0007	LOW_STORAGE – Free storage for the replication instance is low.
Failover	DMS-EVENT-0013	FAILOVER_STARTED – Failover started for a Multi-AZ replication instance.
Failover	DMS-EVENT-0049	FAILOVER_COMPLETED – Failover has been completed for a Multi-AZ replication instance.
Failover	DMS-EVENT-0050	MAZ_INSTANCE_AC-TIVATION_STARTED – Multi-AZ activation has started.
Failover	DMS-EVENT-0051	MAZ_INSTANCE_ACTI-VATION_COMPLETED – Multi-AZ activation completed.
Failure	DMS-EVENT-0031	REPLICATION_IN-STANCE_FAILURE – The replication instance has gone into storage failure.
Failure	DMS-EVENT-0036	INCOMPATIBLE_NET-WORK – The replication instance has failed due to an incompatible network.

The following table shows the possible categories and events for the replication task source type.

Category	DMS Event ID	Description
StateChange	DMS-EVENT-0069	REPLICA-TION_TASK_STARTED – The replication task has started.
StateChange	DMS-EVENT-0077	REPLICA-TION_TASK_STOPPED – The replication task has stopped.
Failure	DMS-EVENT-0078	REPLICA-TION_TASK_FAILED – A replication task has failed.
Deletion	DMS-EVENT-0073	REPLICA-TION_TASK_DELETED – The replication task has been deleted.
Creation	DMS-EVENT-0074	REPLICA-TION_TASK_CREATED – The replication task has been created.

Subscribing to AWS DMS Event Notification

You can create an AWS DMS event notification subscription so you can be notified when an AWS DMS event occurs. The simplest way to create a subscription is with the AWS DMS console. If you choose to create event notification subscriptions using AWS DMS API, you must create an Amazon SNS topic and subscribe to that topic with the Amazon SNS console or API. In this case, you also need to note the topic's Amazon Resource Name (ARN), because this ARN is used when submitting CLI commands or API actions. For information on creating an Amazon SNS topic and subscribing to it, see Getting Started with Amazon SNS.

In a notification subscription, you can specify the type of source you want to be notified of and the AWS DMS source that triggers the event. You define the AWS DMS source type by using a **SourceType** value. You define the source generating the event by using a **SourceIdentifier** value. If you specify both **SourceType** and **SourceIdentifier**, such as SourceType = db-instance and SourceIdentifier = myDBInstance1, you receive all the DB_Instance events for the specified source. If you specify **SourceType** but not **SourceIdentifier**, you receive notice of the events for that source type for all your AWS DMS sources. If you don't specify either **SourceType** or **SourceIdentifier**, you are notified of events generated from all AWS DMS sources belonging to your customer account.

AWS Management Console

To subscribe to AWS DMS event notification by using the console

1. Sign in to the AWS Management Console and choose AWS DMS. Note that if you are signed in as an AWS Identity and Access Management (IAM) user, you must have the appropriate permissions to access AWS DMS.

2. In the navigation pane, choose **Event Subscriptions**.

3. On the **Event Subscriptions** page, choose **Create Event Subscription**.

4. On the **Create Event Subscription** page, do the following:

5. For **Name**, type a name for the event notification subscription.

6. Either choose an existing Amazon SNS topic for **Send notifications to,** or choose **create topic**. You must have either an existing Amazon SNS topic to send notices to or you must create the topic. If you choose **create topic**, you can enter an email address where notifications will be sent.

7. For **Source Type**, choose a source type. The only option is **replication instance**.

8. Choose **Yes** to enable the subscription. If you want to create the subscription but not have notifications sent yet, choose **No**.

9. Depending on the source type you selected, choose the event categories and sources you want to receive event notifications for.

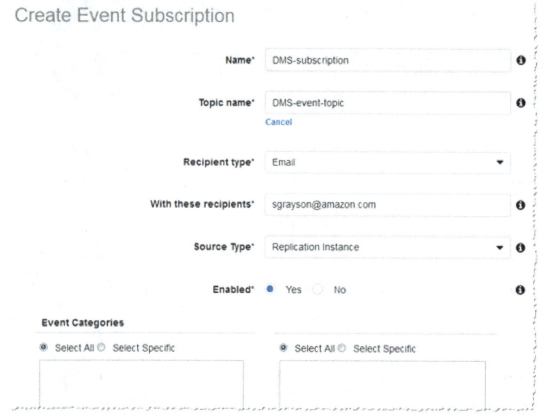

10. Choose **Create.**

The AWS DMS console indicates that the subscription is being created.

AWS DMS API

To subscribe to AWS DMS event notification by using the AWS DMS API

- Call `CreateEventSubscription`.

Troubleshooting Migration Tasks

The following sections provide information on troubleshooting issues with AWS Database Migration Service (AWS DMS).

- Slow Running Migration Tasks
- Task Status Bar Not Moving
- Missing Foreign Keys and Secondary Indexes
- Amazon RDS Connection Issues
- Networking Issues
- CDC Stuck After Full Load
- Primary Key Violation Errors When Restarting a Task
- Initial Load of Schema Fails
- Tasks Failing With Unknown Error
- Task Restart Loads Tables From the Beginning
- Number of Tables Per Task
- Troubleshooting Oracle Specific Issues
- Troubleshooting MySQL Specific Issues
- Troubleshooting PostgreSQL Specific Issues
- Troubleshooting Microsoft SQL Server Specific Issues
- Troubleshooting Amazon Redshift Specific Issues
- Troubleshooting Amazon Aurora MySQL Specific Issues

Slow Running Migration Tasks

There are several issues that may cause a migration task to run slowly, or for subsequent tasks to run slower than the initial task. The most common reason for a migration task running slowly is that there are inadequate resources allocated to the AWS DMS replication instance. Check your replication instance's use of CPU, Memory, Swap, and IOPs to ensure that your instance has enough resources for the tasks you are running on it. For example, multiple tasks with Amazon Redshift as an endpoint are IO intensive. You can increase IOPS for your replication instance or split your tasks across multiple replication instances for a more efficient migration.

For more information about determining the size of your replication instance, see Determining the Optimum Size for a Replication Instance

You can increase the speed of an initial migration load by doing the following:

- If your target is an Amazon RDS DB instance, ensure that Multi-AZ is not enabled for the target DB instance.

- Turn off any automatic backups or logging on the target database during the load, and turn back on those features once the migration is complete.

- If the feature is available on the target, use Provisioned IOPs.

- If your migration data contains LOBs, ensure that the task is optimized for LOB migration. See Target Metadata Task Settings for more information on optimizing for LOBs.

Task Status Bar Not Moving

The task status bar gives an estimation of the task's progress. The quality of this estimate depends on the quality of the source database's table statistics; the better the table statistics, the more accurate the estimation. For a task with only one table that has no estimated rows statistic, we are unable to provide any kind of percentage complete estimate. In this case, the task state and the indication of rows loaded can be used to confirm that the task is indeed running and making progress.

Missing Foreign Keys and Secondary Indexes

AWS DMS creates tables, primary keys, and in some cases unique indexes, but it doesn't create any other objects that are not required to efficiently migrate the data from the source. For example, it doesn't create secondary indexes, non-primary key constraints, or data defaults.

To migrate secondary objects from your database, use the database's native tools if you are migrating to the same database engine as your source database. Use the Schema Conversion Tool if you are migrating to a different database engine than that used by your source database to migrate secondary objects.

Amazon RDS Connection Issues

There can be several reasons why you are unable to connect to an Amazon RDS DB instance that you set as an endpoint. These include:

- Username and password combination is incorrect.
- Check that the endpoint value shown in the Amazon RDS console for the instance is the same as the endpoint identifier you used to create the AWS DMS endpoint.
- Check that the port value shown in the Amazon RDS console for the instance is the same as the port assigned to the AWS DMS endpoint.
- Check that the security group assigned to the Amazon RDS DB instance allows connections from the AWS DMS replication instance.
- If the AWS DMS replication instance and the Amazon RDS DB instance are not in the same VPC, check that the DB instance is publicly accessible.

Error Message: Incorrect thread connection string: incorrect thread value 0

This error can often occur when you are testing the connection to an endpoint. The error indicates that there is an error in the connection string, such as a space after the host IP address or a bad character was copied into the connection string.

Networking Issues

The most common networking issue involves the VPC security group used by the AWS DMS replication instance. By default, this security group has rules that allow egress to 0.0.0.0/0 on all ports. If you modify this security group or use your own security group, egress must, at a minimum, be permitted to the source and target endpoints on the respective database ports.

Other configuration related issues include:

- **Replication instance and both source and target endpoints in the same VPC** — The security group used by the endpoints must allow ingress on the database port from the replication instance. Ensure that the security group used by the replication instance has ingress to the endpoints, or you can create a rule in the security group used by the endpoints that allows the private IP address of the replication instance access.
- **Source endpoint is outside the VPC used by the replication instance (using Internet Gateway)** — The VPC security group must include routing rules that send traffic not destined for the VPC to the Internet Gateway. In this configuration, the connection to the endpoint appears to come from the public IP address on the replication instance.

- **Source endpoint is outside the VPC used by the replication instance (using NAT Gateway)** — You can configure a network address translation (NAT) gateway using a single Elastic IP Address bound to a single Elastic Network Interface which then receives a NAT identifier (nat-#####). If the VPC includes a default route to that NAT Gateway instead of the Internet Gateway, the replication instance will instead appear to contact the Database Endpoint using the public IP address of the Internet Gateway. In this case, the ingress to the Database Endpoint outside the VPC needs to allow ingress from the NAT address instead of the Replication Instance's public IP Address.

CDC Stuck After Full Load

Slow or stuck replication changes can occur after a full load migration when several AWS DMS settings conflict with each other. For example, if the **Target table preparation mode** parameter is set to **Do nothing** or **Truncate**, then you have instructed AWS DMS to do no setup on the target tables, including creating primary and unique indexes. If you haven't created primary or unique keys on the target tables, then AWS DMS must do a full table scan for each update, which can significantly impact performance.

Primary Key Violation Errors When Restarting a Task

This error can occur when data remains in the target database from a previous migration task. If the **Target table preparation mode** parameter is set to **Do nothing**, AWS DMS does not do any preparation on the target table, including cleaning up data inserted from a previous task. In order to restart your task and avoid these errors, you must remove rows inserted into the target tables from the previous running of the task.

Initial Load of Schema Fails

If your initial load of your schemas fails with an error of `Operation:getSchemaListDetails:errType=, status =0, errMessage=, errDetails=,` then the user account used by AWS DMS to connect to the source endpoint does not have the necessary permissions.

Tasks Failing With Unknown Error

The cause of these types of error can be varied, but often we find that the issue involves insufficient resources allocated to the AWS DMS replication instance. Check the replication instance's use of CPU, Memory, Swap, and IOPs to ensure your instance has enough resources to perform the migration. For more information on monitoring, see Data Migration Service Metrics.

Task Restart Loads Tables From the Beginning

AWS DMS restarts table loading from the beginning when it has not finished the initial load of a table. When a task is restarted, AWS DMS does not reload tables that completed the initial load but will reload tables from the beginning when the initial load did not complete.

Number of Tables Per Task

While there is no set limit on the number of tables per replication task, we have generally found that limiting the number of tables in a task to less than 60,000 is a good rule of thumb. Resource use can often be a bottleneck when a single task uses more than 60,000 tables.

Troubleshooting Oracle Specific Issues

The following issues are specific to using AWS DMS with Oracle databases.

- Pulling Data from Views
- Migrating LOBs from Oracle 12c
- Switching Between Oracle LogMiner and BinaryReader
- Error: Oracle CDC stopped 122301 Oracle CDC maximum retry counter exceeded.
- Automatically Add Supplemental Logging to an Oracle Source Endpoint
- LOB Changes not being Captured
- Error: ORA-12899: value too large for column <column-name>
- NUMBER data type being misinterpreted

Pulling Data from Views

You can pull data once from a view; you cannot use it for ongoing replication. To be able to extract data from views, you must add the following code to the **Extra connection attributes** in the **Advanced** section of the Oracle source endpoint. Note that when you extract data from a view, the view is shown as a table on the target schema.

```
1  exposeViews=true
```

Migrating LOBs from Oracle 12c

AWS DMS can use two methods to capture changes to an Oracle database, BinaryReader and Oracle LogMiner. By default, AWS DMS uses Oracle LogMiner to capture changes. However, on Oracle 12c, Oracle LogMiner does not support LOB columns. To capture changes to LOB columns on Oracle 12c, use BinaryReader.

Switching Between Oracle LogMiner and BinaryReader

AWS DMS can use two methods to capture changes to a source Oracle database, BinaryReader and Oracle LogMiner. Oracle LogMiner is the default. To switch to using BinaryReader for capturing changes, do the following:

To use BinaryReader for capturing changes

1. Sign in to the AWS Management Console and select DMS.

2. Select **Endpoints**.

3. Select the Oracle source endpoint that you want to use BinaryReader.

4. Select **Modify**.

5. Select Advanced, and then add the following code to the Extra connection attributes text box:

```
1  useLogminerReader=N
```

6. Use an Oracle developer tool such as SQL-Plus to grant the following additional privilege to the AWS DMS user account used to connect to the Oracle endpoint:

```
1  SELECT ON V_$TRANSPORTABLE_PLATFORM
```

Error: Oracle CDC stopped 122301 Oracle CDC maximum retry counter exceeded.

This error occurs when the needed Oracle archive logs have been removed from your server before AWS DMS was able to use them to capture changes. Increase your log retention policies on your database server. For an Amazon RDS database, run the following procedure to increase log retention. For example, the following code increases log retention on an Amazon RDS DB instance to 24 hours.

```
1 Exec rdsadmin.rdsadmin_util.set_configuration'(archivelog retention 'hours,24);
```

Automatically Add Supplemental Logging to an Oracle Source Endpoint

By default, AWS DMS has supplemental logging turned off. To automatically turn on supplemental logging for a source Oracle endpoint, do the following:

To add supplemental logging to a source Oracle endpoint

1. Sign in to the AWS Management Console and select **DMS**.
2. Select **Endpoints**.
3. Select the Oracle source endpoint that you want to add supplemental logging to.
4. Select **Modify**.
5. Select **Advanced**, and then add the following code to the **Extra connection attributes** text box:

```
1 addSupplementalLogging=Y
```

6. Choose **Modify**.

LOB Changes not being Captured

Currently, a table must have a primary key for AWS DMS to capture LOB changes. If a table that contains LOBs doesn't have a primary key, there are several actions you can take to capture LOB changes:

- Add a primary key to the table. This can be as simple as adding an ID column and populating it with a sequence using a trigger.
- Create a materialized view of the table that includes a system generated ID as the primary key and migrate the materialized view rather than the table.
- Create a logical standby, add a primary key to the table, and migrate from the logical standby.

Error: ORA-12899: value too large for column <column-name>

The error "ORA-12899: value too large for column <column-name>" is often caused by a mismatch in the character sets used by the source and target databases or when NLS settings differ between the two databases. A common cause of this error is when the source database NLS_LENGTH_SEMANTICS parameter is set to CHAR and the target database NLS_LENGTH_SEMANTICS parameter is set to BYTE.

NUMBER data type being misinterpreted

The Oracle NUMBER data type is converted into various AWS DMS datatypes, depending on the precision and scale of NUMBER. These conversions are documented here Using an Oracle Database as a Source for AWS DMS. The way the NUMBER type is converted can also be affected by using Extra Connection Attributes for the source Oracle endpoint. These Extra Connection Attributes are documented in Using Extra Connection Attributes with AWS Database Migration Service.

Troubleshooting MySQL Specific Issues

The following issues are specific to using AWS DMS with MySQL databases.

- CDC Task Failing for Amazon RDS DB Instance Endpoint Because Binary Logging Disabled
- Connections to a target MySQL instance are disconnected during a task
- Adding Autocommit to a MySQL-compatible Endpoint
- Disable Foreign Keys on a Target MySQL-compatible Endpoint
- Characters Replaced with Question Mark
- "Bad event" Log Entries
- Change Data Capture with MySQL 5.5
- Increasing Binary Log Retention for Amazon RDS DB Instances
- Log Message: Some changes from the source database had no impact when applied to the target database.
- Error: Identifier too long
- Error: Unsupported Character Set Causes Field Data Conversion to Fail

CDC Task Failing for Amazon RDS DB Instance Endpoint Because Binary Logging Disabled

This issue occurs with Amazon RDS DB instances because automated backups are disabled. Enable automatic backups by setting the backup retention period to a non-zero value.

Connections to a target MySQL instance are disconnected during a task

If you have a task with LOBs that is getting disconnected from a MySQL target with the following type of errors in the task log, you might need to adjust some of your task settings.

```
1 [TARGET_LOAD ]E: RetCode: SQL_ERROR SqlState: 08S01 NativeError:
2 2013 Message: [MySQL][ODBC 5.3(w) Driver][mysqld-5.7.16-log]Lost connection
3 to MySQL server during query [122502] ODBC general error.
```

```
1  [TARGET_LOAD ]E: RetCode: SQL_ERROR SqlState: HY000 NativeError:
2 2006 Message: [MySQL][ODBC 5.3(w) Driver]MySQL server has gone away
3 [122502] ODBC general error.
```

To solve the issue where a task is being disconnected from a MySQL target, do the following:

- Check that you have your database variable `max_allowed_packet` set large enough to hold your largest LOB.

- Check that you have the following variables set to have a large timeout value. We suggest you use a value of at least 5 minutes for each of these variables.

    - `net_read_timeout`

    - `net_write_timeout`

    - `wait_timeout`

    - `interactive_timeout`

Adding Autocommit to a MySQL-compatible Endpoint

To add autocommit to a target MySQL-compatible endpoint

1. Sign in to the AWS Management Console and select **DMS**.

2. Select **Endpoints**.

3. Select the MySQL-compatible target endpoint that you want to add autocommit to.

4. Select **Modify**.

5. Select **Advanced**, and then add the following code to the **Extra connection attributes** text box:

```
1 Initstmt= SET AUTOCOMMIT=1
```

6. Choose **Modify**.

Disable Foreign Keys on a Target MySQL-compatible Endpoint

You can disable foreign key checks on MySQL by adding the following to the **Extra Connection Attributes** in the **Advanced** section of the target MySQL, Amazon Aurora with MySQL compatibility, or MariaDB endpoint.

To disable foreign keys on a target MySQL-compatible endpoint

1. Sign in to the AWS Management Console and select **DMS**.

2. Select **Endpoints**.

3. Select the MySQL, Aurora MySQL, or MariaDB target endpoint that you want to disable foreign keys.

4. Select **Modify**.

5. Select **Advanced**, and then add the following code to the **Extra connection attributes** text box:

```
1 Initstmt=SET FOREIGN_KEY_CHECKS=0
```

6. Choose **Modify**.

Characters Replaced with Question Mark

The most common situation that causes this issue is when the source endpoint characters have been encoded by a character set that AWS DMS doesn't support. For example, AWS DMS does not support the UTF8MB4 character set.

"Bad event" Log Entries

"Bad event" entries in the migration logs usually indicate that an unsupported DDL operation was attempted on the source database endpoint. Unsupported DDL operations cause an event that the replication instance cannot skip so a bad event is logged. To fix this issue, restart the task from the beginning, which will reload the tables and will start capturing changes at a point after the unsupported DDL operation was issued.

Change Data Capture with MySQL 5.5

AWS DMS change data capture (CDC) for Amazon RDS MySQL-compatible databases requires full image row-based binary logging, which is not supported in MySQL version 5.5 or lower. To use AWS DMS CDC, you must up upgrade your Amazon RDS DB instance to MySQL version 5.6.

Increasing Binary Log Retention for Amazon RDS DB Instances

AWS DMS requires the retention of binary log files for change data capture. To increase log retention on an Amazon RDS DB instance, use the following procedure. The following example increases the binary log retention to 24 hours.

```
1 Call mysql.rds_set_configuration`(binlog retention 'hours, 24);
```

Log Message: Some changes from the source database had no impact when applied to the target database.

When AWS DMS updates a MySQL database column's value to its existing value, a message of `zero rows affected` is returned from MySQL. This behavior is unlike other database engines such as Oracle and SQL Server that perform an update of one row, even when the replacing value is the same as the current one.

Error: Identifier too long

The following error occurs when an identifier is too long:

```
1 TARGET_LOAD E: RetCode: SQL_ERROR SqlState: HY000 NativeError:
2 1059 Message: MySQLhttp://ODBC 5.3(w) Driverhttp://mysqld-5.6.10Identifier
3 name '<name>' is too long 122502 ODBC general error. (ar_odbc_stmt.c:4054)
```

When AWS DMS is set to create the tables and primary keys in the target database, it currently does not use the same names for the Primary Keys that were used in the source database. Instead, AWS DMS creates the Primary Key name based on the tables name. When the table name is long, the auto-generated identifier created can be longer than the allowed limits for MySQL. The solve this issue, currently, pre-create the tables and Primary Keys in the target database and use a task with the task setting **Target table preparation mode** set to **Do nothing** or **Truncate** to populate the target tables.

Error: Unsupported Character Set Causes Field Data Conversion to Fail

The following error occurs when an unsupported character set causes a field data conversion to fail:

```
1 "[SOURCE_CAPTURE ]E: Column '<column name>' uses an unsupported character set [120112]
2 A field data conversion failed. (mysql_endpoint_capture.c:2154)
```

This error often occurs because of tables or databases using UTF8MB4 encoding. AWS DMS does not support the UTF8MB4 character set. In addition, check your database's parameters related to connections. The following command can be used to see these parameters:

```
1 SHOW VARIABLES LIKE '%char%';
```

Troubleshooting PostgreSQL Specific Issues

The following issues are specific to using AWS DMS with PostgreSQL databases.

- JSON data types being truncated
- Columns of a user defined data type not being migrated correctly
- Error: No schema has been selected to create in
- Deletes and updates to a table are not being replicated using CDC
- Truncate statements are not being propagated
- Preventing PostgreSQL from capturing DDL
- Selecting the schema where database objects for capturing DDL are created
- Oracle tables missing after migrating to PostgreSQL
- Task Using View as a Source Has No Rows Copied

JSON data types being truncated

AWS DMS treats the JSON data type in PostgreSQL as an LOB data type column. This means that the LOB size limitation when you use Limited LOB mode applies to JSON data. For example, if Limited LOB mode is set to 4096 KB, any JSON data larger than 4096 KB is truncated at the 4096 KB limit and will fail the validation test in PostgreSQL.

For example, the following log information shows JSON that was truncated due to the Limited LOB mode setting and failed validation.

```
1  03:00:49
2  2017-09-19T03:00:49 [TARGET_APPLY ]E: Failed to execute statement:
3   'UPDATE "public"."delivery_options_quotes" SET "id"=? , "enabled"=? ,
4   "new_cart_id"=? , "order_id"=? , "user_id"=? , "zone_id"=? , "quotes"=? ,
5   "start_at"=? , "end_at"=? , "last_quoted_at"=? , "created_at"=? ,
6   "updated_at"=? WHERE "id"=? ' [1022502] (ar_odbc_stmt
7  2017-09-19T03:00:49 [TARGET_APPLY ]E: Failed to execute statement:
8   'UPDATE "public"."delivery_options_quotes" SET "id"=? , "enabled"=? ,
9   "new_cart_id"=? , "order_id"=? , "user_id"=? , "zone_id"=? , "quotes"=? ,
10  "start_at"=? , "end_at"=? , "last_quoted_at"=? , "created_at"=? ,
11  "updated_at"=? WHERE "id"=? ' [1022502] (ar_odbc_stmt.c:2415)
12
13 03:00:49
14 2017-09-19T03:00:49 [TARGET_APPLY ]E: RetCode: SQL_ERROR SqlState:
15  22P02 NativeError: 1 Message: ERROR: invalid input syntax for type json;,
16  Error while executing the query [1022502] (ar_odbc_stmt.c:2421)
17 2017-09-19T03:00:49 [TARGET_APPLY ]E: RetCode: SQL_ERROR SqlState:
18  22P02 NativeError: 1 Message: ERROR: invalid input syntax for type json;,
19  Error while executing the query [1022502] (ar_odbc_stmt.c:2421)
```

Columns of a user defined data type not being migrated correctly

When replicating from a PostgreSQL source, AWS DMS creates the target table with the same data types for all columns, apart from columns with user-defined data types. In such cases, the data type is created as "character varying" in the target.

Error: No schema has been selected to create in

The error "SQL_ERROR SqlState: 3F000 NativeError: 7 Message: ERROR: no schema has been selected to create in" can occur when your JSON table mapping contains a wild card value for the schema but the source database doesn't support that value.

Deletes and updates to a table are not being replicated using CDC

Delete and Update operations during change data capture (CDC) are ignored if the source table does not have a primary key. AWS DMS supports change data capture (CDC) for PostgreSQL tables with primary keys; if a table does not have a primary key, the WAL logs do not include a before image of the database row and AWS DMS cannot update the table. Create a primary key on the source table if you want delete operations to be replicated.

Truncate statements are not being propagated

When using change data capture (CDC), TRUNCATE operations are not supported by AWS DMS.

Preventing PostgreSQL from capturing DDL

You can prevent a PostgreSQL target endpoint from capturing DDL statements by adding the following **Extra Connection Attribute** statement. The **Extra Connection Attribute** parameter is available in the **Advanced** tab of the source endpoint.

```
1 captureDDLs=N
```

Selecting the schema where database objects for capturing DDL are created

You can control what schema the database objects related to capturing DDL are created in. Add the following **Extra Connection Attribute** statement. The **Extra Connection Attribute** parameter is available in the **Advanced** tab of the target endpoint.

```
1 ddlArtifactsSchema=xyzddlschema
```

Oracle tables missing after migrating to PostgreSQL

Oracle defaults to uppercase table names while PostgreSQL defaults to lowercase table names. When performing a migration from Oracle to PostgreSQL you will most likely need to supply transformation rules under the table mapping section of your task to convert the case of your table names.

Your tables and data are still accessible; if you migrated your tables without using transformation rules to convert the case of your table names, you will need to enclose your table names in quotes when referencing them.

Task Using View as a Source Has No Rows Copied

A View as a PostgreSQL source endpoint is not supported by AWS DMS.

Troubleshooting Microsoft SQL Server Specific Issues

The following issues are specific to using AWS DMS with Microsoft SQL Server databases.

- Special Permissions for AWS DMS user account to use CDC
- SQL Server Change Data Capture (CDC) and Amazon RDS
- Errors Capturing Changes for SQL Server Database
- Missing Identity Columns
- Error: SQL Server Does Not Support Publications
- Changes Not Appearing in Target

Special Permissions for AWS DMS user account to use CDC

The user account used with AWS DMS requires the SQL Server SysAdmin role in order to operate correctly when using change data capture (CDC). CDC for SQL Server is only available for on-premises databases or databases on an EC2 instance.

SQL Server Change Data Capture (CDC) and Amazon RDS

AWS DMS currently does not support change data capture (CDC) from an Amazon RDS SQL Server DB instance. CDC for SQL Server is only available for on-premises databases or databases on an Amazon EC2 instance.

Errors Capturing Changes for SQL Server Database

Errors during change data capture (CDC) can often indicate that one of the pre-requisites was not met. For example, the most common overlooked pre-requisite is a full database backup. The task log indicates this omission with the following error:

```
1 SOURCE_CAPTURE E: No FULL database backup found (under the 'FULL' recovery model).
2 To enable all changes to be captured, you must perform a full database backup.
3 120438 Changes may be missed. (sqlserver_log_queries.c:2623)
```

Review the pre-requisites listed for using SQL Server as a source in Using a Microsoft SQL Server Database as a Source for AWS DMS.

Missing Identity Columns

AWS DMS does not support identity columns when you create a target schema. You must add them after the initial load has completed.

Error: SQL Server Does Not Support Publications

The following error is generated when you use SQL Server Express as a source endpoint:

```
1 RetCode: SQL_ERROR SqlState: HY000 NativeError: 21106
2 Message: This edition of SQL Server does not support publications.
```

AWS DMS currently does not support SQL Server Express as a source or target.

Changes Not Appearing in Target

AWS DMS requires that a source SQL Server database be in either 'FULL' or 'BULK LOGGED' data recovery model in order to consistently capture changes. The 'SIMPLE' model is not supported.

The SIMPLE recovery model logs the minimal information needed to allow users to recover their database. All inactive log entries are automatically truncated when a checkpoint occurs. All operations are still logged, but as soon as a checkpoint occurs the log is automatically truncated, which means that it becomes available for re-use and older log entries can be over-written. When log entries are overwritten, changes cannot be captured, and that is why AWS DMS doesn't support the SIMPLE data recovery model. For information on other required pre-requisites for using SQL Server as a source, see Using a Microsoft SQL Server Database as a Source for AWS DMS.

Troubleshooting Amazon Redshift Specific Issues

The following issues are specific to using AWS DMS with Amazon Redshift databases.

- Loading into a Amazon Redshift Cluster in a Different Region Than the AWS DMS Replication Instance
- Error: Relation "awsdms_apply_exceptions" already exists
- Errors with Tables Whose Name Begins with "awsdms_changes"
- Seeing Tables in Cluster with Names Like dms.awsdms_changes000000000XXXX
- Permissions Required to Work with Amazon Redshift

Loading into a Amazon Redshift Cluster in a Different Region Than the AWS DMS Replication Instance

This can't be done. AWS DMS requires that the AWS DMS replication instance and a Redshift cluster be in the same region.

Error: Relation "awsdms_apply_exceptions" already exists

The error "Relation "awsdms_apply_exceptions" already exists" often occurs when a Redshift endpoint is specified as a PostgreSQL endpoint. To fix this issue, modify the endpoint and change the **Target engine** to "redshift."

Errors with Tables Whose Name Begins with "awsdms_changes"

Error messages that relate to tables with names that begin with "awsdms_changes" often occur when two tasks that are attempting to load data into the same Amazon Redshift cluster are running concurrently. Due to the way temporary tables are named, concurrent tasks can conflict when updating the same table.

Seeing Tables in Cluster with Names Like dms.awsdms_changes000000000XXXX

AWS DMS creates temporary tables when data is being loaded from files stored in S3. The name of these temporary tables have the prefix "dms.awsdms_changes." These tables are required so AWS DMS can store data when it is first loaded and before it is placed in its final target table.

Permissions Required to Work with Amazon Redshift

To use AWS DMS with Amazon Redshift, the user account you use to access Amazon Redshift must have the following permissions:

- CRUD (Select, Insert, Update, Delete)
- Bulk Load
- Create, Alter, Drop (if required by the task's definition)

To see all the pre-requisites required for using Amazon Redshift as a target, see Using an Amazon Redshift Database as a Target for AWS Database Migration Service.

Troubleshooting Amazon Aurora MySQL Specific Issues

The following issues are specific to using AWS DMS with Amazon Aurora MySQL databases.

- Error: CHARACTER SET UTF8 fields terminated by ',' enclosed by '"' lines terminated by '\n'

Error: CHARACTER SET UTF8 fields terminated by ',' enclosed by '"' lines terminated by '\n'

If you are using Amazon Aurora MySQL as a target and see an error like the following in the logs, this usually indicates that you have ANSI_QUOTES as part of the SQL_MODE parameter. Having ANSI_QUOTES as part of the SQL_MODE parameter causes double quotes to be handled like quotes and can create issues when you run a task. To fix this error, remove ANSI_QUOTES from the SQL_MODE parameter.

```
1 2016-11-02T14:23:48 [TARGET_LOAD ]E: Load data sql statement. load data local infile
2 "/rdsdbdata/data/tasks/7XO4FJHCVON7TYTLQ6RX3CQHDU/data_files/4/LOAD000001DF.csv" into table
3 `VOSPUSER`.`SANDBOX_SRC_FILE` CHARACTER SET UTF8 fields terminated by ','
4 enclosed by '"' lines terminated by '\n'( `SANDBOX_SRC_FILE_ID`,`SANDBOX_ID`,
5 `FILENAME`,`LOCAL_PATH`,`LINES_OF_CODE`,`INSERT_TS`,`MODIFIED_TS`,`MODIFIED_BY`,
6 `RECORD_VER`,`REF_GUID`,`PLATFORM_GENERATED`,`ANALYSIS_TYPE`,`SANITIZED`,`DYN_TYPE`,
7 `CRAWL_STATUS`,`ORIG_EXEC_UNIT_VER_ID` ) ; (provider_syntax_manager.c:2561)
```

Reference for AWS Database Migration Service Including Data Conversion Reference and Additional Topics

This reference section includes additional information you may need when using AWS Database Migration Service (AWS DMS), including data type conversion information and additional procedures.

There are several ways to begin a database migration. You can select the AWS DMS console wizard that walks you through each step of the process, or you can do each step by selecting the appropriate task from the navigation pane. You can also use the AWS CLI; for information on using the AWS CLI with AWS DMS, see DMS.

There are a few important things to remember about data types when migrating a database:

- The FLOAT data type is inherently an approximation. The FLOAT data type is special in the sense that when you insert a specific value, it may be represented differently in the database, as it is not an accurate data type, such as a decimal data type like NUMBER or NUMBER(p,s). As a result, the internal value of FLOAT stored in the database might be different than the value that you insert, so the migrated value of a FLOAT might not match exactly the value on the source database.

  Here are some articles on the topic:

  IEEE floating point https://en.wikipedia.org/wiki/IEEE_floating_point

  IEEE Floating-Point Representation https://msdn.microsoft.com/en-us/library/0b34tf65.aspx

  Why Floating-Point Numbers May Lose Precision https://msdn.microsoft.com/en-us/library/c151dt3s.aspx

- The UTF-8 4-byte character set (utf8mb4) is not supported and could cause unexpected behavior in a source database. Plan to convert any data using the UTF-8 4-byte character set before migrating.

- Source Data Types

- Target Data Types

- Data Types for AWS Database Migration Service

- Using Extra Connection Attributes with AWS Database Migration Service

- Using ClassicLink with AWS Database Migration Service

Source Data Types

You can find data type conversion tables for databases used as a source for AWS Database Migration Service following.

- Source Data Types for Oracle
- Source Data Types for Microsoft SQL Server
- Source Data Types for PostgreSQL
- Source Data Types for MySQL
- Source Data Types for SAP ASE
- Source Data Types for MongoDB
- Source Data Types for Amazon S3

Source Data Types for Oracle

The Oracle endpoint for AWS DMS supports most Oracle data types. The following table shows the Oracle source data types that are supported when using AWS DMS and the default mapping to AWS DMS data types.

For additional information about AWS DMS data types, see Data Types for AWS Database Migration Service.

Oracle Data Type	AWS DMS Data Type
BINARY_FLOAT	REAL4
BINARY_DOUBLE	REAL8
BINARY	BYTES
FLOAT (P)	If precision is less than or equal to 24, use REAL4. If precision is greater than 24, use REAL8.
NUMBER (P,S)	When scale is less than 0, use REAL8
NUMBER according to the "Expose number as" property in the Oracle source database settings.	When scale is 0: [See the AWS documentation website for more details] In all other cases, use REAL8.
DATE	DATETIME
INTERVAL_YEAR TO MONTH	STRING (with interval year_to_month indication)
INTERVAL_DAY TO SECOND	STRING (with interval day_to_second indication)
TIME	DATETIME
TIMESTAMP	DATETIME
TIMESTAMP WITH TIME ZONE	STRING (with timestamp_with_timezone indication)
TIMESTAMP WITH LOCAL TIME ZONE	STRING (with timestamp_with_local_timezone indication)
CHAR	STRING
VARCHAR2	STRING
NCHAR	WSTRING
NVARCHAR2	WSTRING
RAW	BYTES
REAL	REAL8
BLOB	BLOB To use this data type with AWS DMS, you must enable the use of BLOB data types for a specific task. AWS DMS supports BLOB data types only in tables that include a primary key.
CLOB	CLOB To use this data type with AWS DMS, you must enable the use of CLOB data types for a specific task. During change data capture (CDC), AWS DMS supports CLOB data types only in tables that include a primary key.
NCLOB	NCLOB To use this data type with AWS DMS, you must enable the use of NCLOB data types for a specific task. During CDC, AWS DMS supports NCLOB data types only in tables that include a primary key.

Oracle Data Type	AWS DMS Data Type
LONG	CLOB The LONG data type is not supported in batch-optimized apply mode (TurboStream CDC mode). To use this data type with AWS DMS, you must enable the use of LOBs for a specific task. During CDC, AWS DMS supports LOB data types only in tables that have a primary key.
LONG RAW	BLOB The LONG RAW data type is not supported in batch-optimized apply mode (TurboStream CDC mode). To use this data type with AWS DMS, you must enable the use of LOBs for a specific task. During CDC, AWS DMS supports LOB data types only in tables that have a primary key.
XMLTYPE	CLOB Support for the XMLTYPE data type requires the full Oracle Client (as opposed to the Oracle Instant Client). When the target column is a CLOB, both full LOB mode and limited LOB mode are supported (depending on the target).

Oracle tables used as a source with columns of the following data types are not supported and cannot be replicated. Replicating columns with these data types result in a null column.

- BFILE
- ROWID
- REF
- UROWID
- Nested Table
- User-defined data types
- ANYDATA

Note
Virtual columns are not supported.

229

Source Data Types for Microsoft SQL Server

Data migration that uses Microsoft SQL Server as a source for AWS DMS supports most SQL Server data types. The following table shows the SQL Server source data types that are supported when using AWS DMS and the default mapping from AWS DMS data types.

For information on how to view the data type that is mapped in the target, see the section for the target endpoint you are using.

For additional information about AWS DMS data types, see Data Types for AWS Database Migration Service.

SQL Server Data Types	AWS DMS Data Types
BIGINT	INT8
BIT	BOOLEAN
DECIMAL	NUMERIC
INT	INT4
MONEY	NUMERIC
NUMERIC (p,s)	NUMERIC
SMALLINT	INT2
SMALLMONEY	NUMERIC
TINYINT	UINT1
REAL	REAL4
FLOAT	REAL8
DATETIME	DATETIME
DATETIME2 (SQL Server 2008 and later)	DATETIME
SMALLDATETIME	DATETIME
DATE	DATE
TIME	TIME
DATETIMEOFFSET	WSTRING
CHAR	STRING
VARCHAR	STRING
VARCHAR (max)	CLOB TEXT To use this data type with AWS DMS, you must enable the use of CLOB data types for a specific task. For SQL Server tables, AWS DMS updates LOB columns in the target even for UPDATE statements that don't change the value of the LOB column in SQL Server. During CDC, AWS DMS supports CLOB data types only in tables that include a primary key.
NCHAR	WSTRING
NVARCHAR (length)	WSTRING
NVARCHAR (max)	NCLOB NTEXT To use this data type with AWS DMS, you must enable the use of NCLOB data types for a specific task. For SQL Server tables, AWS DMS updates LOB columns in the target even for UPDATE statements that don't change the value of the LOB column in SQL Server. During CDC, AWS DMS supports CLOB data types only in tables that include a primary key.
BINARY	BYTES
VARBINARY	BYTES

SQL Server Data Types	AWS DMS Data Types
VARBINARY (max)	BLOB IMAGE For SQL Server tables, AWS DMS updates LOB columns in the target even for UPDATE statements that don't change the value of the LOB column in SQL Server. To use this data type with AWS DMS, you must enable the use of BLOB data types for a specific task. AWS DMS supports BLOB data types only in tables that include a primary key.
TIMESTAMP	BYTES
UNIQUEIDENTIFIER	STRING
HIERARCHYID	Use HIERARCHYID when replicating to a SQL Server target endpoint. Use WSTRING (250) when replicating to all other target endpoints.
XML	NCLOB For SQL Server tables, AWS DMS updates LOB columns in the target even for UPDATE statements that don't change the value of the LOB column in SQL Server. To use this data type with AWS DMS, you must enable the use of NCLOB data types for a specific task. During CDC, AWS DMS supports NCLOB data types only in tables that include a primary key.
GEOMETRY	Use GEOMETRY when replicating to target endpoints that support this data type. Use CLOB when replicating to target endpoints that don't support this data type.
GEOGRAPHY	Use GEOGRAPHY when replicating to target endpoints that support this data type. Use CLOB when replicating to target endpoints that do not support this data type.

AWS DMS does not support tables that include fields with the following data types:

- CURSOR
- SQL_VARIANT
- TABLE

Note
User-defined data types are supported according to their base type. For example, a user-defined data type based on DATETIME is handled as a DATETIME data type.

Source Data Types for PostgreSQL

The following table shows the PostgreSQL source data types that are supported when using AWS DMS and the default mapping to AWS DMS data types.

For additional information about AWS DMS data types, see Data Types for AWS Database Migration Service.

PostgreSQL Data Types	AWS DMS Data Types
INTEGER	INT4
SMALLINT	INT2
BIGINT	INT8
NUMERIC (p,s)	If precision is from 0 through 38, then use NUMERIC. If precision is 39 or greater, then use STRING.
DECIMAL(P,S)	If precision is from 0 through 38, then use NUMERIC. If precision is 39 or greater, then use STRING.
REAL	REAL4
DOUBLE	REAL8
SMALLSERIAL	INT2
SERIAL	INT4
BIGSERIAL	INT8
MONEY	NUMERIC(38,4) Note: The MONEY data type is mapped to FLOAT in SQL Server.
CHAR	WSTRING (1)
CHAR(N)	WSTRING (n)
VARCHAR(N)	WSTRING (n)
TEXT	NCLOB
BYTEA	BLOB
TIMESTAMP	TIMESTAMP
TIMESTAMP (z)	TIMESTAMP
TIMESTAMP with time zone	Not supported
DATE	DATE
TIME	TIME
TIME (z)	TIME
INTERVAL	STRING (128)—1 YEAR, 2 MONTHS, 3 DAYS, 4 HOURS, 5 MINUTES, 6 SECONDS
BOOLEAN	CHAR (5) false or true
ENUM	STRING (64)
CIDR	STRING (50)
INET	STRING (50)
MACADDR	STRING (18)
BIT (n)	STRING (n)
BIT VARYING (n)	STRING (n)
UUID	STRING
TSVECTOR	CLOB
TSQUERY	CLOB
XML	CLOB
POINT	STRING (255) "(x,y)"
LINE	STRING (255) "(x,y,z)"
LSEG	STRING (255) "((x1,y1),(x2,y2))"
BOX	STRING (255) "((x1,y1),(x2,y2))"
PATH	CLOB "((x1,y1),(xn,yn))"
POLYGON	CLOB "((x1,y1),(xn,yn))"

PostgreSQL Data Types	AWS DMS Data Types
CIRCLE	STRING (255) ”(x,y),r”
JSON	NCLOB
ARRAY	NCLOB
COMPOSITE	NCLOB
INT4RANGE	STRING (255)
INT8RANGE	STRING (255)
NUMRANGE	STRING (255)
STRRANGE	STRING (255)

Source Data Types for MySQL

The following table shows the MySQL database source data types that are supported when using AWS DMS and the default mapping from AWS DMS data types.

Note

The UTF-8 4-byte character set (utf8mb4) is not supported and could cause unexpected behavior in a source database. Plan to convert any data using the UTF-8 4-byte character set before migrating.

For additional information about AWS DMS data types, see Data Types for AWS Database Migration Service.

MySQL Data Types	AWS DMS Data Types
INT	INT4
MEDIUMINT	INT4
BIGINT	INT8
TINYINT	INT1
DECIMAL(10)	NUMERIC (10,0)
BINARY	BYTES(1)
BIT	BOOLEAN
BIT(64)	BYTES(8)
BLOB	BYTES(66535)
LONGBLOB	BLOB
MEDIUMBLOB	BLOB
TINYBLOB	BYTES(255)
DATE	DATE
DATETIME	DATETIME
TIME	STRING
TIMESTAMP	DATETIME
YEAR	INT2
DOUBLE	REAL8
FLOAT	REAL(DOUBLE) The supported FLOAT range is -1.79E+308 to -2.23E-308, 0 and 2.23E-308 to 1.79E+308 If the FLOAT values are not in the range specified here, map the FLOAT data type to the STRING data type.
VARCHAR (45)	WSTRING (45)
VARCHAR (2000)	WSTRING (2000)
VARCHAR (4000)	WSTRING (4000)
VARBINARY (4000)	BYTES (4000)
VARBINARY (2000)	BYTES (2000)
CHAR	WSTRING
TEXT	WSTRING (65535)
LONGTEXT	NCLOB
MEDIUMTEXT	NCLOB
TINYTEXT	WSTRING (255)
GEOMETRY	BLOB
POINT	BLOB
LINESTRING	BLOB
POLYGON	BLOB
MULTIPOINT	BLOB
MULTILINESTRING	BLOB
MULTIPOLYGON	BLOB
GEOMETRYCOLLECTION	BLOB

Note
If the DATETIME and TIMESTAMP data types are specified with a "zero" value (that is, 0000-00-00), you need to make sure that the target database in the replication task supports "zero" values for the DATETIME and TIMESTAMP data types. Otherwise, they are recorded as null on the target.

The following MySQL data types are supported in full load only:

MySQL Data Types	AWS DMS Data Types
ENUM	STRING
SET	STRING

Source Data Types for SAP ASE

Data migration that uses SAP ASE as a source for AWS DMS supports most SAP ASE data types. The following table shows the SAP ASE source data types that are supported when using AWS DMS and the default mapping from AWS DMS data types.

For information on how to view the data type that is mapped in the target, see the section for the target endpoint you are using.

For additional information about AWS DMS data types, see Data Types for AWS Database Migration Service.

SAP ASE Data Types	AWS DMS Data Types
BIGINT	INT8
BINARY	BYTES
BIT	BOOLEAN
CHAR	STRING
DATE	DATE
DATETIME	DATETIME
DECIMAL	NUMERIC
DOUBLE	REAL8
FLOAT	REAL8
IMAGE	BLOB
INT	INT4
MONEY	NUMERIC
NCHAR	WSTRING
NUMERIC	NUMERIC
NVARCHAR	WSTRING
REAL	REAL4
SMALLDATETIME	DATETIME
SMALLINT	INT2
SMALLMONEY	NUMERIC
TEXT	CLOB
TIME	TIME
TINYINT	UINT1
UNICHAR	UNICODE CHARACTER
UNITEXT	NCLOB
UNIVARCHAR	UNICODE
VARBINARY	BYTES
VARCHAR	STRING

AWS DMS does not support tables that include fields with the following data types:

- User-defined type (UDT)

Source Data Types for MongoDB

Data migration that uses MongoDB as a source for AWS DMS supports most MongoDB data types. The following table shows the MongoDB source data types that are supported when using AWS DMS and the default mapping from AWS DMS data types. For more information about MongoDB data types, see https://docs.mongodb.com/manual/reference/bson-types.

For information on how to view the data type that is mapped in the target, see the section for the target endpoint you are using.

For additional information about AWS DMS data types, see Data Types for AWS Database Migration Service.

MongoDB Data Types	AWS DMS Data Types
Boolean	Bool
Binary	BLOB
Date	Date
Timestamp	Date
Int	INT4
Long	INT8
Double	REAL8
String (UTF-8)	CLOB
Array	CLOB
OID	String
REGEX	CLOB
CODE	CLOB

Source Data Types for Amazon S3

Data migration that uses Amazon S3 as a source for AWS DMS will need to map data from S3 to AWS DMS data types. For more information, see Defining External Tables for S3 as a Source for AWS DMS.

For information on how to view the data type that is mapped in the target, see the section for the target endpoint you are using.

For additional information about AWS DMS data types, see Data Types for AWS Database Migration Service.

AWS DMS Data Types—Amazon S3 as Source
BYTERequires `ColumnLength`. For more information, see Defining External Tables for S3 as a Source for AWS DMS.
DATE
TIME
DATETIME
TIMESTAMP
INT1
INT2
INT4
INT8
NUMERIC Requires `ColumnPrecision` and `ColumnScale`. For more information, see Defining External Tables for S3 as a Source for AWS DMS.
REAL4
REAL8
STRINGRequires `ColumnLength`. For more information, see Defining External Tables for S3 as a Source for AWS DMS.
UINT1
UINT2
UINT4
UINT8
BLOB
CLOB
BOOLEAN

Target Data Types

You can find data type conversion tables for databases used as a target for AWS Database Migration Service following.

- Target Data Types for Oracle
- Target Data Types for Microsoft SQL Server
- Target Data Types for PostgreSQL
- Target Data Types for MySQL
- Target Data Types for SAP ASE
- Target Data Types for Amazon Redshift
- Target Data Types for Amazon DynamoDB

Target Data Types for Oracle

A target Oracle database used with AWS DMS supports most Oracle data types. The following table shows the Oracle target data types that are supported when using AWS DMS and the default mapping from AWS DMS data types. For more information about how to view the data type that is mapped from the source, see the section for the source you are using.

AWS DMS Data Type	Oracle Data Type
BOOLEAN	NUMBER (1)
BYTES	RAW (length)
DATE	DATETIME
TIME	TIMESTAMP (0)
DATETIME	TIMESTAMP (scale)
INT1	NUMBER (3)
INT2	NUMBER (5)
INT4	NUMBER (10)
INT8	NUMBER (19)
NUMERIC	NUMBER (p,s)
REAL4	FLOAT
REAL8	FLOAT
STRING	With date indication: DATE With time indication: TIMESTAMP With timestamp indication: TIMESTAMP With timestamp_with_timezone indication: TIMESTAMP WITH TIMEZONE With timestamp_with_local_timezone indication: TIMESTAMP WITH LOCAL TIMEZONE With interval_year_to_month indication: INTERVAL YEAR TO MONTH With interval_day_to_second indication: INTERVAL DAY TO SECOND If length > 4000: CLOB In all other cases: VARCHAR2 (length)
UINT1	NUMBER (3)
UINT2	NUMBER (5)
UINT4	NUMBER (10)
UINT8	NUMBER (19)
WSTRING	If length > 2000: NCLOB In all other cases: NVARCHAR2 (length)
BLOB	BLOB To use this data type with AWS DMS, you must enable the use of BLOBs for a specific task. BLOB data types are supported only in tables that include a primary key
CLOB	CLOB To use this data type with AWS DMS, you must enable the use of CLOBs for a specific task. During CDC, CLOB data types are supported only in tables that include a primary key.
NCLOB	NCLOB To use this data type with AWS DMS, you must enable the use of NCLOBs for a specific task. During CDC, NCLOB data types are supported only in tables that include a primary key.

AWS DMS Data Type	Oracle Data Type
XMLTYPE	The XMLTYPE target data type is only relevant in Oracle-to-Oracle replication tasks. When the source database is Oracle, the source data types are replicated "as is" to the Oracle target. For example, an XMLTYPE data type on the source is created as an XMLTYPE data type on the target.

Target Data Types for Microsoft SQL Server

The following table shows the Microsoft SQL Server target data types that are supported when using AWS DMS and the default mapping from AWS DMS data types. For additional information about AWS DMS data types, see Data Types for AWS Database Migration Service.

AWS DMS Data Type	SQL Server Data Type
BOOLEAN	TINYINT
BYTES	VARBINARY(length)
DATE	For SQL Server 2008 and later, use DATE. For earlier versions, if the scale is 3 or less use DATETIME. In all other cases, use VARCHAR (37).
TIME	For SQL Server 2008 and later, use DATETIME2 (%d). For earlier versions, if the scale is 3 or less use DATETIME. In all other cases, use VARCHAR (37).
DATETIME	For SQL Server 2008 and later, use DATETIME2 (scale). For earlier versions, if the scale is 3 or less use DATETIME. In all other cases, use VARCHAR (37).
INT1	SMALLINT
INT2	SMALLINT
INT4	INT
INT8	BIGINT
NUMERIC	NUMBER (p,s)
REAL4	REAL
REAL8	FLOAT
STRING	If the column is a date or time column, then do the following: [See the AWS documentation website for more details] If the column is not a date or time column, use VARCHAR (length).
UINT1	TINYINT
UINT2	SMALLINT
UINT4	INT
UINT8	BIGINT
WSTRING	NVARCHAR (length)
BLOB	VARBINARY(max) IMAGE To use this data type with AWS DMS, you must enable the use of BLOBs for a specific task. AWS DMS supports BLOB data types only in tables that include a primary key.
CLOB	VARCHAR(max) To use this data type with AWS DMS, you must enable the use of CLOBs for a specific task. During CDC, AWS DMS supports CLOB data types only in tables that include a primary key.
NCLOB	NVARCHAR(max) To use this data type with AWS DMS, you must enable the use of NCLOBs for a specific task. During CDC, AWS DMS supports NCLOB data types only in tables that include a primary key.

Target Data Types for PostgreSQL

The PostgreSQL database endpoint for AWS DMS supports most PostgreSQL database data types. The following table shows the PostgreSQL database target data types that are supported when using AWS DMS and the default mapping from AWS DMS data types. Unsupported data types are listed following the table.

For additional information about AWS DMS data types, see Data Types for AWS Database Migration Service.

AWS DMS Data Type	PostgreSQL Data Type
BOOL	BOOL
BYTES	BYTEA
DATE	DATE
TIME	TIME
TIMESTAMP	If the scale is from 0 through 6, then use TIMESTAMP. If the scale is from 7 through 9, then use VARCHAR (37).
INT1	SMALLINT
INT2	SMALLINT
INT4	INTEGER
INT8	BIGINT
NUMERIC	DECIMAL (P,S)
REAL4	FLOAT4
REAL8	FLOAT8
STRING	If the length is from 1 through 21,845, then use VARCHAR (length in bytes). If the length is 21,846 through 2,147,483,647, then use VARCHAR (65535).
UINT1	SMALLINT
UINT2	INTEGER
UINT4	BIGINT
UINT8	BIGINT
WSTRING	If the length is from 1 through 21,845, then use VARCHAR (length in bytes). If the length is 21,846 through 2,147,483,647, then use VARCHAR (65535).
BCLOB	BYTEA
NCLOB	TEXT
CLOB	TEXT

Note

When replicating from a PostgreSQL source, AWS DMS creates the target table with the same data types for all columns, apart from columns with user-defined data types. In such cases, the data type is created as "character varying" in the target.

Target Data Types for MySQL

The following table shows the MySQL database target data types that are supported when using AWS DMS and the default mapping from AWS DMS data types.

For additional information about AWS DMS data types, see Data Types for AWS Database Migration Service.

AWS DMS Data Types	MySQL Data Types
BOOLEAN	BOOLEAN
BYTES	If the length is from 1 through 65,535, then use VARBINARY (length). If the length is from 65,536 through 2,147,483,647, then use LONGLOB.
DATE	DATE
TIME	TIME
TIMESTAMP	"If scale is => 0 and =< 6, then: DATETIME (Scale) If scale is => 7 and =< 9, then: VARCHAR (37)"
INT1	TINYINT
INT2	SMALLINT
INT4	INTEGER
INT8	BIGINT
NUMERIC	DECIMAL (p,s)
REAL4	FLOAT
REAL8	DOUBLE PRECISION
STRING	If the length is from 1 through 21,845, then use VARCHAR (length). If the length is from 21,846 through 2,147,483,647, then use LONGTEXT.
UINT1	UNSIGNED TINYINT
UINT2	UNSIGNED SMALLINT
UINT4	UNSIGNED INTEGER
UINT8	UNSIGNED BIGINT
WSTRING	If the length is from 1 through 32,767, then use VARCHAR (length). If the length is from 32,768 through 2,147,483,647, then use LONGTEXT.
BLOB	If the length is from 1 through 65,535, then use BLOB. If the length is from 65,536 through 2,147,483,647, then use LONGBLOB. If the length is 0, then use LONGBLOB (full LOB support).
NCLOB	If the length is from 1 through 65,535, then use TEXT. If the length is from 65,536 through 2,147,483,647, then use LONGTEXT with ucs2 for CHARACTER SET. If the length is 0, then use LONGTEXT (full LOB support) with ucs2 for CHARACTER SET.
CLOB	If the length is from 1 through 65535, then use TEXT. If the length is from 65536 through 2147483647, then use LONGTEXT. If the length is 0, then use LONGTEXT (full LOB support).

Target Data Types for SAP ASE

The following table shows the SAP ASE database target data types that are supported when using AWS DMS and the default mapping from AWS DMS data types.

For additional information about AWS DMS data types, see Data Types for AWS Database Migration Service.

AWS DMS Data Types	SAP ASE Data Types
BOOLEAN	BIT
BYTES	VARBINARY (Length)
DATE	DATE
TIME	TIME
TIMESTAMP	If scale is => 0 and =< 6, then: BIGDATE-TIME If scale is => 7 and =< 9, then: VAR-CHAR (37)
INT1	TINYINT
INT2	SMALLINT
INT4	INTEGER
INT8	BIGINT
NUMERIC	NUMERIC (p,s)
REAL4	REAL
REAL8	DOUBLE PRECISION
STRING	VARCHAR (Length)
UINT1	TINYINT
UINT2	UNSIGNED SMALLINT
UINT4	UNSIGNED INTEGER
UINT8	UNSIGNED BIGINT
WSTRING	VARCHAR (Length)
BLOB	IMAGE
CLOB	UNITEXT
NCLOB	TEXT

AWS DMS does not support tables that include fields with the following data types. Replicated columns with these data types will show as null.

- User-defined type (UDT)

Target Data Types for Amazon Redshift

The Amazon Redshift endpoint for AWS DMS supports most Amazon Redshift data types. The following table shows the Amazon Redshift target data types that are supported when using AWS DMS and the default mapping from AWS DMS data types.

For additional information about AWS DMS data types, see Data Types for AWS Database Migration Service.

AWS DMS Data Types	Amazon Redshift Data Types
BOOLEAN	BOOL
BYTES	VARCHAR (Length)
DATE	DATE
TIME	VARCHAR(20)
DATETIME	If the scale is => 0 and =< 6, then: TIMESTAMP (s) If the scale is => 7 and =< 9, then: VARCHAR (37)
INT1	INT2
INT2	INT2
INT4	INT4
INT8	INT8
NUMERIC	If the scale is => 0 and =< 37, then: NUMERIC (p,s) If the scale is => 38 and =< 127, then: VARCHAR (Length)
REAL4	FLOAT4
REAL8	FLOAT8
STRING	If the length is => 1 and =< 65535, then: VARCHAR (Length in Bytes) If the length is => 65536 and =< 2147483647, then: VARCHAR (65535)
UINT1	INT2
UINT2	INT2
UINT4	INT4
UINT8	NUMERIC (20,0)
WSTRING	If the length is => 1 and =< 65535, then: NVARCHAR (Length in Bytes) If the length is => 65536 and =< 2147483647, then: NVARCHAR (65535)
BLOB	VARCHAR (Max LOB Size *2) Note: The maximum LOB size cannot exceed 31 KB.
NCLOB	NVARCHAR (Max LOB Size) Note: The maximum LOB size cannot exceed 63 KB.
CLOB	VARCHAR (Max LOB Size) Note: The maximum LOB size cannot exceed 63 KB.

Target Data Types for Amazon DynamoDB

The Amazon DynamoDB endpoint for Amazon AWS DMS supports most Amazon DynamoDB data types. The following table shows the Amazon AWS DMS target data types that are supported when using AWS DMS and the default mapping from AWS DMS data types.

For additional information about AWS DMS data types, see Data Types for AWS Database Migration Service.

When AWS DMS migrates data from heterogeneous databases, we map data types from the source database to intermediate data types called AWS DMS data types. We then map the intermediate data types to the target data types. The following table shows each AWS DMS data type and the data type it maps to in DynamoDB:

AWS DMS Data Type	DynamoDB Data Type
String	String
WString	String
Boolean	Boolean
Date	String
DateTime	String
INT1	Number
INT2	Number
INT4	Number
INT8	Number
Numeric	Number
Real4	Number
Real8	Number
UINT1	Number
UINT2	Number
UINT4	Number
UINT8	Number
CLOB	String

Data Types for AWS Database Migration Service

AWS Database Migration Service uses built-in data types to migrate data from one database to another. The following table shows the built-in data types and their descriptions.

AWS DMS Data Types	Description
STRING	A character string.
WSTRING	A double-byte character string.
BOOLEAN	A Boolean value.
BYTES	A binary data value.
DATE	A date value: year, month, day.
TIME	A time value: hour, minutes, seconds.
DATETIME	A timestamp value: year, month, day, hour, minute, second, fractional seconds. The fractional seconds have a maximum scale of 9 digits.
INT1	A one-byte, signed integer.
INT2	A two-byte, signed integer.
INT4	A four-byte, signed integer.
INT8	An eight-byte, signed integer.
NUMERIC	An exact numeric value with a fixed precision and scale.
REAL4	A single-precision floating-point value.
REAL8	A double-precision floating-point value.
UINT1	A one-byte, unsigned integer.
UINT2	A two-byte, unsigned integer.
UINT4	A four-byte, unsigned integer.
UINT8	An eight-byte, unsigned integer.
BLOB	Binary large object. This data type can be used only with Oracle endpoints.
CLOB	Character large object.
NCLOB	Native character large object.

Using Extra Connection Attributes with AWS Database Migration Service

You can specify additional connection attributes when creating an endpoint for AWS Database Migration Service. The following database engine specific sections show possible settings.

MySQL

[See the AWS documentation website for more details]

PostgreSQL

[See the AWS documentation website for more details]

Oracle

[See the AWS documentation website for more details]

SQL Server

[See the AWS documentation website for more details]

Amazon Redshift

[See the AWS documentation website for more details]

SAP Adaptive Server Enterprise (ASE)

[See the AWS documentation website for more details]

Note
If the user name or password specified in the connection string contains non-Latin characters (for example, Chinese), the following property is required: `charset=gb18030`

Using ClassicLink with AWS Database Migration Service

You can use ClassicLink, in conjunction with a proxy server, to connect an Amazon RDS DB instance that is not in a VPC to a AWS DMS replication server and DB instance that reside in a VPC.

The following procedure shows how to use ClassicLink to connect an Amazon RDS source DB instance that is not in a VPC to a VPC containing an AWS DMS replication instance and a target DB instance.

- Create an AWS DMS replication instance in a VPC. (All replication instances are created in a VPC).

- Associate a VPC security group to the replication instance and the target DB instance. When two instances share a VPC security group, they can communicate with each other by default.

- Set up a proxy server on an EC2 Classic instance.

- Create a connection using ClassicLink between the proxy server and the VPC.

- Create AWS DMS endpoints for the source and target databases.

- Create an AWS DMS task.

To use ClassicLink to migrate a database on a DB instance not in a VPC to a database on a DB instance in a VPC

1. Step 1: Create an AWS DMS replication instance.

   To create a AWS DMS replication instance and assign a VPC security group:

   1. Sign in to the AWS Management Console and choose AWS Database Migration Service. Note that if you are signed in as an AWS Identity and Access Management (IAM) user, you must have the appropriate permissions to access AWS DMS. For more information on the permissions required for database migration, see IAM Permissions Needed to Use AWS DMS.

   2. On the **Dashboard** page, choose **Replication Instance**. Follow the instructions at Step 2: Create a Replication Instance to create a replication instance.

   3. After you have created the AWS DMS replication instance, open the EC2 service console. Select **Network Interfaces** from the navigation pane.

   4. Select the *DMSNetworkInterface*, and then choose **Change Security Groups** from the **Actions** menu.

   5. Select the security group you want to use for the replication instance and the target DB instance.

2. Step 2: Associate the security group from the last step with the target DB instance.

To associate a security group with a DB instance

1. Open the Amazon RDS service console. Select **Instances** from the navigation pane.

2. Select the target DB instance. From **Instance Actions**, select **Modify**.

3. For the **Security Group** parameter, select the security group you used in the previous step.

4. Select **Continue**, and then **Modify DB Instance**.

5. Step 3: Set up a proxy server on an EC2 Classic instance using NGINX. Use an AMI of your choice to launch an EC2 Classic instance. The example below is based on the AMI Ubuntu Server 14.04 LTS (HVM).

   To set up a proxy server on an EC2 Classic instance

   1. Connect to the EC2 Classic instance and install NGINX using the following commands:

```
1 Prompt> sudo apt-get update
2 Prompt> sudo wget http://nginx.org/download/nginx-1.9.12.tar.gz
3 Prompt> sudo tar -xvzf nginx-1.9.12.tar.gz
```

```
 4 Prompt> cd nginx-1.9.12
 5 Prompt> sudo apt-get install build-essential
 6 Prompt> sudo apt-get install libpcre3 libpcre3-dev
 7 Prompt> sudo apt-get install zlib1g-dev
 8 Prompt> sudo ./configure --with-stream
 9 Prompt> sudo make
10 Prompt> sudo make install
```

2. Edit the NGINX daemon file, /etc/init/nginx.conf, using the following code:

```
 1 # /etc/init/nginx.conf - Upstart file
 2
 3 description "nginx http daemon"
 4 author "email"
 5
 6 start on (filesystem and net-device-up IFACE=lo)
 7 stop on runlevel [!2345]
 8
 9 env DAEMON=/usr/local/nginx/sbin/nginx
10 env PID=/usr/local/nginx/logs/nginx.pid
11
12 expect fork
13 respawn
14 respawn limit 10 5
15
16 pre-start script
17         $DAEMON -t
18         if [ $? -ne 0 ]
19                 then exit $?
20         fi
21 end script
22
23 exec $DAEMON
```

1. Create an NGINX configuration file at /usr/local/nginx/conf/nginx.conf. In the configuration file, add the following:

```
 1 # /usr/local/nginx/conf/nginx.conf - NGINX configuration file
 2
 3 worker_processes  1;
 4
 5 events {
 6     worker_connections  1024;
 7 }
 8
 9 stream {
10   server {
11     listen <DB instance port number>;
12 proxy_pass <DB instance identifier>:<DB instance port number>;
13   }
14 }
```

2. From the command line, start NGINX using the following commands:

```
1 Prompt> sudo initctl reload-configuration
2 Prompt> sudo initctl list | grep nginx
3 Prompt> sudo initctl start nginx
```

6. Step 4: Create a ClassicLink connection between the proxy server and the target VPC that contains the target DB instance and the replication instance

   Use ClassicLink to connect the proxy server with the target VPC

   1. Open the EC2 console and select the EC2 Classic instance that is running the proxy server.

   2. Select **ClassicLink** under **Actions**, then select **Link to VPC**.

   3. Select the security group you used earlier in this procedure.

   4. Select **Link to VPC**.

7. Step 5: Create AWS DMS endpoints using the procedure at Step 3: Specify Source and Target Endpoints. You must use the internal EC2 DNS hostname of the proxy as the server name when specifying the source endpoint.

8. Step 6: Create a AWS DMS task using the procedure at Step 4: Create a Task.

Release Notes for AWS Database Migration Service

This topic describes the release notes for versions of AWS Database Migration Service (AWS DMS).

AWS Database Migration Service (AWS DMS) 2.4.1 Release Notes

The following tables shows the features and bug fixes for version 2.4.1 of AWS Database Migration Service (AWS DMS).

New feature or enhancement	Description
JSONB support for PostgreSQL sources	Introduced support for JSONB migration from PostgreSQL as a source. JSONB is treated as a LOB data type and will require appropriate LOB settings to be used.
HSTORE support for PostgreSQL sources	Introduced support for HSTORE data type migration from PostgreSQL as a source. HSTORE is treated as a LOB data type and will require appropriate LOB settings to be used.
Additional copy command parameters for Redshift as a target	Introduced support for the following additional copy parameters via the extra connection attributes – [See the AWS documentation website for more details]

Issues Resolved

Date reported	Description
12th July 2017	Fixed an issue where migration task is hung before the full load phase starts when reading from an Oracle table with TDE column encryption enabled.
3rd October 2017	Fixed an issue where a JSON column from a PostgreSQL source would not migrate as expected.
5th October 2017	Fixed an issue when DMS migration task shows 0 source latency when archive redo log file is not found on the source Oracle instance. This fix will linearly increase source latency under such conditions.
20th November 2017	Fixed an issue with LOB migration where a TEXT column in PostgreSQL was migrating to a CLOB column in Oracle with extra spaces after each character in the LOB entry.
20th November 2017	Fixed an issue with a migration task not stopping as expected after an underlying replication instance upgrade from version 1.9.0 to 2.4.0.
30th November 2017	Fixed an issue where a DMS migration task does not properly capture changes made by a copy command run on a source PostgreSQL instance.

Date reported	Description
11th December 2017	Fixed an issue where a migration task failed when reading change data from a non-existent bin log from a MySQL source.
11th December 2017	Fixed an issue where DMS is reading change data from a non-existent table from a MySQL source.
20th December 2017	Includes several fixes and enhancements for the data validation feature.
22nd December 2017	Fixed an issue with maxFileSize parameter for Redshift targets. This parameter was wrongly being interpreted as bytes instead of kilobytes.
4th January 2018	Fixed a memory allocation bug for a DynamoDB as a target migration tasks. In certain conditions, AWS DMS was not allocating enough memory if the object mapping being used contained a sort key.
10th January 2018	Fixed an issue with Oracle 12.2 as a source where DMLs were not captured as expected when ROWDEPENDENCIES are used.

AWS Database Migration Service (AWS DMS) 2.4.0 Release Notes

The following tables shows the features and bug fixes for version 2.4.0 of AWS Database Migration Service (AWS DMS).

New feature or enhancement	Description
Replicating Oracle index tablespaces	Adds functionality to support replication of Oracle index tablespaces. More details about index tablespaces can be seen here.
Cross account S3 access support	Adds functionality to support canned ACLs to support cross account access with S3 endpoints. More details about canned ACLs can be seen here. Usage: Set extra connect attribute in S3 endpoint – `CannedAclForObjects=value` Possible values – [See the AWS documentation website for more details]

Issues Resolved

Date reported	Description
24th August 2017	Fixed an issue with PostgreSQL target where the fraction part in the TIME datatype was handled incorrectly.

Date reported	Description
7th August 2017	Fixed an issue which caused unexpected behavior with migration tasks with Oracle as a source when the source is down for more than 5 minutes. This issue caused the ongoing replication phase to hang even after the source became available.
19th July 2017	Fixed an issue where replication task runs in a retry loop forever when source PostgreSQL instance runs out of replication slots. With this fix, the task will fail with an error reporting that DMS could not create a logical replication slot.
27th July 2017	Fixed an issue in the replication engine where the enum MySQL data type caused task failure with a memory allocation error.
14th September 2017	Fixed an issue were incorrect values were being written to TOAST fields in PostgreSQL based targets during updates in the CDC phase.
8th October 2017	Fixed an issue from version 2.3.0 where ongoing replication with MySQL 5.5 sources would not work as expected.
12th October 2017	Fixed an issue with reading changes from a SQL Server 2016 source during the on-going replication phase. This fix needs to be used in conjunction with the following extra connect attribute in the source SQL Server endpoint – `IgnoreTxnCtxValidityCheck=true`

AWS Database Migration Service (AWS DMS) 2.3.0 Release Notes

The following tables shows the features and bug fixes for version 2.3.0 of AWS Database Migration Service (AWS DMS).

New feature or enhancement	Description
S3 as a source	Using Amazon S3 as a Source for AWS DMS
SQL Azure as a source	Using Microsoft Azure SQL Database as a Source for AWS DMS
Platform – AWS SDK update	Update to AWS SDK in the replication instance to 1.0.113. AWS SDK is used for certain endpoints like Redshift and S3 to upload data on customer's behalf into these endpoints. Usage - Unrestricted
Oracle Source – Support replication of tablespace in Oracle	Ability to migrate tablespaces from an Oracle source eliminating the need to pre-create tablespaces in the target before migration. Usage – Use the `ReadTableSpaceName` setting in the extra connect attributes in the Oracle source endpoint and set it to true to support tablespace replication. This is set to false by default.

New feature or enhancement	Description
Oracle Source – CDC support for Oracle active data guard standby as a source	Ability to use Oracle active data guard standby instance as a source for replicating ongoing changes to a supported target eliminating the need to connect to an active database which may be in production. Usage – Use the `StandbyDelayTime` setting in the extra connect attributes in the Oracle source endpoint and specify time in minutes to specify the delay in standby sync.
PostgreSQL Source – add WAL heartbeat	Added a WAL heartbeat (run dummy queries) for replication from a PostgreSQL source so idle logical replication slots do not hold on to old WAL logs which may result in storage full situations on the source. This heartbeat keeps restart_lsn moving and prevents storage full scenarios. Usage - wherever applicable – [See the AWS documentation website for more details]
All endpoints – Maintain homogeneous replication with transformation	Ability to do like to like migrations for homogeneous migration tasks (from a table structure/data type perspective) came in 2.2.0. However, DMS would still convert datatypes internally when a task was launched with table transformations. This feature maintains datatypes from source on target for homogeneous lift and shift migrations even when transformations are used. Usage – Unrestricted for all homogeneous migrations.
All endpoints – fail task when no tables are found	Ability to force Replication Task Failure When Include Transformation Rules Finds No Matches Usage – Flip `FailOnNoTablesCaptured` task setting to true.
Oracle source – stop task when archive redo log is missing	Ability to come out of a retry loop and stop task when archive redo log on the source is missing. Usage – Use the `RetryTimeoutInMinutes` extra connect attribute to specify stop timeout in minutes.

Issues resolved

Date reported	Description
5th January 2017	*MySQL: Server ID collision when using multiple tasks on same MySQL source:* Fixed a server ID collision issue when launching multiple DMS tasks to the same MySQL instance (version 5.6+)

Date reported	Description
21st February 2017	**MongoDB: Issue with create table when _id is a string:** Fixed an issue where create table fails for nestingLevel=ONE when _id in MongoDB is a String in the document. Before this fix, _id (when it is a String) was being created as a LONGTEXT (MySQL) or CLOB (Oracle) which causes a failure when it tries to make it a primary key.
5th May 2017	Oracle: NULL LOBs migrating as empty:Fixed an issue where NULL LOBs were migrating as empty when using full LOB mode with an Oracle source.
5th May 2017	**MySQL: Too many connections error when starting CDC from timestamp:** Fixed an issue where a MySQL as a source task fails with a too many connections error when custom CDC start time is older than 24 hours.
24th May 2017	DMS: Task starting for too long:Fixed an issue where task was starting for too long when multiple tasks were launched on the replication instance at once.
19th July 2017	**DynamoDB: Issue with updates/deletes to DynamoDB from Oracle:** Fixed an issue where updates/deletes from Oracle to DynamoDB were not being migrated well
8th August 2017	**Oracle: Oracle as a source – unexpected behavior during CDC:** Fixed an issue which caused unexpected behavior during CDC when an Oracle source database instance went down for more than 5 minutes during a migration.
27th August 2017	**MongoDB: Full load task crash:** Fixed an issue where full load task crashes when nestingLevel=NONE and _id is not ObjectId.
7th July 2017	**PostgreSQL: Error message about using all available connection slots not showing up** Fixed an issue to log an error in the default logging level when all available connection slots to PostgreSQL are used up and DMS cannot get more slots to continue with replication.
12th August 2017	**Redshift: Nulls being migrated as amazon_null:** Fixed an issue where nulls from any source where being migrated as amazon_null causing issues when inserted into non-varchar datatypes in Redshift.

Document History

The following table describes the important changes to the documentation since the last release of the AWS Database Migration Service.

- **API version:** 20160101
- **Latest documentation update:** November 27, 2017

Change	Description	Date Changed
New feature	Added support for using AWS DMS with AWS Snowball to migrate large databases. For more information, see Migrating Large Data Stores Using AWS Database Migration Service and AWS Snowball.	November 17, 2017
New feature	Added support for task assessment report and data validation. For more information about the task assessment report, see Creating a Task Assessment Report. For more information about data validation, see Data Validation Task Settings.	November 17, 2017
New feature	Added support for AWS CloudFormation templates. For more information, see AWS DMS Support for AWS CloudFormation.	July 11, 2017
New feature	Added support for using Amazon Dynamo as a target. For more information, see Using an Amazon DynamoDB Database as a Target for AWS Database Migration Service.	April 10, 2017
New feature	Added support for using MongoDB as a source. For more information, see Using MongoDB as a Source for AWS DMS.	April 10, 2017
New feature	Added support for using Amazon S3 as a target. For more information, see Using Amazon S3 as a Target for AWS Database Migration Service.	March 27, 2017
New feature	Adds support for reloading database tables during a migration task. For more information, see Reloading Tables During a Task.	March 7, 2017

Change	Description	Date Changed
New feature	Added support for events and event subscriptions. For more information, see Working with Events and Notifications.	January 26, 2017
New feature	Added support for SSL endpoints for Oracle. For more information, see SSL Support for an Oracle Endpoint.	December 5, 2016
New feature	Added support for using Change Data Capture (CDC) with an Amazon RDS PostgreSQL DB instance. For more information, see Setting Up an Amazon RDS PostgreSQL DB Instance as a Source.	September 14, 2016
New region support	Added support for the Asia Pacific (Mumbai), Asia Pacific (Seoul), and South America (São Paulo) regions. For a list of supported regions, see What Is AWS Database Migration Service?.	August 3, 2016
New feature	Added support for ongoing replication. For more information, see Ongoing Replication.	July 13, 2016
New feature	Added support for secured connections using SSL. For more information, see Using SSL With AWS Database Migration Service.	July 13, 2016
New feature	Added support for SAP Adaptive Server Enterprise (ASE) as a source or target endpoint. For more information, see Using a SAP ASE Database as a Source for AWS DMS and Using a SAP ASE Database as a Target for AWS Database Migration Service.	July 13, 2016
New feature	Added support for filters to move a subset of rows from the source database to the target database. For more information, see Using Source Filters.	May 2, 2016
New feature	Added support for Amazon Redshift as a target endpoint. For more information, see Using an Amazon Redshift Database as a Target for AWS Database Migration Service.	May 2, 2016
General availability	Initial release of AWS Database Migration Service.	March 14, 2016

Change	Description	Date Changed
Public preview release	Released the preview documentation for AWS Database Migration Service.	January 21, 2016

AWS Glossary

For the latest AWS terminology, see the AWS Glossary in the *AWS General Reference*.